Draughtsmanship
Architectural and Building Graphics

FRASER REEKIE
FRIBA, FRSA, FRTPI, Dip Arch, Dip TP (RIBA)
Chartered Architect   Chartered Town Planner

Edward Arnold

© R. FRASER REEKIE 1976
First published in 1946 by
Edward Arnold (Publishers) Ltd
41 Bedford Square, London WC1B 3DQ
Reprinted 1947, 1949, 1952, 1956, 1957, 1959, 1961, 1963, 1965
Second edition 1969
Reprinted 1970, 1971, 1973, 1975
Third edition 1976
Reprinted 1978, 1980 (twice), 1981, 1982

ISBN: 0 7131 3368 6

*Illustrations not otherwise credited prepared
by author*

___
By the same author
DESIGN IN THE BUILT ENVIRONMENT
BACKGROUND TO ENVIRONMENTAL PLANNING

Printed in Hong Kong by
Wing King Tong Co Ltd

Author's Preface to Third Edition

A new edition of this book has been called for in order to make those changes which always become necessary from time to time as a result of developments in professional and industrial practice and, in this case, further teaching experience.

Since the preparation of the second edition seven years ago, there have been continued technological advances in the processes of design and construction. The overall effect has been to make evident a greater need than ever before for skills in relevant graphic techniques. The primary purpose of this book remains that of providing information and guidance with regard to these means of communication, for students in any way connected with planning, architecture, surveying and building.

In a general sense there is little I can add to what I wrote as prefaces to the first and second editions. These are reprinted in the following pages and they should be read in conjunction with these remarks. One of the changes that has taken place since the times in which they were written has been the proliferation of drafting aids, as can be seen in the now profusely illustrated catalogues of suppliers of drawing office materials. It is never possible to include all such equipment in a book or to give a picture of every latest item, but descriptions of basic types, of which it is helpful to have some knowledge, have been included. Future products for a long time to come are likely only to be variations.

Cognisance has also been taken of computer graphics. Although for reasons of cost and difficulties of availability their use up to the present has been confined mainly to large firms and government agencies, it is possible that with wider educational recognition of the capabilities of computers and with the expansion of computer services, there will be increased acceptance and utilisation in the future. It is desirable that there is an awareness of this trend.

The chapter on Freehand Drawing, formerly 'Freehand Sketches', has been re-written with added examples to give more emphasis to what manifestly has become of greater importance at all levels in all branches of technical and professional activities.

The opportunity has also been taken to rearrange sections of the book in a more logical order while including new and revised text material as required by the changes referred to above. A number of new illustrations have been added.

Production or working drawings, as in previous editions, have not been included in detail, not only because the limitations of page size make legible reproduction impossible, but also—a more important reason—because practice varies from country to country, from place to place and from office to office. It is intended that there should be an awareness of fundamentals, but it would be beyond the scope of this book, which is essentially concerned with graphic techniques rather than drawings *per se*, to attempt a comprehensive survey of such drawings. From various inquiries that have recently been made, it is interesting to find that the majority of working drawings are still being produced on traditional lines.

As the book is used internationally, references to the imperial system of measurement are retained.

In conclusion, I would like to say to those who are starting their studies that fluency in draughtsmanship is not merely a practical means of communication—sometimes the only adequate means—and of making and keeping records, but also a generator and refiner of ideas in the creative process and, not least, a continual source of pleasure to oneself and one's fellows.

Acknowledgements

I have no space to list with my grateful thanks the names of all the people in different parts of the world and at various times who have told me of their interest in the book and the many who have assisted me in the preparation of successive editions. It has been especially satisfying to learn that the book not only helped some when they were students but that it continued to be useful to them in their subsequent careers.

With regard to this edition, I would like to express particular thanks to the following, who gave of their time to discuss techniques and who provided new material:

David G. Campion BA(Arch) DipTP FRIBA MBCS
Frank A. Evans MBE FRSA AFAS
Tony K. McCarthy ARIBA DipRP(Edin) FRSA
Graham Moss MPhil(Edin) DipTP MRTPI RIBA ARIAS
Howard Tozer BArch RIBA DipArch

Author's Preface to
Original Edition

Author's Preface to Second Edition

Since the original edition of this book was prepared, many changes and developments have taken place in the practice of architecture and related professions, and in organization and methods in the construction industry. They include the adoption of the metric system, the use of modular co-ordination and industrialised and system-building techniques for certain types of buildings, improved procedures in design and in building-team management, and increased employment of and adaptation to modern scientific and technological processes and aids, such as computers.

Professional and technical education, too, has changed. For the professions, higher standards of entry are required and there is an upgrading of course content and examinations to degree level. Similar advances have been made in general and specialist building training to meet needs created by the growing complexity and scale of operations, and to equip architectural and other technicians for their careers as essential contributors to the efficiency of the professions and the industry.

With this background in mind, this new edition of *Draughtsmanship* has been prepared to make it more useful for all concerned with building. Some of the original edition which is still valid has been retained but much has been rewritten and enlarged by adding new material and illustrations. In the crowded syllabuses of universities, polytechnics and schools, less time than formerly can be spared for instruction and practice in graphics, but drawings in one form or another will always be the chief means of communication in design and construction; this book may therefore be all the more valuable in providing basic knowledge and principles, and an awareness of current practices and likely trends.

R. Fraser Reekie

Author's Preface to Original Edition

The purpose of this book is to describe the technique of draughtsmanship and the methods of preparing drawings used in connection with the lay-out, design, and construction of buildings.

It is written mainly for the student, particularly the beginner, but it is also intended as a reference book for the more accomplished.

For several years I have been concerned in the teaching of draughtsmanship, and I have discovered that anyone with normal vision and the ability to use his hands intelligently can be taught to draw very well in a short time. The only people who never learn to draw or who draw badly, apart from those with some physical handicap, are those who are not interested—although how anyone can fail to be interested in drawing, especially if proposing to take up or actually engaged in work connected with building, is difficult to understand.

However, while it is true that no one can learn to draw by reading a book and that the real way is to start drawing and to keep on drawing as much as possible, the process can be made a good deal easier by knowing the methods which up to the present have been found successful; and the various conventions in common use. But I am not a lover of unnecessary standardisation and I would not like to see all draughtsmen producing exactly similar drawings. Therefore, while I have tried to include what I believe to be the most useful information and advice, I have deliberately besprinkled the text with such qualifying words and phrases as 'usually', 'generally', 'in most cases', and so on, with the intention of avoiding any feeling that draughtsmanship is a matter of hard and fast rules. Such a belief, simpler though it might make life in some respects, does not give rise to satisfactory work, and I strongly emphasise the suggestion made frequently throughout the book that only by the continual study of drawings of all types, non-technical as well as technical, and by experiment and practice can first-class proficiency be achieved.

Of course, the broad principles of good drawing are unchanging: suitability in accordance with purpose, accuracy, legibility and neatness, economy in time and labour; but there are always opportunities for new and better ideas in satisfying them, especially with regard to architectural renderings. Let the beginner, however, be in no hurry to impart a personal 'style' to his work—it may result in mere eccentricity and affectation. A good foundation, the habit of simple, direct drawing, should be laid first. Real individual character comes with practice and cannot be forced.

I have assumed that readers, whether or not attending classes or receiving practical experience in their profession, are in a position to study other subjects and have an elementary knowledge at least of some of the common terms used in building. Most of them used in this book will, I think, be clear from the context, but any doubtful ones should be looked up in an appropriate technical dictionary. The study of geometry and geometrical drawing should in particular proceed concurrently with the study of draughtsmanship, and for this reason I have not dealt with the working out in detail of the examples included here.

I have been greatly assisted in the preparation of this work by suggestions and criticisms from my colleagues and professional associates and, not least, by the successful and not-so-successful efforts of my students. I also wish to express thanks to those who prepared drawings specially or who loaned drawings for inclusion in the examples illustrated and whose work is acknowledged individually elsewhere, and to J. D. W. Ball, Esq., of the British Standards Institution, and Harcourt Hanrott, Esq., of the Drawing Office Materials Manufacturers and Dealers Association.

R. Fraser Reekie

Contents

1
Drawing Equipment

The following notes deal with the principal items of drawing equipment required by the student and the draughtsman.

There are many different kinds of most of the articles mentioned. A full description of all would be tedious and is unnecessary. The aim here is to cover everything essential and to give guidance as regards general selection and use.

The beginner is advised to purchase the best available instruments that he can afford; the experienced draughtsman usually requires no such reminder. While it is possible for the latter to make good drawings with very little or even improvised equipment when the occasion arises, it is foolish for the novice to handicap himself at the outset by inadequate or inferior articles. It is also advisable to purchase drawing-office equipment and materials from reputable manufacturers and dealers.

In Britain many items are covered by British Standards Institute recommendations, e.g. drawing boards and Tee squares BS 4867, set-squares BS 2459, instruments BS 1709, scales BS 1347, drawing inks BS 2490, cartridge paper BS 1343, tracing paper BS 1340, detail paper BS 1342, but these are primarily for the guidance of manufacturers and suppliers.

Drawing boards

Drawing boards are made in sizes to correspond with standard drawing paper sizes. The most suitable for general use are:

A1   920 mm × 650 mm $(36'' \times 25\frac{1}{2}'')$
A0   1270 mm × 920 mm $(50'' \times 36'')$

which supersede the former standard sizes of: imperial, $32'' \times 23''$ (813 mm × 585 mm), and double elephant, $42'' \times 32''$ (1067 mm × 813 mm). Boards of these old sizes and a larger size called antiquarian, $54'' \times 32''$ (1372 mm × 813 mm), are still common and can be used for the appropriate smaller A sizes of paper. Various other sizes of boards are made to suit drafting machines which are referred to later in this chapter.

1

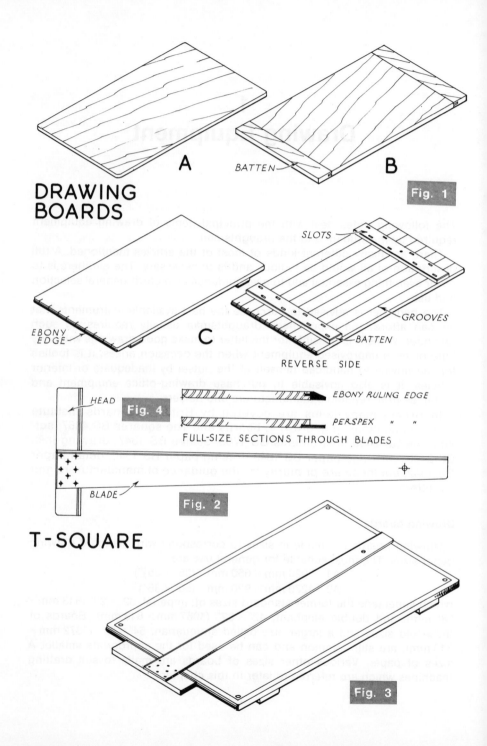

DRAWING BOARDS

A

BATTEN

B

Fig. 1

SLOTS

EBONY EDGE

C

GROOVES

BATTEN

REVERSE SIDE

HEAD

Fig. 4

EBONY RULING EDGE

PERSPEX " "

FULL-SIZE SECTIONS THROUGH BLADES

BLADE

Fig. 2

T-SQUARE

Fig. 3

Fig. 1 illustrates three types of drawing boards. Types A and B, not bigger than size A1, are suitable for the student as they are light for carrying about and are relatively inexpensive. Such boards can be obtained with metal edges. Type C, which is best for office use, is usually made from spruce and has beech battens secured by screws in elongated washers to allow for expansion and contraction. The back of the board is grooved to resist warping. Some larger boards have a recessed electronic calculator in the top right-hand corner.

It is important with all types of drawing boards that the faces are perfectly flat and smooth, and that they will not twist or buckle with normal use. Edges should be at right-angles to one another. Wooden boards should have a firm even grain free from knots, and should be soft enough to take drawing pins or staples easily and allow their removal without difficulty. Boards with composition surfaces can have paper attached by means of spring clips or strips of drafting tape as described later.

Small drawing boards accepting paper up to A3 size are now becoming generally available. They are precision made with smooth plastic surfaces, are light and easily transportable and are often supplied with a carrying case. Some incorporate adjustable supports so that they can be set up on a level table or desk at one of several slopes. They are provided with positive sliding drawing heads or rules, operating rather like T-squares, for drawing horizontal lines and with matching set-squares of ingenious multi-purpose design. Alternatively, they can be fitted with miniature drafting machines. They usually have devices for holding drawing paper in position as pins or staples cannot be used and adhesive tapes tend to spoil the surface of the board.

Care of drawing boards

The value of a good drawing board can only be maintained by careful treatment. The surface should be protected from knocks and scratches. If left on the table, it should be covered with a cloth; if put against a wall the working side should face inwards and the ebony edge should be at the top. It should not be exposed to heat or moisture. Drawing pins should not be stuck in unnecessarily, and using the board as a backing on which to cut paper or card is harmful to the surface.

T-squares

T-squares or Tee squares, Fig. 2, are described in shape by the name. They are used in conjunction with the board for drawing horizontal lines,

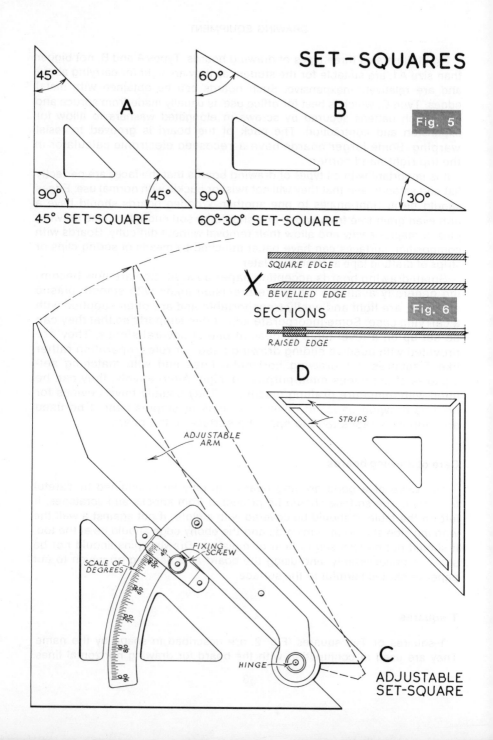

SET-SQUARES

45° SET-SQUARE

60°-30° SET-SQUARE

Fig. 5

45°

A

90°   45°

60°

B

90°   30°

SQUARE EDGE

BEVELLED EDGE

Fig. 6

SECTIONS

RAISED EDGE

D

STRIPS

ADJUSTABLE
ARM

FIXING
SCREW

SCALE OF
DEGREES

HINGE

C

ADJUSTABLE
SET-SQUARE

Fig. 3, the head of the T-square being held against the left-hand side of the board by right-handed persons (reverse T-squares to operate against the right-hand side of the board are made for the left-handed draughtsmen).

Sizes correspond to the lengths of the drawing boards listed above:

A1   920 mm blade   (36″)

A0   1270 mm blade   (50″)

and for the old sizes: imperial, 32″; double elephant, 42″; antiquarian, 54″.

T-squares are best when made of mahogany with ebony or clear plastic ruling edges (Fig. 4).

In Britain the blade usually tapers, which makes the T-square more manageable when lifted by the head. In the U.S.A. and on the Continent the blade is more often with parallel edges. They have necessarily to be made of thin strips of wood for lightness, but this renders them liable to fracture. They should therefore be handled with care and should not be left lying about in 'bridging' positions or leaning against walls. They should either be left flat or hung on pegs. Damage is also likely to arise in two other ways by careless handling; a loosening of the fixing between head and blade, and indentations along the ruling edge. The former results from using the T-square as a hammer with which to knock in drawing pins; the latter by using the blade as a straight-edge in cutting paper. Loose blades can often be tightened up with a screwdriver, but care must be taken to see that a true right-angle is formed with the head. Blades that have become dented can be re-shot; a remedy which should not be attempted by the amateur. Most drawing equipment suppliers will carry out this and other repairs.

It is important to keep the underside of the blade smooth and clean, and this is best achieved by wiping it periodically with a soft cloth and a few drops of petrol or similar spirit. Water can be used, but is less effective and may cause warping. The underside is less likely to collect dust in traversing the paper if the tapered edge is rounded off, as shown in Fig. 4.

Set-squares

Set-squares are used for drawing vertical and inclined lines. They are triangles of clear plastic about 2 mm thick and are of three basic kinds, as illustrated in Fig. 5: A–45 degrees, B–60–30 degrees, C–adjustable. The last supersedes the two others as it can be set to any angle. In recent years somewhat complex set-squares with sides at 90, 60, 45 and 30 degrees, and with divisions like a protractor (Fig. 14) for other angles, plus scales and apertures for circles, lettering and various symbols, etc. have appeared. Some even manage to include a selection

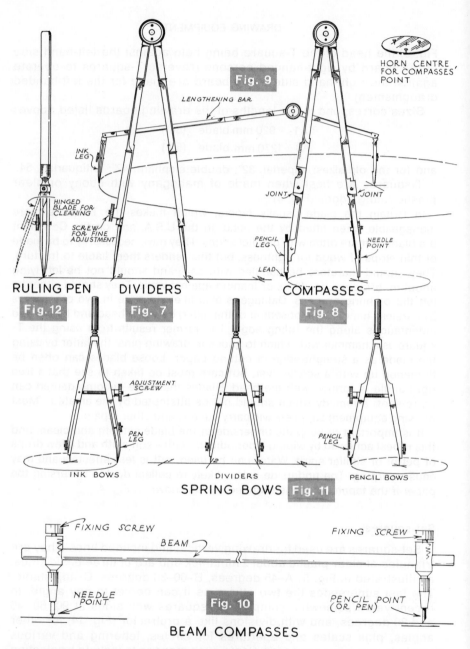

HORN CENTRE FOR COMPASSES' POINT

LENGTHENING BAR

INK LEG

HINGED BLADE FOR CLEANING

SCREW FOR FINE ADJUSTMENT

JOINT

JOINT

PENCIL LEG

NEEDLE POINT

LEAD

RULING PEN   **DIVIDERS**   **COMPASSES**

Fig. 12   Fig. 7   Fig. 8

ADJUSTMENT SCREW

PEN LEG

PENCIL LEG

INK BOWS   DIVIDERS   PENCIL BOWS

SPRING BOWS Fig. 11

Fig. 9

FIXING SCREW   BEAM   FIXING SCREW

NEEDLE POINT   Fig. 10   PENCIL POINT (OR PEN)

BEAM COMPASSES

DRAWING INSTRUMENTS

of french curves! While useful for small drawings made under restricted conditions, e.g. away from the drawing office, it is doubtful if they have any other advantages over conventional equipment.

For general use, the length of the longest side should be about 230–300 mm and the edges should be square, Fig. 6, not bevelled. The square edge is less likely to cause smudging when ink lines are ruled.

A type of set-square specially designed to prevent smudging is illustrated in Fig. 5D. It consists of the ordinary type of set-square with additional thin strips stuck on both sides a short distance back from the edges, which are thus raised above the paper. A similar type has stepped edges.

As with T-squares, it is important to protect set-squares from damage. Dents are caused by hard knocks, and cutting with a razor-blade, etc., along the edges can easily ruin them. They should be kept scrupulously clean because dirty set-squares quickly transfer the dirt to the drawing in almost ineradicable lines and patches. Petrol, etc., can be used for cleaning, but soap and water is also effective and does not harm plastic. Particular care should be paid to cleaning the edges of set-squares.

Drawing instruments

Chief amongst the personal equipment of the draughtsman is a set of instruments, and special attention should be taken in the selection and care of them. There is normally a wide range of kinds and patterns to choose from, and they can be bought separately or in sets. It is probably more economical to purchase the pieces individually in the beginning. Sets, in cases, usually contain one or more inessential items, and it is probably easier to test the instruments if they are bought singly. Cases are, of course, useful for keeping the instruments, which require to be protected when not in use. A suitable carrying-case can be made cheaply, however, by folding and sewing a piece of chamois leather to form a series of pockets. This can be rolled up and tied with tapes.

The most useful types of instruments described below are based on good typical examples.

All instruments should be carefully examined to see that they function properly. Needle points of compasses and dividers, ruling pens and pen compasses should be checked.

Dividers

Fig. 7 illustrates a pair of dividers used for dividing lines into equal units by trial and error and for multiplying or transferring distances. A convenient size is about 140 mm long. A spring screw attachment to one leg for fine

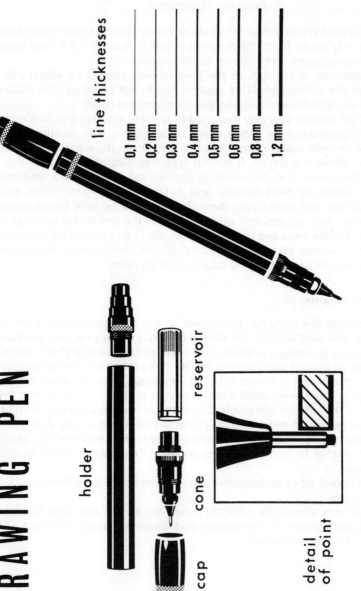

DRAWING PEN

line thicknesses

0.1 mm
0.2 mm
0.3 mm
0.4 mm
0.5 mm
0.6 mm
0.8 mm
1.2 mm

holder

reservoir

cone

cap

detail of point

Plate 1   Example of reservoir-type drawing pen for use with black and coloured inks.
(Illustration of Rotring Variant pen by courtesy of Hartley Reece & Co.)

adjustment is an advantage. The hinge should move easily but should not be loose.

Compasses

Fig. 8 shows a common pattern of compasses, which are used for drawing circles and arcs. One leg terminates in a needle point and the other leg can be fitted with pencil or pen. An additional needle-pointed leg can also be obtained for converting this instrument into another pair of dividers for emergency use. For large circles and arcs a lengthening bar, Fig. 9, is valuable.

Both legs of the compasses are jointed so that they can be bent to keep the point more or less perpendicular to the paper.

Needle points are removable and are usually shouldered at one end — this end is best for use in drawing circles, as the point does not penetrate the paper too far. The instrument should be held at the top — see illustration of dividers in Fig. 7, and pressure must be only sufficient to keep the centre from slipping and to maintain a smooth, even line for the curve. The two points of the compasses must be carefully adjusted. The pencil lead should be the same grade as the ordinary pencil being used on the same drawing. A 12 mm length can be cut from the bottom of the pencil for the purpose. It should be sharpened to a fine chisel point and arranged tangential to the circumference, although for small circles a round point is probably better.

Pens are capable of adjustment in the manner of ruling pens described later. The thickness of the ink line should be tested at the side of the paper before the required curve is drawn. To avoid blots thick lines should be built up rather than drawn by opening the pen widely.

Special compass/pen attachments are available for use with the Rotring Variant drawing pen described below and with pump compasses, for drawing small circles.

Beam compasses

For drawing larger circles than are possible with ordinary compasses and the lengthening bar, beam compasses, as illustrated in Fig. 10, can be used. They consist of a centre point and a fitting, with interchangeable pencil and pen legs, which are screwed to a bar to give the radius required.

The Roller beam compasses, an alternative type, can be used for the same purpose.

Spring bows and pump compasses

Small dividers and pencil and pen compasses for accurate and fine work are called spring bows and are illustrated in Fig. 11. Adjustment is made by

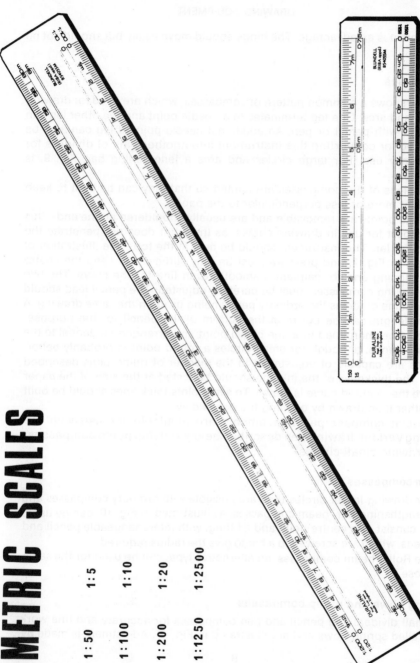

Plate 2 Metric scales. Illustration shows arrangement of scales on each side.

means of a screw either at the side, as shown, or in the middle of the instrument. There are a number of variations of these instruments including precision-made pump compasses and rapid adjustment compasses. It should be mentioned, however, that for general work small circles and arcs are drawn through templates, see p.14.

Drawing pens (sometimes called technical pens)

Straight lines in ink are ruled in conjunction with the T-square and set-square by means of special drawing pens, such as the Rotring Graphos or the Rotring Variant (Plate 1). These pens are based on the fountain-pen principle, with ink reservoirs so that they can be used for long periods without refilling. Interchangeable nibs or drawing elements are used for different thicknesses of lines, usually ranging from 0.2 mm to 1.2 mm — the consistency of line is a great advantage. The pens can also be used for the freehand drawing of lines and for freehand and stencil lettering (see Chapter 4 for reference to guided pen lettering). The Graphos pen has special nibs for freehand lettering.

Instructions for use and care come with the pens, and it is only necessary here to emphasise how important it is to follow these instructions, which should be kept readily available for reference, especially in regard to cleaning. Much of the speed and convenience to be gained by using these pens can be lost if they are not properly looked after but are allowed to become clogged or encrusted with ink, so that undue time has to be wasted in making them work — with all the exasperation this can cause!

Fig. 12 shows the old type of ruling pen, which has frequently to be filled, either by means of the dropper from the ink bottle, Fig. 19, or by dipping an ordinary freehand pen into the bottle and transferring the ink to the blades. It is better not to put much ink between the blades; practice will indicate how much is satisfactory. The thickness of line required is obtained by means of the adjustment screw and by testing at the side of the drawing paper or on a scrap of similar paper. Ruling pens, filled by means of small brushes, are essential for ruling lines in chinese white or other opaque water colours, see Chapter 9.

All kinds of drawing pens should be held perfectly upright against the edge of T-square or set-square, and should be drawn smoothly with even pressure from left to right or in an upwards direction. It may be found convenient to build up thick lines from two or three close rulings of thinner lines, but care must be taken at ends and corners that they do not become ragged.

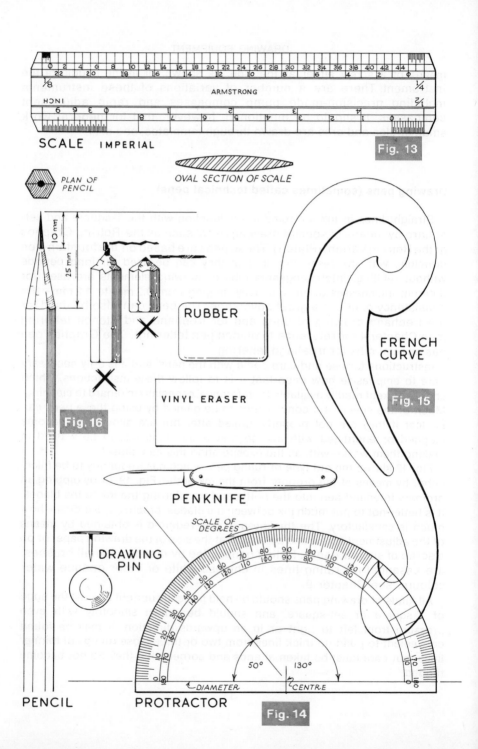

SCALE IMPERIAL

Fig. 13

OVAL SECTION OF SCALE

ARMSTRONG

PLAN OF PENCIL

10 mm

25 mm

RUBBER

VINYL ERASER

Fig. 16

PENKNIFE

FRENCH CURVE

Fig. 15

DRAWING PIN

SCALE OF DEGREES

50°   130°

DIAMETER   CENTRE

PENCIL   PROTRACTOR

Fig. 14

Scales

Scales are thin narrow strips of white or yellow plastic, or boxwood or ivory, with divisions along each edge, usually on both sides. These divisions are in various recognised proportions to actual distances and dimensions, and can therefore be used for making new drawings 'to scale' (see Chapter 5) or for measuring, by 'scaling', as it is termed, existing drawings.

Plate 2 shows the two sides of the R.I.B.A. Approved Scale for metric drawings, and this is the scale now commonly used by architects. There are two lines of divisions along each edge in the proportions of 1 : 1 or 1 : 10/1 : 100, 1 : 20/1 : 200, 1 : 5/1 : 50, 1 : 250/1 : 2500.

Fig. 13 shows the appearance of one side of a scale for use in connection with drawings in which distances are related to feet and inches. It is 'Armstrong' divided, i.e. with $\frac{1}{8}''$, $\frac{1}{4}''$, $\frac{1}{2}''$, and 1" divisions on one side and $\frac{3}{8}''$, $\frac{3}{4}''$, $1\frac{1}{2}''$, and 3" divisions on the other, the end unit in each case being subdivided into twelve parts. There are also special conversion scales which enable distances on drawings made in accordance with imperial dimensions or measurements to be 'read' in metric, and vice versa. Other kinds of scales are available for land survey and town planning drawings.

Scales are usually 300 mm (12") or 150 mm (6") long. The longer is often more convenient in use, but the shorter can be carried in the breast pocket.

Scales are best if oval on section for architectural drawings so that the edges can be brought close to the surface of the paper for marking off or measuring distances. For surveying drawings the flat section is better. Scales should never be used for ruling lines or for any other purpose for which they are not intended; the edges are soon chipped and broken.

See Chapter 5 for descriptions of the scales used for various kinds of drawings.

Protractors

A protractor, Fig. 14, is used for measuring or for setting out angles. It is a semi-circular piece of metal or clear plastic with the arc divided into degrees, reading both to left and right, and with the centre and diameter indicated. The illustration shows how measurements are made. The protractor is placed so that the centre coincides with the apex of the angle and the diameter lies along one line, the position of the other line on the scale giving the reading.

The most convenient sizes have diameters from 100 mm to 150 mm. The transparent protractor is to be preferred, but, for architectural drawings, the instrument is superseded by the adjustable set-square. They are, however, used in the plotting of surveys.

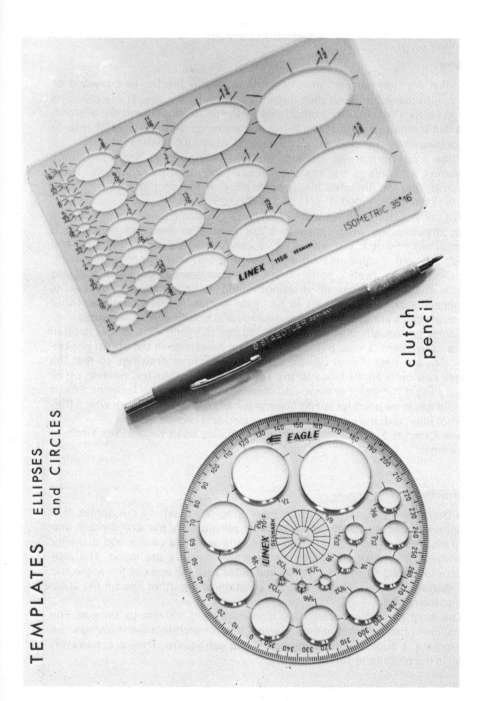

TEMPLATES ELLIPSES and CIRCLES

clutch pencil

Plate 3 Clutch pencil, and clear plastic templates for drawing ellipses and circles of various sizes. Metric and imperial templates are available.

French curves

Fig. 15. illustrates a typical french curve. Made of clear plastic like set-squares, they can be used for drawing irregular or complex curved lines which cannot be conveniently made up of arcs of circles. Many shapes are available, but one is usually sufficient for architectural drawing. They are not essential, and with practice curved lines can be drawn freehand more rapidly and often with better effect. Long, slow curves can be drawn by a series of blended straight lines with acceptable accuracy.

Another device is the flexible ruler consisting of a length of pliable plastic which can be bent to any required curve. Patience is needed to get the correct curvature, but once set the ruler is particularly useful for repetition work.

Small circles and ellipses, or parts thereof, can often be more easily drawn with the help of plastic templates which are available for figures of various metric and imperial sizes.

Pencils

Ordinary drawing pencils are made of cedarwood with 'leads' of compressed clay and graphite, and are about 175 mm (7″) long. The hexagonal type is more easily held in the fingers and the pencil does not roll off the board or table. The value of a pencil is, generally, proportionate to its cost. The best should always be used for drawing. It is false economy to buy cheap pencils, the leads of which are gritty or crumbly and make good draughtsmanship impossible.

Leads are made in varying degrees of hardness and softness, ranging from 9H, the hardest, to 6B, the softest. The extreme grades are very little used. Most drawing can be carried out perfectly well in HB or F. Setting out lines and fine work may be done in H; rough sketching in B. Beginners, particularly, should not use pencils harder than H on cartridge and similar drawing papers. It is a common error to resort to a hard pencil because the point lasts longer and the line is less likely to smudge; properly used, an HB pencil will keep its point just as long and will give a much better line whilst permitting greater freedom of wrist action. Hard pencils bite into the paper and make harsh wiry lines. Smudging is due to carelessness and the student should learn to avoid rubbing the lines of his drawing. This matter has to be stressed, but no real progress in drawing can be made while hard pencils are used. References will be made later to the use of other types of pencil for particular purposes.

When a pencil has been reduced to about half its original length by sharpening, the 'balance' tends to be destroyed and it becomes difficult to control in the fingers. The short length should then be put in a holder, of which there are many types, and so can be used down to the last half-inch. Drawing with a short stub of pencil should not be attempted. In an emergency, a strip of paper can be rolled around the end and gummed, to increase the length and make the pencil more manageable.

Pencil points should be long, round, and evenly tapering, as shown in Fig. 16. The exposed lead should be about 10 mm ($\frac{3}{8}''$) long, and the wood cut back a further 10–15 mm ($\frac{3}{8}''$–$\frac{5}{8}''$). The point must be round, and then, if the pencil is slowly revolved as lines are drawn, it will wear away evenly and remain sharp for some time. So-called chisel points are useless except for compasses. Satisfactory lines cannot be drawn with blunt or jagged points.

The best way of sharpening a pencil is by means of an ordinary penknife. The pencil is held in the left hand, below table-level and pointing downwards so that chips and lead dust fall to the floor and not on the drawing paper, and with the penknife in the right hand inclined cuts are made firmly and regularly to remove the wood around the point. The final sharpening is done with the penknife blade held more or less at right-angles to the lead—this reduces the risk of a sudden cut going right through the point. The fingers should be wiped or blown clean afterwards as a certain amount of dust usually adheres to them and would otherwise get transferred to the paper. Pencils should not be sharpened with the lead held against a thumb—a sure way to make hands and clothes dirty—nor should safety-razor blades be used—they are much too sharp and difficult to control. Sandpaper pads, which unfortunately are sold for sharpening pencil points, are an abomination and should never be used. Not only are they invariably too coarse to produce anything like a good point, but they make an intolerable amount of dust which is rapidly transferred to fingers, clothes, and drawing paper.

Mechanical pencil sharpeners which can be screwed either to the table or wall are generally efficient and save a certain amount of labour, although the points usually need a final touch of the penknife. The small sharpeners that can be held in the fingers are much improved nowadays and are quite useful, although care must be taken that lead dust and shavings fall into a waste basket or are otherwise safely disposed of.

It must be realised that pencils require frequent sharpening when in continuous use, and the beginner should start with a good stock and not be surprised if they wear out quickly.

A popular alternative to the ordinary pencil is the clutch pencil of similar shape and size, consisting of a metal lead holder, into which 2 mm leads of varying degrees, usually from 4B to 6H, or various colours can be inserted. A push button operates the clutch and enables the lead to be withdrawn or fully protected as required. The main advantage of the clutch pencil is that balance is always constant, but it is heavier than the wooden pencil, which is preferred by many architects. A lead pointer is incorporated in the push

16

button, although its use is a potential source of black dust on fingers and paper; it is better to use a special pointing machine. See Plate 3.

Erasers

Alterations, corrections, and the removal of unwanted pencil lines are best made by rubbing with a soft rubber or vinyl eraser. Erasers should be large enough to be easily gripped, but very large rubbers last too long and as the outside surface becomes hard and useless in time, it is probably better to keep to small sizes. When the surface of the eraser is affected it can be cut away or, if not too bad, rubbed clean on an odd scrap of paper—a procedure which is usually necessary if the eraser has not been used for some time.

When a large area of paper has to be cleansed the so-called gum eraser is probably quicker and more gentle to the surface.

For removing soft pencil shading, charcoal and pastel, which are smeared by an ordinary eraser, a special putty rubber must be used.

Ink lines on drawing paper are removed by hard erasers of shape shown in Fig. 17. As usually only a small portion of an ink drawing has to be removed and the surrounding lines disturbed as little as possible, the rubbing is best done through a thin metal or celluloid rubbing shield, Fig. 18, which has openings to suit areas to be erased. Ink lines on tracing paper are best removed by scraping gently backwards and forwards with a safety razor blade held vertically between finger and thumb.

Electrically operated erasers are sometimes installed in large drawing offices. The machine is suspended over the drawing table and is drawn down to the surface of the paper and a small motor rotates rapidly a piece of pencil rubber or ink eraser.

The small particles of rubber which result from rubbing out should be carefully removed from the surface of the paper by blowing or by lightly flicking with a clean, smooth duster. Some draughtsmen can effectively remove the particles with sweeps of the palm of the hand. It is important, however the job is done, to remove every single crumb and, if the drawing is in pencil, not to smear the line.

A special ink eraser, which removes drawing inks from tracing paper and drafting film (but which cannot be used on paper) by chemical process is available. It has the advantage that clean new lines can be immediately drawn over the erased area.

Drawing ink

Waterproof black ink is used for line drawings. It can be taken from small (1-oz.) glass bottles, such as illustrated in Fig. 19, with dropper

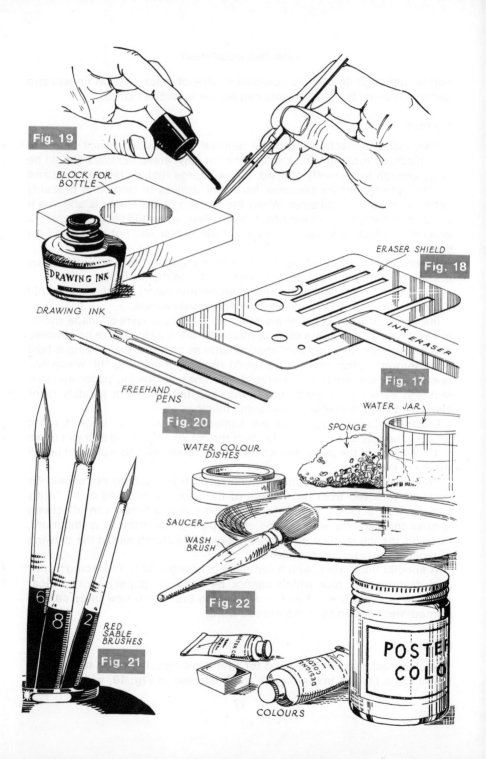

Fig. 19

BLOCK FOR BOTTLE

DRAWING INK

ERASER SHIELD

Fig. 18

INK ERASER

Fig. 17

FREEHAND PENS

Fig. 20

WATER COLOUR DISHES

WATER JAR

SPONGE

SAUCER

WASH BRUSH

Fig. 22

RED SABLE BRUSHES

Fig. 21

POSTER COLO

COLOURS

or pipette for filling ruling pens and other instruments, from plastic bottles for Variant and similar pens, or from special cartridges for Graphos pens, etc. The processes of manufacture vary and the products are not equally good. Some inks are sticky and do not run freely; others are uneven in quality and deteriorate rapidly. A little experimenting will soon reveal the most satisfactory. Not all inks are suitable for the drawing pens described earlier in this chapter or for use on all kinds of film, and the makers' recommendations should be followed.

Containers should always be kept closed, except when pens or instruments are being filled, to keep out dust and to lessen the risk of accidental spills. A useful hint in avoiding the latter is to stand the bottle in a circular hole in a block of wood or cardboard lid of a suitable size. Special iron and rubber bottle-holders are sold for the same purpose. In warm weather it may be found that the ink will run more freely if it is slightly diluted with clean, preferably distilled, water. Bottles should not be shaken once they are in use or any sediment which may have collected at the bottom will be disturbed. Inks should never be mixed and dirty pens must not be used – chemical action may be set up and the ink become lumpy.

Drawing inks are also obtainable in about twenty different colours.

Chinese stick ink

This is referred to later in Chapter 9.

Freehand pens

Every draughtsman requires some good freehand pens. Most manage very well with two, one for very thin lines and the other for medium lines, Fig. 20. Thick lines should always be built up. The ordinary 'mapping' pen is suitable for fine work and small lettering, and an ordinary penholder fitted with a sharp and flexible steel nib (such as Gillott's No. 303) to suit the draughtsman's hand will usually suffice for other purposes. Most pens have to be worn in with use, and then, when working well, become a valued possession.

Lettering pens and stencils

These are described later in Chapter 4

Colours

Water-colours are extensively used for drawings of all types, from the conventional indication of materials on constructional drawings to full colour perspectives. For all purposes the colours are usually taken from tubes or pans; sticks and cakes are not often seen. Using colours from pans is thought to be more economical, but if left for any length of time the material becomes hard and is difficult to soften again quickly. Tube colours keep softer longer and are more quickly mixed and blended, but a certain amount is wasted every time they are used as it is impossible to calculate exactly how much to squeeze out. Tube colours keep cleaner; pans, especially if in a colour box, often get others colours mixed with them.

Further references are made to the use of water-colours later in this book, and some pigments are named. The beginner should purchase colours as required and so build up a working range gradually instead of starting out with an arbitrary selection, many of which may never be used. At the same time, only experience can reveal the possibilities of each, so a little exploration is to be encouraged.

A colour box is not a necessity and may be a nuisance; the colours can be kept quite well in any small box.

Artists' quality water-colours should always be used for work of any importance. Other qualities are more or less adulterated and good results cannot be obtained.

Poster colours

These, in small or medium size pots and tubes, also play a large part in the colouring of many types of drawings. For similar purposes, but for better results, designers' quality gouache colours can be substituted. Further references are made later to technique.

Care and common sense will avoid the wasting and spoiling of colours. Caps should be replaced on tubes and jars promptly after use to prevent the contents becoming hard and unusable. Dirty brushes and dirty water should never be allowed to touch fresh colour. When mixing colours the brush must be rinsed clean before a new colour is taken up. The water jar should be large, with a wide mouth, preferably of clear glass, so that it can be seen when the water gets muddy. The water should be changed when it becomes discoloured.

Dishes

Two or three large saucers and about half a dozen good-sized water-colour dishes, as sold in sets or nests, are required for mixing colours and holding washes. They should be glazed and white; coloured and patterned dishes affect the apparent hue of the pigments. Little jars or tins should not be used as heavy colours deposit particles of pigment at the bottom and they are not properly stirred up in the wash. Slopes and slant slabs are not much used as they do not hold a sufficient quantity of liquid for large drawings. Dishes should be thoroughly cleansed after use.

Brushes

Most requirements are met by three red sable brushes, sizes 2, 6, and 8, in metal ferrules and wood handles, Fig. 21, and one camel-hair 'wash brush' in a quill, Fig. 22.

Brushes vary in quality and must be carefully selected. A poor brush can be a serious hindrance to success. Sable brushes should come to a fine point and should have plenty of spring in the hairs. The point of a brush can be tested by dipping it in water and drawing the hairs along the palm of the hand, turning it round at the same time. The hairs should come easily to a fine point — if not, the brush should be rejected. The 'spring' can be tested by gently pressing the hairs against the hand or other firm surface and feeling how they straighten again when the pressure is released. A brush without spring is of little value. The spring is soon destroyed, incidentally, by rough usage.

Wash brushes hold a good quantity of water, but do not come to a point, and for this reason some draughtsmen prefer a large-size red sable, say No. 12.

Brushes must be kept clean. Colour should never be allowed to dry in the hairs. Brushes should be wiped carefully on a clean rag after washing and left standing upright in a jar, as illustrated in Fig. 21. They must not be left with the hairs in the water jar. If they have to be carried about they should be tightly held by a rubber band to a stiff strip of card somewhat longer than the longest brush or put in a plastic tube so that the hairs are protected.

Drawing pins and other fixings

Small, flat-headed pins are best for fixing the paper to the board in most cases. Large ones are unsatisfactory as they catch the T-square. They should be well-made of brass with sharp round points. The type with the 'point' stamped out of the head is of little use.

As the heads should hold the paper, the pins must be pressed well into the board. Four pins, one at each corner, should be sufficient if put in about 12 mm from the edge of the sheet. Whenever a drawing is re-pinned the previous pin-holes, unless enlarged or torn, should be used again. Pins can usually be taken out easily by finger and thumb-nail, but the blade of an old penknife can be inserted under the head to prise it up in the case of a stubborn one.

Other means of holding the paper to the board are spring steel clips, staples, and Scotch drafting tape. Clips are not always secure and sometimes get in the way of border lines, etc. Staples, the smallest size is best, are quick and convenient for fastening the paper and do not interfere with the running of T-square and set-square, but are a nuisance to get out, although the blade of the old penknife employed with dexterity facilitates matters. Drafting tape

TRACING PAPER

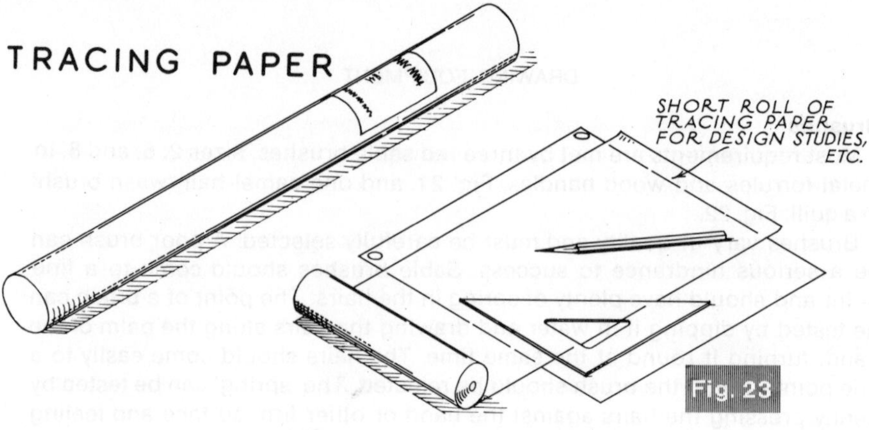

SHORT ROLL OF TRACING PAPER FOR DESIGN STUDIES, ETC.

Fig. 23

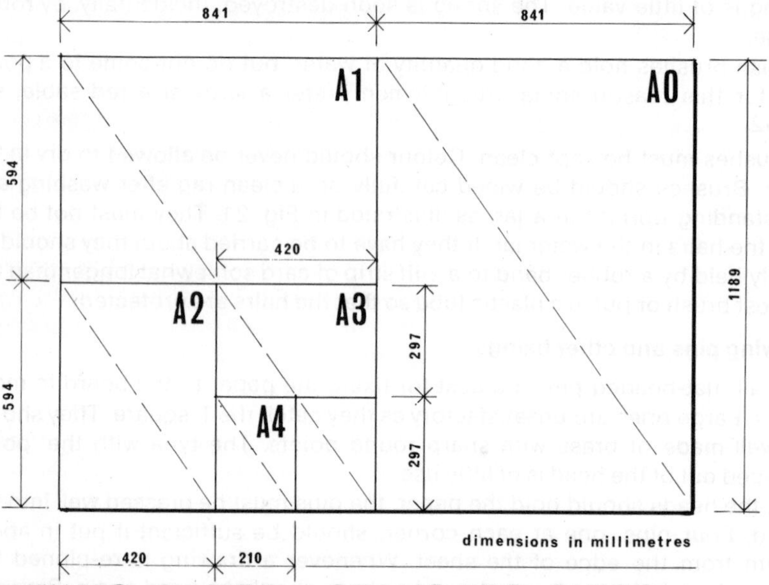

841

841

A1

A0

594

1189

420

A2

A3

297

594

A4

297

420

210

dimensions in millimetres

Fig. 24

DRAWING PAPER - STANDARD SIZES

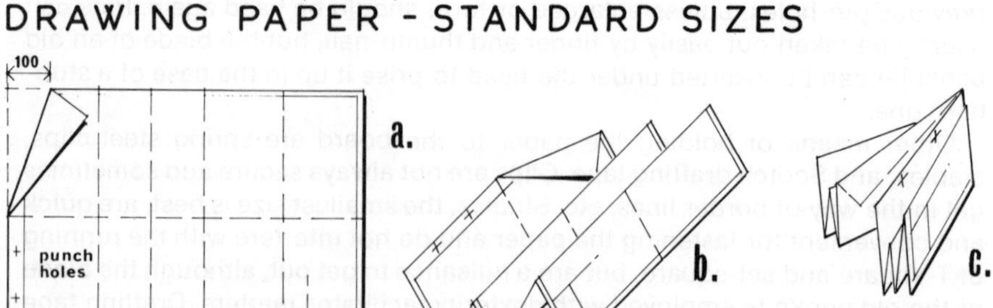

100

punch holes

a.

210   =   =   184   184

b.

c.

FOLDING FOR FILING

A1

Fig. 25

tends to be an untidy and rather messy fixing method except for short-term use. For holding one piece of tracing paper over another, especially where the piece if relatively small and pins cannot be used because they would damage the sheet below as well as get in the way of T-square and set-square, transparent self-adhesive tape, such as Sellotape, is most suitable as it can be peeled away on completion without affecting the paper.

Drawing papers

There are two main classifications of drawing papers: (1) machine-made papers, such as cartridge, which are used for exercises and line drawings, and (2) handmade or mouldmade papers used for rendered drawings. Mention is made of other types of paper, where necessary, in later chapters.

Cartridge

This is sold in rolls and A-size sheets, including pads of 30 sheets up to A2 size, as well as in the old standard sizes of antiquarian, double elephant, and imperial. Fig. 24 shows A sheet sizes drawn to a comparative scale.

The paper is made in three thicknesses: 'thin', 'medium', and 'stout'. The 'thin' is usually too flimsy to be of much value. It is also obtainable in rolls either unmounted or mounted on cotton or holland. The rolls can be conveniently cut into the various standard sheets or used for extra large drawings, and are probably more economical for the busy office.

Unmounted cartridge paper has right and wrong sides which can be distinguished by examination – the wrong side has a slightly but regularly pitted surface, and the cut edge of the sheet is usually turned down towards the wrong side.

The surface is fairly satisfactory for pencil drawing and the 'stout' quality will take ink moderately well, but it is not really suitable for colour washes except those of a most limited nature. White cartridge paper, which is usually of better quality, is to be preferred to that which is cream in colour.

Handmade and mouldmade papers

These are obtainable in sheets of standard sizes, and usually in three surfaces: HP (Hot Pressed) – smooth; NOT – medium; R – rough. The first-named is the kind most used for pencil and ink drawings and various types of renderings, particularly work in wash. All the papers can be 'stretched' as later described in Chapter 9, and some can be obtained already mounted on stiff card or board. Water colour paper is also sold in pads.

Ordinary drawing board and tee-square (right foreground). Less precise but simple, versatile and portable. Cheaper. *Parallel motion (right background).* Special drawing board with straight-edge, counterbalanced by weights, moving up and down for ruling horizontal lines. Ordinary set squares can be used for vertical and angled lines.

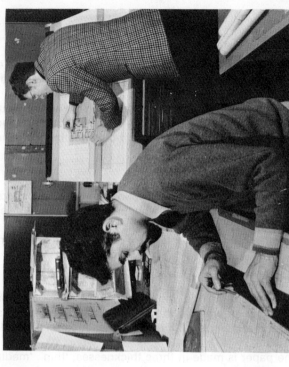

Drafting machine (left). Such machines are of various sizes and can be fixed to any drawing board of corresponding size. The arms maintain horizontal and vertical ruling edges, or can be set to any angle. Interchangeable arms provide alternative scales. Ordinary scales and set-squares are not required.

Plate 4 Basic types of drawing board.

Plastic-coated card

For particularly fine pencil line and pen and ink drawings some draughtsmen prefer an extremely smooth plastic-coated card, such as CS10. Great care is needed, however, in working with this medium as ink lines are easily smudged. Any removal of lines must be made by gently rubbing with a soft eraser.

Sizes of drawings

The advantages of standardised sizes for drawings are that they enable a more economical use of drawing and tracing paper, sensitised paper and cloth for prints, etc., to be made, and that the binding together and storing of the drawings becomes easier.

Standardisation is almost automatic when A sizes are used and sheets of different size can be folded to a common size for filing in folders, for example A1 sheet as illustrated by Fig. 25.

For folding for transmission by post or for loose storage drawings can be similarly folded. In all cases the title block appears uppermost for ready reference.

The folding of drawings is not, of course, to be recommended for general use. Drawings should preferably be kept flat. If rolled for carrying, the roll should be as loose as possible. Drawings and prints to be used in quantity surveyors' offices should always be dispatched rolled, not folded.

Tracing paper, cloth and film

These materials are specially treated paper and linen, and polyester film of transparent or semi-transparent nature; when placed over an original drawing they allow the lines underneath to be clearly seen and so copied or traced. The tracings thus made can then be used as negatives for the making of any number of further copies by the photo-printing processes described in Chapter 7. Drawings can of course be made directly on the materials in question. Almost all production drawings are negatives of one kind or another.

Tracing paper is most economical if purchased in rolls, but for final drawings it is increasingly the practice in offices and in schools of architecture to use pre-cut sheets in the A sizes, often with printed border lines, title blocks, and sometimes modular or other grids, etc. Tracing paper can be roughly classified into three categories: thin, medium and stout, and two surfaces: smooth and rough. Different makes vary, however, so that it is difficult to particularise as to the most suitable; personal preference plays some part in selection. Thin papers are usually good enough for preliminary sketches but are too flimsy for final negatives. Smooth surfaces are best for

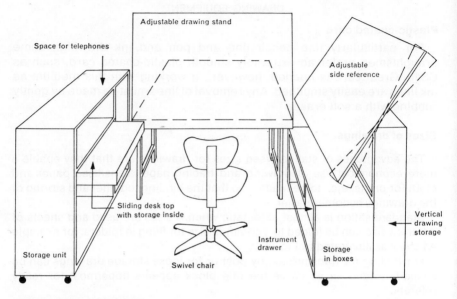

MOVABLE WORK PLACE

Labels: Adjustable drawing stand; Space for telephones; Adjustable side reference; Sliding desk top with storage inside; Vertical drawing storage; Storage unit; Instrument drawer; Storage in boxes; Swivel chair

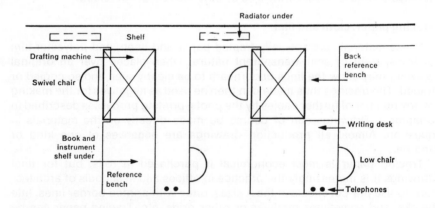

FIXED WORK PLACE

Labels: Radiator under; Shelf; Drafting machine; Back reference bench; Swivel chair; Writing desk; Book and instrument shelf under; Low chair; Reference bench; Telephones

Plate 5 Examples of drawing-table arrangements reproduced by permission from the RIBA *Handbook of Architectural Practice and Management*, Part 2.670—Equipment of Drawing Offices.

pencil drawings, as the rough kinds wear down the leads and tend to smudge and smear. Further remarks on technique are made in Chapter 7. For roughing out designs and many other uses rolls in short widths are handy, Fig. 23.

Tracing cloth is nearly always supplied in rolls, although short lengths can be purchased. The material is usually tinted blue, but white is also available. It is much more expensive than tracing paper, and is used mainly for master negatives in ink, but to a lesser extent than formerly as it is being superseded by film. Film is also expensive but has superior transparency and is stated to be stretch-proof and waterproof. It should be used in accordance with the manufacturers' recommendations, for example in regard to type of backing sheets, preparation before inking, and use of erasers.

Detail paper

This paper, which is supplied in rolls and pads of 100 sheets (called layout pads) up to A2 size, is like thick tracing paper and is used chiefly for preliminary sketch drawings and lay-outs, and for final large-scale details. It is transparent enough for copying by tracing yet is white enough for original work to show up clearly and takes coloured pencils or felt and fibre pens satisfactorily. Acceptable dye-line prints can usually be obtained, especially from ink or strong pencil lines. Detail paper is also commonly used for computer graphic output.

Backing sheets

Drawing boards should be covered with backing sheets, over which the actual drawing paper or tracing media is placed to provide a firm, even working surfaces. This is particularly important if boards have become pitted, scored, damaged or worn.

Thick white cartridge paper is a satisfactory material, cheap enough to be discarded as it becomes soiled; drawing pins can be used. Other and harder materials for backing sheets of a semi-permanent nature are thick, flexible plastic sheets usually with a green surface and cellulose-acetate sheets, which can be printed to standard lay-outs and grids.

In connection with backing sheets, a useful device to minimise the marking of drawings by rubbing of the T-square is the fixing of a strip of folded drawing or tracing paper — three or four thicknesses are sufficient — about 20 mm wide along the left-hand edge of the board. Fixing by drawing pins or staples at the ends only is best.

Drawing boards with an integral plastic surface do not normally require backing sheets, but for working on tracing paper a white under sheet is an advantage.

Drawing tables

It is beyond the scope of this book to deal in detail with major items of drawing office equipment: for this information reference can be made to the appropriate British Standard Institution's publications, to Part 2.670 of the R.I.B.A. *Handbook of Architectural Practice and Management*, and to manufacturers' catalogues.

However, the two most common working arrangements are: the drawing table, about 920 mm high, with level top on which the drawing board is placed, usually tilted slightly by means of a block or tapered sub-frame, and used in conjunction with a T-square and set-squares; or one of the various types of drawing boards mounted on a stand or secured at the front of a table and, although capable of adjustment, used in an almost upright position in combination with a parallel motion sliding horizontal rule and/or drafting machine (Plate 4).

The first arrangement has the merits of simplicity, economy, adaptability and mobility — it is little trouble to transport the ordinary board and T-square — which are certainly advantageous for the student. Drawings have to be made standing or sitting on a high stool, which many people prefer for freedom of movement, but a real disadvantage of the arrangement is that as the board cannot be tilted more than 15 degrees without the T-square and set-squares slipping down, there is often difficulty in working comfortably at the top of larger boards. Although there are ways of mitigating this problem, the second arrangement does overcome it and also enables the draughtsman, if he so wishes, to work sitting in a swivel chair (Plate 5); this arrangement, provided the board is kept upright, is also more economical in floor space. But it is virtually a fixed arrangement more suited to the office than the studio.

In all cases there should be nearby horizontal surfaces for the laying out of reference drawings and other papers and for placing instruments, together with drawers and cupboards for storage.

Minor items of equipment

In addition to the essential equipment already described, the following should be readily available for use as the need arises:

1. A good pair of scissors. Cutting knives, e.g. a Stanley knife for thick card and a lighter knife, of which there are many kinds, for thin card and paper. In this connection, a metal rule or straight-edge is useful.
2. A magnifying glass for examining small scale maps and drawings and for executing fine draughting.
3. Rolls of drafting tape – Scotch tape and masking tape are the same thing – and of Sellotape or similar. Arrowmounts, obtainable from photographic shops; these are small adhesive squares for the invisible mounting of photographs, but they are also

28

DRAWING EQUIPMENT

useful for mounting drawings on paper (unless very flimsy) and thin card without the risk of cockling or distortion that the application of gums or pastes might cause. However, conventional gums and pastes are needed, and aerosol spray adhesives for heavier or other appropriate purposes.

4. A supply of pre-printed gridded paper, i.e. divided into squares of 2mm or larger, for use under sheets in freehand approximate scale drawings on tracing or detail paper. Pads of tracing paper with fold-under grids are useful in many situations.
5. A handy scratch pad for notes, memos, rough calculations, testing pens, etc.
6. A clean duster.
7. For the safe-keeping or transporting of personal drawings a good portfolio, while not a necessity, is desirable. The simplest kind can be made from two equal rectangular pieces of stout cardboard of adequate size loosely connected down one pair of long sides and provided with tapes at intervals along the other edges for tying together. They can, however, be purchased ready-made as can more elaborate flexible zip-around portfolios. The latter are only suitable for mounted drawings. Plastic and cardboard stoppered tubes of various sizes can be used for mailing or carrying rolled drawings.

2
Line Drawing

Pencil drawing

Line drawing in pencil should be mastered first; it is the best introduction to drawing in any medium.

Almost everyone has 'drawn' with a pencil from an early age, but little benefit is usually derived from this kind of intermittent and undirected practice. Only bad habits seem to be formed. It is wise, therefore, on setting out to make a serious study of draughtsmanship, to forget any previous ideas of drawing, and to start as if pencil and paper had never been handled before.

In the previous chapter something was said about the materials required and the use of various instruments. Preliminary exercises in pencil drawing can be carried out with the aid of drawing board, T-square and set-squares, H and HB pencils, and good quality cartridge paper.

The first step is to learn how to draw straight lines. Straight lines in pencil should be *firm*, *clean*, and of *even strength*. Start by pinning down the paper, right side up, squarely on the board. Sharpen an HB pencil, as previously described. Give the T-square a wipe with a duster and place it on the board with the head against the left-hand edge — if you are left-handed you can get a special T-square which can be held against the right-hand edge of the board, but most left-handed draughtsmen seem to manage quite well in the ordinary way. Holding the T-square steady in a position towards the top of the sheet, draw with the pencil along the ruling edge from left to right, pressing the point on the paper sufficiently to make a clear line, but not so hard as to make a groove. Turn the pencil slowly round in the fingers as you move it along. The completed line should be exactly the same thickness and strength throughout its length. Make sure that the pencil keeps the same angle with the T-square from start to finish or the line will be wavy.

Now move the T-square down the paper and repeat the operation. If necessary, try to improve on the first line. Draw a number of parallel lines in this way until you are satisfied with the quality of the lines. If you find the line becoming 'woolly', Fig. 26, it is probably because the pencil needs

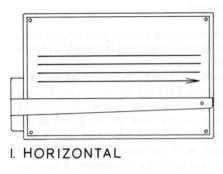

1. HORIZONTAL

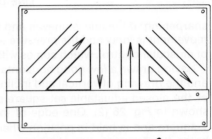

2. VERTICAL AND 45°

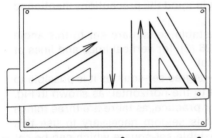

3. VERTICAL, 30° AND 60°

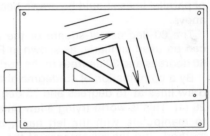

4. 15° AND 75°

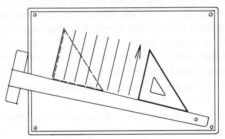

5. PARALLEL *TO ANY GIVEN LINE*

LINES SHOULD BE FIRM, CLEAN, AND OF EVEN QUALITY

NOT COARSE AND 'WOOLLY'

NOR DOUBLE AND BROKEN

STRAIGHT LINES

sharpening; if the line is uneven and broken, it may be that your arm or wrist movement is jerky and the pressure erratic; to correct this is merely a matter of muscular control, which comes with practice.

Having drawn a few good horizontal lines, pass on to the use of set-squares and the drawing of vertical and inclined lines. Take the 45-degree set-square or the closed adjustable set-square and with this practise drawing lines, as shown in Fig. 26 (2). One edge of the set-square rests on the blade of the T-square and is held in position where required by the left-hand, which also holds the T-square firm. Lines are drawn with the pencil along the other edges of the set-square in the directions indicated by the arrows. A number of parallel lines should be drawn bearing in mind the precautions mentioned above.

The 60-degree set-square or the adjustable set-square set to this angle can be used similarly, as shown in Fig. 26 (3), for vertical lines and lines at 60 degrees and 30 degrees to the horizontal.

By a combination of 45-degree and 60-degree set-squares it is possible to draw lines at 15 degrees and 75 degrees to the horizontal, as shown in Fig. 26 (4). This is worth trying a few times for practice, as there are three things to manipulate with the left hand, but it is seldom necessary to use this method, and the advantages of the adjustable set-square which can be set to these and any angle in such cases is obvious.

When a number of lines are to be drawn parallel to an inclined line, as may occur in the setting-out of roof-tiling, etc., the method shown in Fig. 26 (5) can be used. Place a set-square along the inclined line so that another of its edges is at right-angles to the line. Then gently bring up the T-square until it is against this edge of the set-square, hold it tightly, and then, by moving the set-square along the T-square to the required positions, lines parallel to the first one can be drawn. This method should be practised with lines at varying angles.

Remember in all cases to keep the pencil well sharpened and held properly against the ruling edge.

The second step in learning to use the pencil is to combine lines so as to construct figures and shapes, e.g. squares, rectangles, etc. Fig. 27 (1, 2 and 3) shows the setting-up of a rectangle. Two parallel horizontal lines are first drawn any suitable distance apart, say, 50–60 mm. The lines should be faint though clear and regular. Their exact length is not important. On the lower line two points, A and B, are marked (in the example the distance between A and B is made the same as the distance between the lines, so the resulting figure is a square). Using the set-square, two vertical lines are now drawn through A and B to cross the first two lines. These also are faint lines and are termed *construction lines*, and to bring out the required figure they have to be strengthened where necessary. This is shown in Fig.

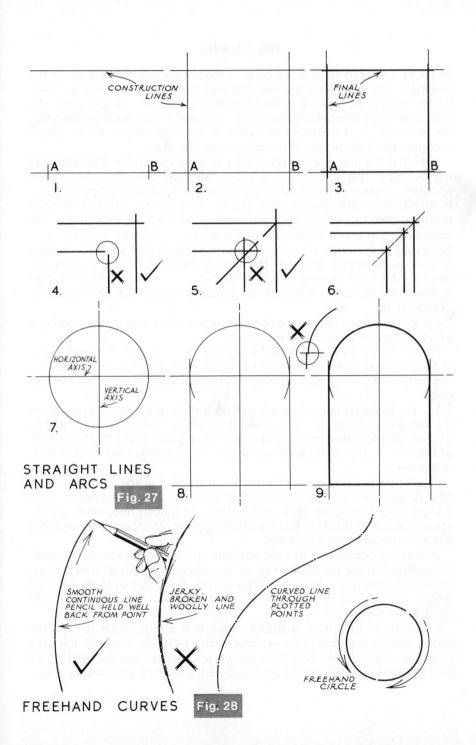

CONSTRUCTION
LINES

FINAL
LINES

| A | B | A | B | A | B |

1.   2.   3.

4.   5.   6.

HORIZONTAL
AXIS

VERTICAL
AXIS

7.

STRAIGHT LINES
AND ARCS   **Fig. 27**

8.   9.

SMOOTH
CONTINUOUS LINE
PENCIL HELD WELL
BACK FROM POINT

JERKY.
BROKEN AND
WOOLLY LINE

CURVED LINE
THROUGH
PLOTTED
POINTS

FREEHAND
CIRCLE

FREEHAND   CURVES   **Fig. 28**

27 (3) by a thickening of those parts of the lines which actually define the rectangle, but in a pencil drawing the lines need not necessarily be made thicker as long as they are made stronger, i.e. 'blacker', by going over the faint lines and putting more pressure on the pencil. Care must be taken that the 'lining in', as it is sometimes called, is done exactly over the construction lines and that irregular or double lines do not result.

Note that the final lines cross slightly where they meet at the corners of the rectangle. This is done to give added definition to the shape and to give a sharper, cleaner appearance to the drawing. It is a widely adopted custom in architectural draughtsmanship, but is not generally used for finished town-planning, surveying, and engineering drawing because of possible confusion, and junctions are accurately made in works of these kinds. In architectural drawings, however, it seldom happens that an exact meeting of lines is necessary, and it is therefore a waste of time, apart from the tendency for such corners to look 'rounded'. Nevertheless, the lines must certainly not fall short, although the crossing should not be irregular or exaggerated.

Fig. 27 (4) shows the crossing of lines at a junction to a larger size, and also a bad example where the lines fail to meet.

Fig. 27 (5) shows the making of a junction of three lines. It is inadvisable in finished drawings to make them all cross. It is generally better to let the two outer ones cross and to bring in the third accurately to the meeting point.

Fig. 27 (6) shows the right-angle junctions of several pairs of lines. When the first pair of lines has been drawn it is helpful to draw a faint line at 45 degrees through the junction and so provide a guide to the meeting points of the others. This also saves setting out the spacing of the lines in both directions.

In addition to being made to cross at junctions, the lines can be made a little stronger at these points by putting more pressure on the pencil. Such a slight emphasis to the ends of final lines can quickly become an unconscious habit with practice, and the effect is greatly to increase the legibility and attractiveness of the drawings.

In drawing circles and arcs the positions of the centres should be established first and the principal axes, i.e. horizontal and vertical lines passing through the centres, should be lightly drawn. Along one of these lines the length of the radius in each case can be marked and the curve drawn with compasses, Fig. 27 (7).

If arcs are to be joined to straight lines, it is always better to draw the curves first. In the case of an example such as Fig. 27 (8 and 9), the axes should be drawn lightly first, then the arc with compasses also lightly, and then the vertical lines from the points where the arc cuts the horizontal axis.

The strengthening of the lines should be done in the same order, i.e. the arc, or semi-circle as it is, first, and then the vertical lines.

When the above elementary steps in draughtsmanship have been mastered, a sound basis has been laid for the making of any drawing in line. A word might be said here on freehand drawing, although this is dealt with further in a later chapter, as a certain amount comes into almost every drawing. The main principle is to get the same quality and strength in the freehand lines as in those drawn with instruments. The tendency to be guarded against is the coarsening of the freehand lines. It is a matter of practice, but keep the pencil well sharpened and try to draw smooth, *continuous* freehand lines with even pressure. Avoid 'sketchy' lines made with jerky movements. Hold the pencil well back from the point for long, flowing curves. Sometimes, when the curve is long and sinuous, it is easier to draw if a number of points along its length are first lightly plotted. Small freehand circles can be best drawn as two curves, as indicated by the arrows in Fig. 28.

Keeping the drawing clean

It is important to keep drawings as clean as possible and to preserve the surface of the paper, especially if colour is to be used. To these ends the following points should be constantly kept in mind:

1. Use clean equipment and instruments and good pencils.
2. Keep hands clean and touch the paper with the fingers as little as possible.
3. Avoid unnecessary rubbing of the surface of the paper with T-squares and set-squares. Move them by lifting rather than by sliding. A piece of paper folded two or three times to make a narrow strip about 1″ wide and pinned along the left-hand side of the board is helpful in lifting the T-square blade just clear of the paper and so reducing friction.
4. Sharpen pencils away from the drawing board and table.
5. Make any erasures carefully and remove all rubber crumbs by blowing or lightly flicking with clean handkerchief or hand.
6. If much drawing is to be done on several small areas of the sheet, cover the whole of it with tracing or detail paper in which suitable flap 'windows' through which to work can be cut.

Inking-in

If a drawing is to be finished in ink, it is always better to draw it first completely in pencil, taking just as much care as if it were to be so finished. The inking then becomes a straightforward process without innumerable breaks for the working-out of details and the correcting of mistakes, and time is thereby probably saved in the long run. There is no excuse for making a care-less, dirty pencil drawing on the grounds that it is subsequently to be inked-in.

The methods of using drawing pens and other instruments have already been described. The sequence in inking-in should generally be as follows:

1. Centre lines.
2. Circles and arcs — drawn with ink compasses.
3. Horizontal lines.
4. Vertical and inclined lines.
5. Hatching and blacking-in of sectional parts, etc.
6. Dimensions lines.
7. Freehand lines, arrows and arrow-heads, dimension figures, notes.
8. Titles, etc.

To avoid being held up while some lines are drying, it may not be possible to keep strictly to this sequence, but systematic working reduces the chances of errors and omissions. As with pencil drawing, main outlines should be strengthened for increased definition and meeting lines should slightly cross in the case of architectural drawings.

If erasures are necessary, an ink rubber (page 17) can be used *gently* until the lines or blots are removed. For small areas or short lines a sharp razor-blade held vertically to the surface of the paper and moved quickly backwards and forwards will do the job. The surface must not be roughened or subsequent ink lines will run and become ragged, although this tendency can be overcome to some extent by smoothing the affected area by pressure from a hard, rounded object such as a table-knife handle.

When the inking has been completed and checked, a soft pencil rubber should be used over the sheet to remove any dirt and pencil lines.

Geometrical drawing

Having acquired the elementary technique of line drawing, the next require-ment is practice and yet more practice. Geometrical drawing is an excellent way of obtaining this practice and at the same time a knowledge of various constructions and figures continually used in the making of technical drawings.

Division of lines

Fig. 29 shows a number of ways of dividing straight lines into equal parts.
1. By trial and error, using dividers. This is a fairly quick way and with

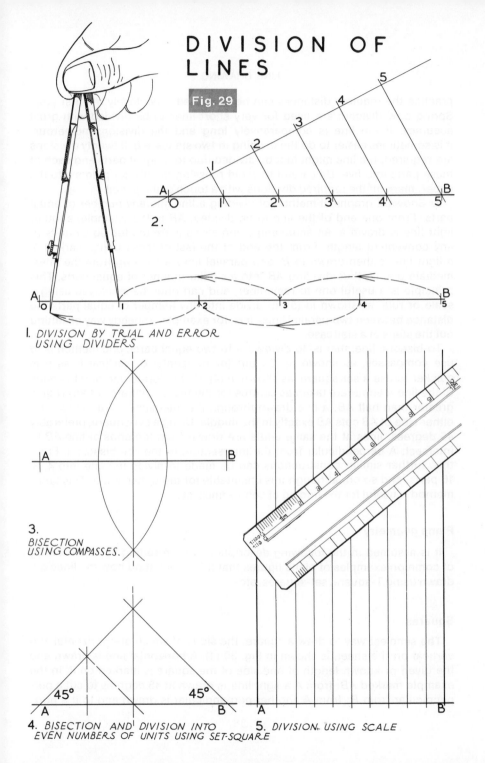

DIVISION OF LINES

Fig. 29

1. DIVISION BY TRIAL AND ERROR USING DIVIDERS

2.

3. BISECTION USING COMPASSES.

4. BISECTION AND DIVISION INTO EVEN NUMBERS OF UNITS USING SET-SQUARE

5. DIVISION USING SCALE

practice the required distances can be estimated very closely the first time. Spring-bow dividers are used for very short lines to be divided with great accuracy. If the line is comparatively long and the divisions numerous, it is sometimes easier to do the dividing in two stages, e.g. if twenty divisions are required, the line might first be divided into four equal parts and each of these parts into five. Be careful to avoid pressing the divider points into the paper: mark off the required divisions with a touch of the pencil.

2. Shows a graphical method of dividing a line into any number of equal parts. From one end of the line to be divided, *AB* in the example, another light line is drawn at an acute angle and along it are plotted equal units of any convenient length. From the end of the last of these units, marked 5, a light line is then drawn to *B*, and parallel lines are drawn from the intermediate points, thus dividing *AB* into a similar number of equal parts. This principle is a useful one to remember, and can often be employed using a scale or rule, as shown in (5), to divide into any number of equal parts the distance between two parallel lines. It is, for example, a speedy way of setting out the steps of a staircase.

To bisect a line, that is, to divide it into two equal parts, one method is to use compasses, as shown in (3), but for horizontal or vertical lines it is quicker to use a set-square, as shown in (4). By the former method the ends of the line *A* and *B* are taken as centres for the two similar arcs of any radius greater than half *AB*; a line drawn through the intersections of the arcs on either side of *AB* cuts *AB* exactly in the middle. Using a set-square, preferably 45 degrees, lines at the same angle are drawn from the ends of line *AB* to intersect. A perpendicular from the intersection to the line bisects it. From this, further similar constructions can be made to divide the line into 4, 8, 16 parts, and so on, although it is unsuitable for more than eight. This latter method is useful for the finding of centre-lines, etc.

Plane geometry

It is assumed in the following descriptions of the setting up and drawing of common examples of plane figures that it is understood how the lines are drawn using T-square, set-squares, etc.

Squares

The simplest way to draw a square, the sides of which are horizontal and vertical on the sheet, is shown in Fig. 30 (1). A horizontal line is drawn and the given or known length of one side of the square is marked on it, in the example marked *AB*; from *A* a light line is drawn at 45 degrees to cut a perpendicular from *B*; from *A* another perpendicular is drawn and to it a hori-

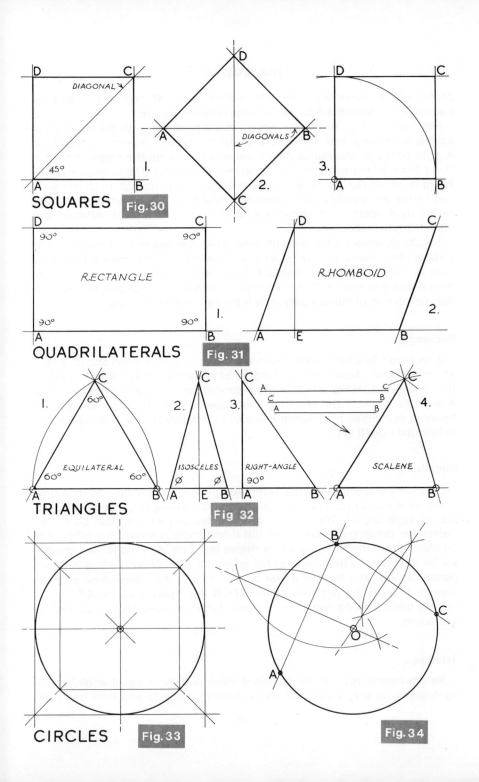

SQUARES   Fig.30

QUADRILATERALS   Fig. 31

TRIANGLES   Fig 32

CIRCLES   Fig.33

Fig.34

zontal line is drawn from the intersection of the 45-degree line and the perpendicular from B, i.e. C. ABCD is the required square.

Alternatively, Fig. 30 (3), the square could be drawn with the aid of compasses or dividers. Having drawn side AB and erected a perpendicular from A, with centre A and radius AB an arc is drawn to cut the perpendicular at D. A horizontal line through D and a perpendicular from B complete the figure. There is, of course, no need to draw a complete arc from B to D; it is sufficient if the arc merely cuts the perpendicular from A. Similarly, AD could be set off by dividers or, in some case, marked off from a scale, although this often leads to inaccuracy.

Fig. 30 (2) shows a square with sides at 45 degrees to the horizontal and vertical. This could be drawn by first drawing side AC, then a horizontal from A and a 45-degree line from C to cut it at B, and then 45-degree lines from A and B to meet at D. A line joining C and D is vertical and, incidentally, the intersection of the two diagonals is the centre of the square.

Rectangles

A rectangle is a four-sided figure with equal opposite sides and its angles all right-angles. Assuming the lengths of its sides are known, one side is first drawn, AB, in Fig. 31 (1), and perpendiculars are erected from A and B. Along one of these the length of the adjoining side AD is set off, and the figure is completed by drawing a line from D parallel to AB, cutting the perpendicular from B at C.

Rhomboid

Of other parallelograms, the setting-up of which is similar, the rhomboid is shown in Fig. 31 (2). The rhomboid is a figure having equal opposite sides, but no right-angles. The lengths of the sides and angles must be known before the drawing can be made, but if one angle is known the others can be calculated. One side, say AB, is drawn and from A at the known angle is set off AD equal to the length of the adjoining side. From D a line is drawn parallel to AB, and from B a line parallel to AD; the intersection of these lines at C gives the required figure, ADCB. A perpendicular to AB from D gives a line DE along which the distance between sides AB and DC can be measured.

Triangles

An equilateral triangle (three equal sides and three equal angles, each 60 degrees), is very simply set up by drawing one side and from each end

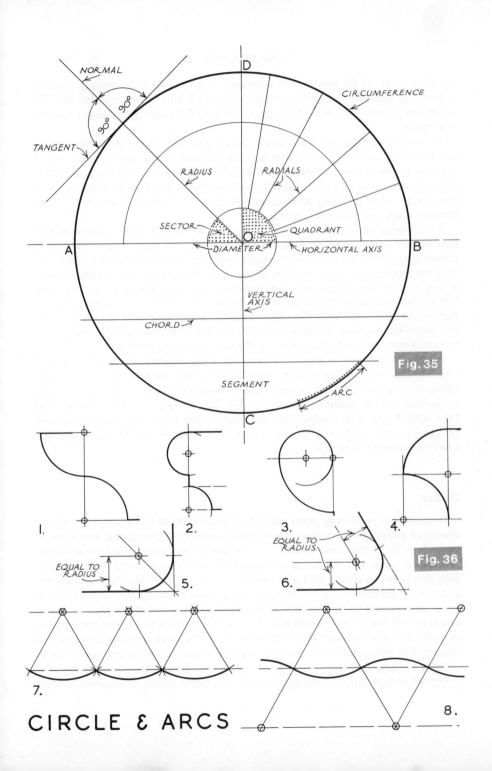

NORMAL

90° 90° 90°

TANGENT

CIRCUMFERENCE

RADIUS

RADIALS

SECTOR

QUADRANT

A

DIAMETER

HORIZONTAL AXIS

B

VERTICAL AXIS

CHORD

Fig. 35

SEGMENT

ARC

C

1. 2. 3. 4.

EQUAL TO RADIUS

EQUAL TO RADIUS

5. 6.

Fig. 36

EQUAL TO RADIUS

7.

8.

CIRCLE & ARCS

drawing lines at 60 degrees to intersect, Fig. 32 (1). Alternatively, having drawn one side *AB*, arcs with centres at *A* and *B* and radius equal to *AB* can be drawn to intersect at *C*. Joining *A* and *B* to *C* by straight lines completes the figure.

An isosceles triangle (two equal sides and two equal angles) can be similarly constructed. By drawing first the unequal side and from each end of it drawing lines at the known equal angles to intersect, Fig. 32(2), or, alternatively, having drawn one side *AB*, with centres *A* and *B* and radius equal to the equal sides drawing arcs to intersect at *C*. Joining *A* and *B* to *C* by straight lines completes the figure.

A right-angled triangle (having two sides at right-angles to each other) can be set up by drawing one side adjacent to the right-angle, erecting a perpendicular of required length at one end and by joining the two free ends. This method applies if the lengths of the two sides at right-angles are known. If only one of these sides and the third side is known, the method is to draw the known side adjacent to the right-angle; at one end of it to erect a perpendicular and then with the other end as centre and with radius equal to the other known side to draw an arc to cut the perpendicular. A line drawn from the intersection to the centre of the arc completes the figure.

To draw a scalene triangle (one having three unequal sides and unequal angles), the lengths of the sides being known, the method—which is applicable to any triangle and is particularly useful when no side is horizontal or vertical on the sheet—is shown in Fig. 32 (4). Any side *AB* is drawn and then with *A* and *B* as centres and with radii equal to the lengths of the other two sides, arcs are drawn to intersect at *C*. Joining *A* and *B* to *C* by straight lines completes the figure.

Circles

Reference has already been made to the drawing of circles and the advisability of establishing centres by lightly drawing the horizontal and vertical axes. Fig. 33 shows how circles can be drawn around and within squares. In the first case, the middle of the square is found by drawing its diagonals; with this point as centre and with radius equal to half the length of a diagonal a circle can be drawn to pass through the corners of the square. In the second case, the middle of the square is found as before, but the radius is made equal to half the length of one side, that is, the pencil point of the compasses is made to pass through the intersections of the axes and the sides of the square. It is obvious from the foregoing how squares can be drawn within or outside circles.

Fig. 34 shows the plotting of a centre of a circle which is required to pass through the points *A*, *B*, and *C*. *AB* and *BC* are both bisected by the method described in Fig. 31 (3). The point *O*, the intersection of the bisectors, is the centre of the circle.

Fig. 35 illustrates various terms descriptive of parts of circles and of lines in relation to circles. Brief definitions, in addition to those previously mentioned, are:

Arc	— A part of the circumference.
Chord	— A straight line, shorter than the diameter, terminated by the circumference at both ends.
Circumference	— A curve line equidistant from a point, the *centre*, confining the circle.
Diameter	— A straight line passing through the centre of the circle and terminated at both ends by the circumference.
Normal	— A straight line drawn from any point on the circumference in a direction radial to the centre of the circle.
Quadrant	— A quarter of a circle in shape and area.
Radius	— A straight line drawn from the centre of a circle to the circumference. (Plural — *radii*).
Radial	— A line in the direction of a radius, e.g. the joint lines of a masonry arch.
Sector	— A part of a circle.
Segment	— A part of a circle contained between a chord and its arc.
Semi-circle	— A half-circle in shape and area; the part on either side of a diameter.
Tangent	— A straight line touching the circumference of a circle at one point at right-angles to a normal at that point. In drawing a tangent to an arc, it is better to draw a radius to the tangential point first and then to draw the tangent at right-angles to it, rather than to judge the meeting of the straight line and curve by eye. See Fig. 29.

In Fig. 36 (1, 2, 3, 4, 7 and 8) are examples of combinations of arcs, and of arcs and straight lines. The construction lines are shown and the centres indicated so that the setting-up can be followed and similar exercises practised. The important point to observe is the part played by the construction lines in making easier the accurate joining of the lines.

Fig. 36 (5) shows the junction of a quadrant arc with two lines at right angles. This is often done by trial and error with unsatisfactory results. The correct method is to draw a light line at 45 degrees from the intersection of the two straight lines and another parallel to one of them and away from it a distance equal to the radius of the required arc. The meeting of this line with the 45-degree line gives the centre for the curve. If, however, the size of the arc is to be judged by eye, the 45-degree line will be helpful in locating the centre of it.

When the arc is to connect two straight lines not at right-angles, as Fig. 36 (6), the method is to draw lines parallel to each of the straight lines at distance away from them equal to the radius of the required arc. The point of intersection is the centre of the arc.

Ellipse

The ellipse comes frequently into architectural drawing, not only as a curve or shape in itself, but also in the representation of circles in various projections, etc. There are several methods of setting up the figure; some locate points on the curve which has to be completed freehand; others give centres from which curves approximating to an ellipse can be drawn. Fig. 37 (1 and 2) are examples of the former; Fig. 37 (3 and 4) of the latter.

1. The ellipse is constructed in a lightly drawn rectangle, *EFGH*, with sides equal to the major and minor axes, *AB* and *CD*. The half major axis *AO* is divided into a number of equal parts, three in the example (the number depends on the size of the drawing, but as few as possible is advised), and *EA* is also divided equally into a similar number of parts. Lines are then drawn from *C* through the divisions on *AO* to intersect corresponding lines drawn from *D* to the divisions on *EA*. The curve of a quarter of the ellipse has now to be drawn carefully and smoothly through the points of intersection. The rest of the ellipse can be completed by repeating the construction or by plotting or transferred tracing from the curve already drawn.

2. The trammel method is preferred by most draughtsmen as it avoids the numerous construction lines of the foregoing and other methods. The major and minor axes are first drawn, *AB* and *DC*, intersecting at *O*. A straight strip of card or stout paper (the trammel) is then taken, placed with its edge along the major axis and with a pencil half the length of the axis, e.g. *OB*, is marked on it. The trammel is then placed with its edge along the minor axis so that half the axis, *OD*, can be marked on it within and from one end of the previous marking. By placing the trammel on the drawing so that the two marks separated by the difference between the two axes falls on the axes as shown, then by moving the trammel but always keeping those marks on the axes, the third mark can be made to trace the curve of the ellipse, and a series of light pencil dots gives the plotting.

The construction of ellipses in the ways described above is only satisfactory where the required sizes are sufficiently large for reasonably accurate setting out. For small curves, unless one's freehand is particularly good, it is easier and better to draw through plastic guides or templates, which are obtainable for various imperial and metric sizes and proportions.

3. The construction of half of a pseudo-ellipse formed of arcs struck from three centres is illustrated. *AB* is the major axis and *AD*, less than half *AB*, is the estimated radius of the first part of the curve, *D* being the centre for the arc, which is continued to cut the minor axis at *E*. *DE* is then bisected and the bisector is continued to cut the line of the minor axis at *O*, which is the centre for the arc *FG* (radius *OE* drawn through *D*). *HB* is equal to *AD*.

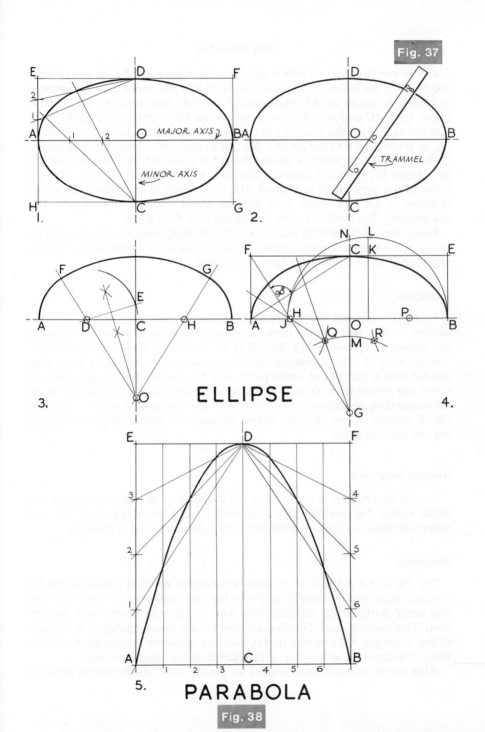

Fig. 37

E D F

2
1
A 1 2 B A O B

MAJOR AXIS

MINOR AXIS

H C G
I.

D

O

TRAMMEL

A O B

C

2.

F G

E

A D C H B

O

3.

ELLIPSE

N L
F C K E

H

A J O P B

Q R

M

G

4.

E D F

3 4

2 5

6

A C B
1 2 3 4 5 6

5.

PARABOLA

Fig. 38

4. The construction of half a pseudo-ellipse formed of arcs struck from five centres. *AB* is the major axis and *OC* is half the minor axis. A rectangle *AFEB* is first set up on *AB*, the sides *AF* and *EB* being equal to *OC*. A line is drawn from *AC* and at right-angles to it a line *FG* is drawn cutting *AB* at *H*. *H* is the centre for the first part of the curve. Then, with centre *O* and radius *OC* an arc is drawn to cut *AB* at *J*. With *JB* as diameter a semi-circle is drawn, from the centre of which a perpendicular is erected to cut the semi-circle at *L*. Along *CG* from *O* a distance *OM* equal to *KL*, the vertical from *EF* to the curve of the semi-circle is marked, and with centre *G* and radius *GM* an arc is drawn to cut arcs struck from centres *A* and *B* with radius equal to *ON*, see drawing. The centres for the curves are *G, H, P, Q* and *R*.

There are other settings out of pseudo-ellipses. They are much used for brick and masonry arches. Careful draughtsmanship is essential, the construction lines being made as light as possible.

Parabola

Parabolic lines and shapes are often required to be drawn, and the simplest setting-up for most general purposes when the required 'height' and 'width' are known is shown in Fig. 38. *AB* is the 'width' or base-line and *CD* the 'height' or axis. The rectangle *AEFB* is constructed; *AE* and *FB* are then divided into a number of equal parts, and *AC* and *CB* are similarly divided. Lines are drawn from *D* to the points of division on *AE* and on *FB* to cut corresponding perpendiculars drawn from the points of division on *AC* and *CB*. A smooth curve carefully drawn through the points of intersection is the required parabola.

Regular polygons

A brief description is given below of the setting-up of the pentagon (five equal sides), the hexagon (six equal sides), and the octagon (eight equal sides), as these are the polygons most commonly required in drawing.

Pentagon

Fig. 39(1). If it is required to draw a pentagon within a known circle, the simplest practical method is to divide the circumference of the circle into five equal parts using dividers, and then to join the points with straight lines. This method can, of course, be used for any regular polygon. If the base of the pentagon is to be horizontal, then the divisions should start from the top of the circle, i.e. where the vertical axis cuts the circumference.

If the length of the sides is known, an old but accurate method is shown in

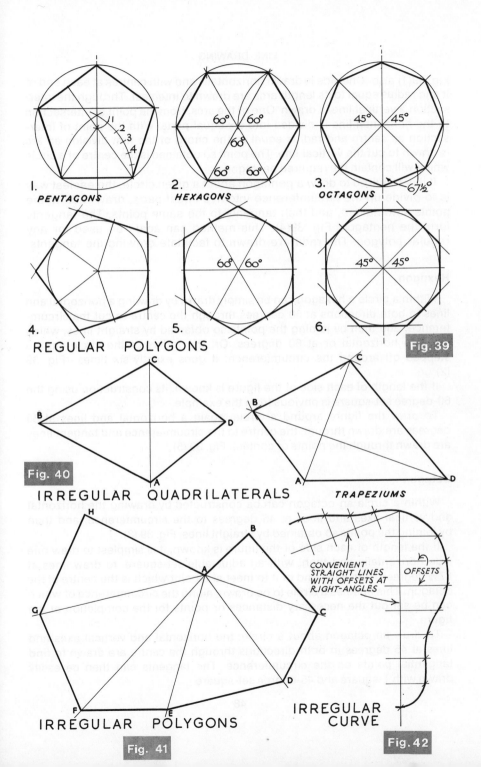

1.
PENTAGONS

2.
HEXAGONS
60° 60° 60° 60° 60° 60°

3.
OCTAGONS
45° 45° 67½°

4.

5.
60° 60°

6.
45° 45°

REGULAR POLYGONS

Fig. 39

B C D A B C D A

Fig. 40

IRREGULAR QUADRILATERALS   TRAPEZIUMS

H B A G C F E D

IRREGULAR POLYGONS

CONVENIENT STRAIGHT LINES WITH OFFSETS AT RIGHT-ANGLES
OFFSETS

IRREGULAR CURVE

Fig. 41   Fig. 42

Fig. 39(1) also. One side is drawn horizontally and with centres at each end of it and radius equal to its length arcs are drawn to intersect. Through the intersection a vertical line is drawn. One of the arcs, from the point of intersection to the horizontal line is divided into six equal parts. With the point of intersection as centre and radius equal to the chord of the first division an arc is drawn to cut the vertical line. The point so obtained is the centre of a circle which will contain the required pentagon.

If it is required to draw a pentagon about a given circle, the easiest way is to divide up the circumference into five equal parts, draw radii to the points so obtained, and then tangents to the same points. The tangents form the pentagon, Fig. 39(4). This method can again be used for any regular polygon. The radii are drawn to facilitate drawing the tangents.

Hexagon

Within a circle a hexagon can be simply drawn by drawing a horizontal and lines in both directions at 60 degrees through the centre to cut the circumference, and then by joining the points so obtained by straight lines, which are also horizontal or at 60 degrees. Or, the radius of the circle can be stepped off around the circumference: it goes exactly six times—Fig. 39 (2).

If the length of each side of the figure is known, its construction using the 60-degree set-square is obvious from the example.

To draw the figure around a circle, again a horizontal and lines at 60 degrees are drawn through the centre to the circumference and tangent lines are drawn through the points of contact, Fig. 39 (5).

Octagon

Within a circle an octagon can be constructed by drawing the horizontal and vertical axes and lines at 45 degrees to the circumference, and then by joining the points so obtained by straight lines, Fig. 39 (3).

If the length of each side of the figure is known, it is simplest to draw one side horizontally and then, with an adjustable set-square, to draw lines at 67½ degrees from each end of it to meet at a point which is the centre of the octagon. This enables a circle to be drawn, along the circumference of which can be set out the necessary distances or points for the completion of the figure.

To draw an octagon about a circle, the horizontal and vertical axes and lines at 45 degrees in both directions through the centre are drawn to find tangential points on the circumference. The tangents can then be easily drawn with T-square and 45-degree set-square.

Irregular quadrilaterals

Two examples of these figures are illustrated in Fig. 40. In the case of the former, the 'kite' shape can be set up by drawing the diagonals first and measuring the required distances along them from the point of intersection. In the latter case, which is likely to be a matter of copying or plotting a survey, the lengths of the sides would have to be known and also either the angles between them or the lengths of the diagonals. If the angles are known, then the setting-up can be done with the aid of a protractor or adjustable set-square, the lengths of the lines being measured or transferred from an original by dividers.

If the lengths of the diagonals are known, the setting-out can be made on the basis of triangulation. In the example illustrated, Fig. 40, side AD is drawn first; then, with centre A and radius equal to the length of the diagonal, an arc is drawn to intersect an arc drawn with centre D and radius equal to the length of known side DC. This establishes the position of point C, and by a similar process, using AC as the base-line, the triangle ABC can be drawn.

Irregular polygons

The drawing of an irregular polygon such as illustrated in Fig. 41 can be made on similar lines to the methods described above for irregular quadrilaterals. If the lengths of the sides and the angles between them are known, as is the case in the plotting of certain types of surveys, the setting-up is made by systematically measuring off lines and angles. If the lengths of the sides and the distances from one corner, point A here, to all other corners are known, the method is to construct the triangles so formed.

Irregular curves

The drawing of irregular curves, when copied from other drawings, is best done by plotting offsets from convenient straight lines which follow the general direction of the curve. This is illustrated in Fig. 42. The offsets are taken at right-angles to the straight lines. They need not necessarily be spaced at regular intervals, although it is sometimes more convenient to do so.

If the curve is part of a survey, the lines and offsets will have been determined in the measuring and the drawing is therefore a straightforward matter of plotting the data to scale.

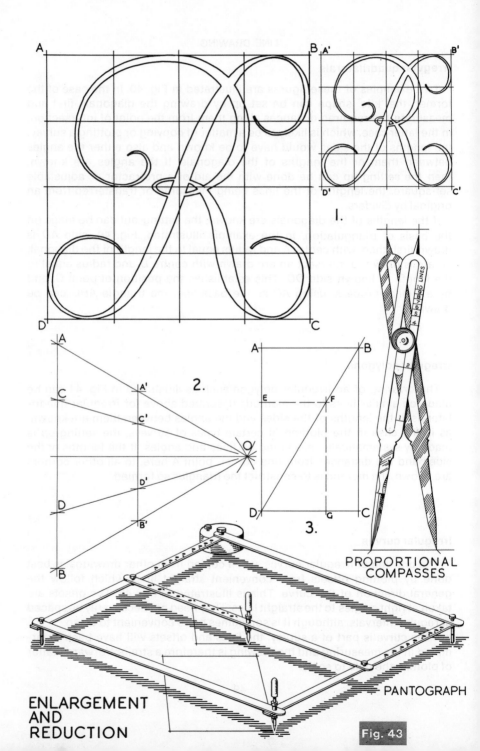

1.

2.

3.

PROPORTIONAL
COMPASSES

PANTOGRAPH

ENLARGEMENT
AND
REDUCTION

Fig. 43

Enlargement and reduction of drawings

There are various methods of enlarging or reducing a line drawing. Some of the most useful are:

Fig. 43 (1). If, for example, the drawing consists of irregular or complex lines, draw over it a square grid of light lines (or, if the drawing is to be protected, draw the grid on a piece of tracing paper and place over the original), and then for the new drawing make a similar grid but proportionately larger or smaller as required. With this grid as a guide it is comparatively easy to make the copy to the size wanted.

Fig. 43 (2). If a line and its divisions, e.g. a scale, is to be enlarged or reduced in other than a simple mathematical proportion this is a useful method to employ. Line *AB* with points *C* and *D* along it is to be reduced; with centres *A* and *B* and radius equal to *AB* two arcs are drawn to intersect at *O*, and lines are drawn from *O* to *A*, *B*, *C* and *D*. The new length of the line is now measured along *OA* from *O*, and a line *A'B'* is drawn parallel to *AB* to which it corresponds. Where this line cuts *CO* and *DO* points *C'* and *D'* corresponding to *C* and *D* on the original are found.

Fig. 43 (3). The proportional enlargement or reduction of rectangles is made by drawing a diagonal so that the alteration of the length of one side automatically gives the required length of the adjacent one. Example: *ABCD* is the rectangle; *BD* is a diagonal. *EFGD* is a proportionately reduced rectangle.

Proportional Compasses. These instruments consist of two slotted pieces of metal with points at each end joined by a centre screw, which can be so set that the distance between the long points is equal to that between the short points or is two, three, four or more times that distance up to ten. They can therefore be used for enlarging or reducing simple drawings in such ratios, although they seem to find little favour with present-day draughtsmen.

Pantograph: an instrument for enlarging or reducing drawings in various ratios. By following the lines of the original with one marker, the other traces them to a larger or smaller scale, as the case may be, and in the proportionate ratio to which the instrument has been set. The illustration shows a simple type. The Eidograph is a somewhat similar instrument, but, having only one point of support, is steadier in action. The cost of these instruments is only justified if dealing with a large number of town plans and surveys.

3
Projections

Orthographic projection

Orthographic projection is the method of showing solid objects which are actually three-dimensional in two-dimensional drawings by means of related views called plans, elevations and sections. Most drawings of buildings are of this nature.

The principle, which although difficult to explain in words, is readily understood when a drawing in orthographic projection is seen, is illustrated by Figs. 44 and 45. Fig. 44 shows a block or rectangle prism, *ABCDEFGH*. Adjacent to it and parallel to its sides are three co-ordinated planes, that is, planes at right-angles to one another. They are horizontal plane, vertical plane 1, and vertical plane 2. If the face of the prism *ABCD* is projected on to vertical plane 1 it appears thereon as a rectangle; similarly, if face *EACG* is projected on to vertical plane 2 it also appears as a rectangle; and likewise with face *EFBA* on to the horizontal plane. Now, if it is imagined that the co-ordinate planes are 'hinged', then if the horizontal plane is swung downwards, as it were, through an angle of 90 degrees, and if vertical plane 2 is swung round through an angle of 90 degrees, the three projections will lie in the same plane and the result is as shown in Fig. 45, which is an *orthographic projection* of the prism showing related plan and two elevations.

In practice, of course, such a projection is made by drawing first the plan, then the elevation of the front face immediately above and then the end elevation at the side.

The projection, as illustrated, is known as *First Angle Projection*, each view being so placed that it represents the side of the object remote from it in the adjacent view. It is the British engineering and Continental standard (excluding Dutch) practice. What is known as *Third Angle Projection* would result in the views being arranged with the plan over elevation 1 and the elevation of face *BFHD*, corresponding to elevation 2, on the left-hand side of elevation 1. Third Angle projection has the advantage of placing the features of adjacent views in juxtaposition, and thus makes it easier than in First

ORTHOGRAPHIC
PROJECTION

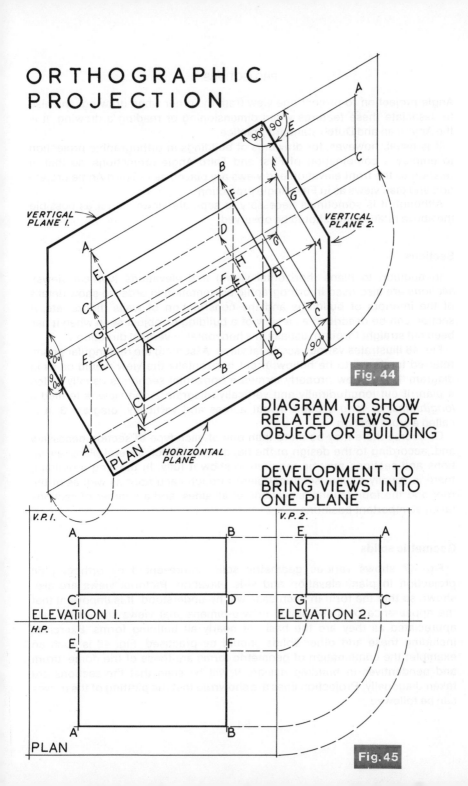

VERTICAL PLANE I.

VERTICAL PLANE 2.

PLAN

HORIZONTAL PLANE

Fig. 44

DIAGRAM TO SHOW
RELATED VIEWS OF
OBJECT OR BUILDING

DEVELOPMENT TO
BRING VIEWS INTO
ONE PLANE

V.P.I.

A   B

C   D

ELEVATION I.

V.P.2.

E   A

G   C

ELEVATION 2.

H.P.

E   F

PLAN

A   B

Fig. 45

Angle projection to project one view from the other when drawing, and also to associate these features when dimensioning or reading a drawing. It is the American and Dutch standard practice.

It is usual, however, for drawings of buildings in orthographic projection to employ a combination of First and Third Angle projections, so that in relation to the front elevation end views are placed as in Third Angle projection and plan views as in First Angle projection.

Although it is sometimes necessary to separate views, so far as possible the above relationship should be observed.

Sections

In addition to plans (horizontal views) and elevations (vertical views), *sections* are also used in orthographic presentation in order to show details of the interiors of buildings and the construction of walls, floors, etc. A section can be described as a view of a building or object seen when it has been cut straight through, usually in a horizontal or vertical direction.

Fig. 46 illustrates various sectional views. Assuming the rectangular prism, referred to above, to be hollow, if cut horizontally the view would be as in diagram 1. This view properly termed a horizontal section is usually called a plan. If cut longitudinally and vertically, diagram 2, the view is termed a *longitudinal or long section*. If cut across and vertically, diagram 3, it is called a *cross section*.

Of course there may be more than one of each type of section necessary and, according to the design of the building or object, several plans, elevations and sections may be required to show it fully. In drawing a building there is usually a plan (sectional plan) through each floor as well as of the roof and the foundations, elevations of all sides, and a number of sections taken at important positions.

Geometric solids

Fig. 47 shows various geometric solids represented by orthographic projection in plan, elevation and side elevation. Pictorial views are also shown so that the form in each case will be understood. It is important that the appearance of these solids in two-dimensional views should be fully appreciated as they are the basis of nearly all building forms. Exercises including these and other solids should be practised. Fig. 48 is such an example; the combination of geometric forms are those of the dome, drum and pendentives in building design. It will be seen that the sections are taken diagonally. Projection lines are shown so that the plotting of the curves can be followed.

SECTIONS

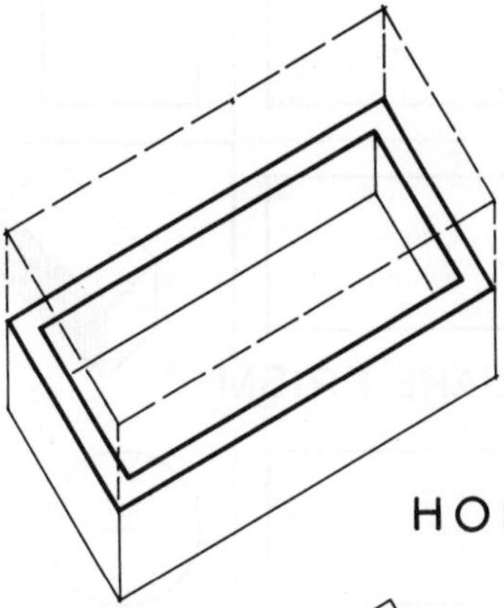

I.

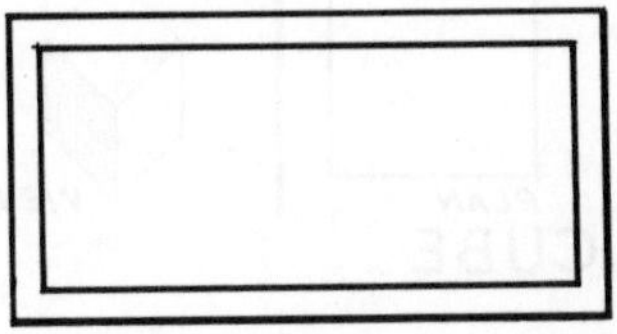

HORIZONTAL SECTION
USUALLY CALLED 'PLAN'

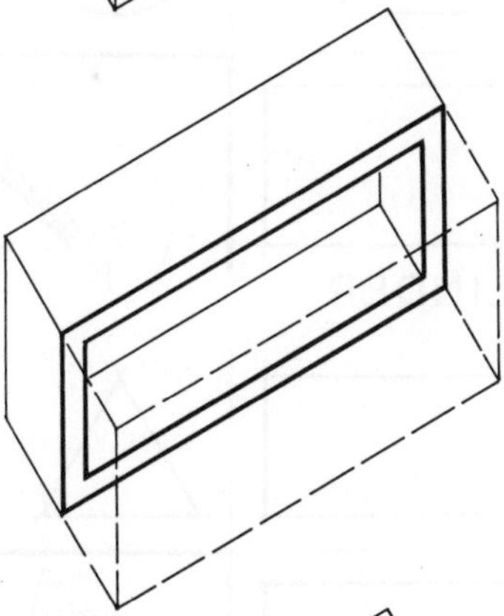

2.

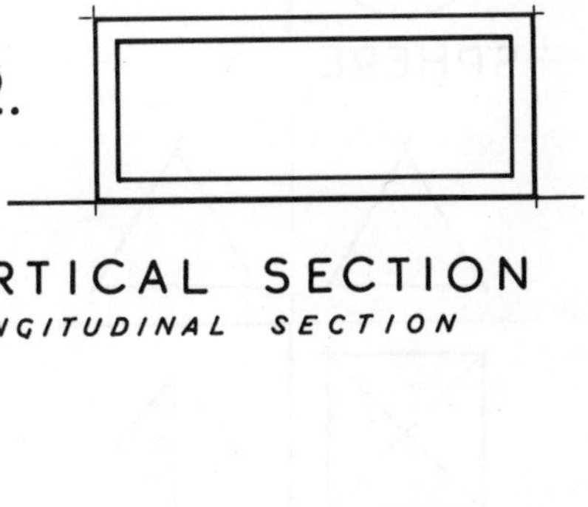

VERTICAL SECTION
LONGITUDINAL SECTION

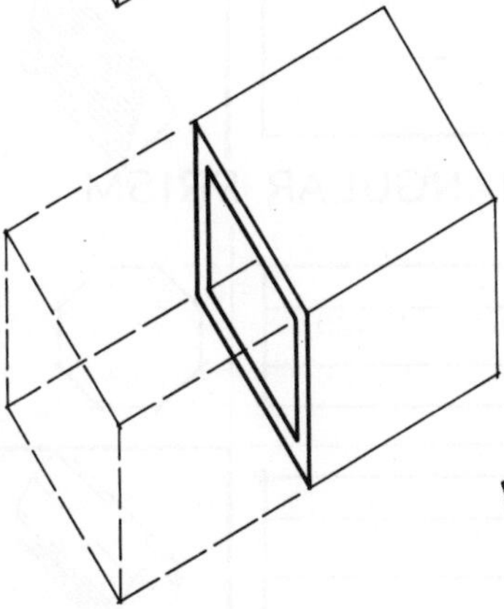

3.

VERTICAL SECTION
CROSS SECTION

Fig. 46

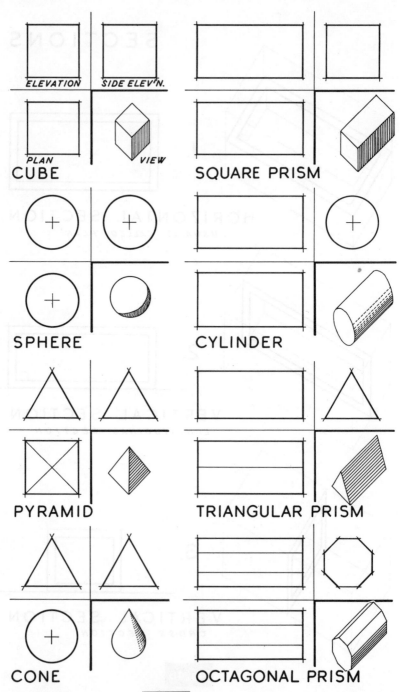

ELEVATION · SIDE ELEV'N.

PLAN · VIEW

CUBE

SQUARE PRISM

SPHERE

CYLINDER

PYRAMID

TRIANGULAR PRISM

CONE

OCTAGONAL PRISM

Fig. 47

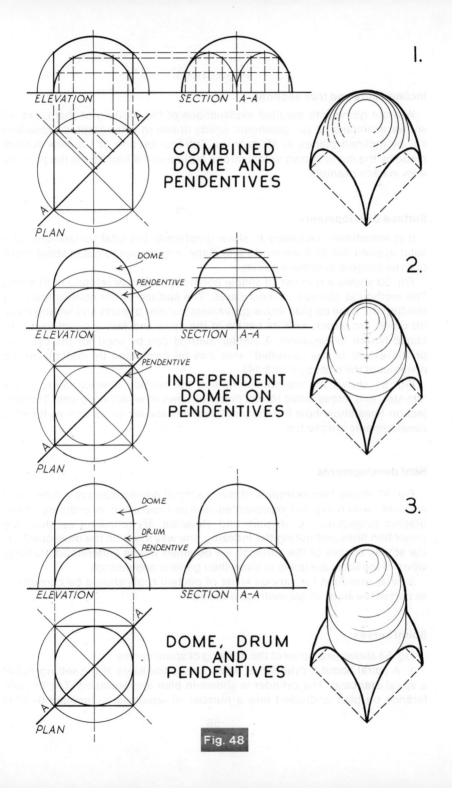

1.

ELEVATION   SECTION A-A

COMBINED
DOME AND
PENDENTIVES

PLAN

A

2.

DOME
PENDENTIVE

ELEVATION   SECTION A-A

PENDENTIVE

INDEPENDENT
DOME ON
PENDENTIVES

PLAN

A

3.

DOME
DRUM
PENDENTIVE

ELEVATION   SECTION A-A

DOME, DRUM
AND
PENDENTIVES

PLAN

A

Fig. 48

Inclined cuts and true sections

Without going into detailed explanations of the plotting of them, Fig. 49 shows examples of six geometric solids drawn in orthographic projection cut by inclined planes at 45 degrees. The true section or the new surface made by the cut is shown with a strong outline and is hatched in the pictorial view in each example.

Surface developments

It is sometimes necessary to show graphically the total surface area of a solid opened out as it were into one plane, e.g. shapes to cut in sheet metal or to be covered in some material.

Fig. 50 shows a number of simple geometric solids developed in this way. The method is obvious in most cases. The surface of the cone is found by dividing the base on plan into a convenient number of parts and setting these off on an arc struck with its centre at the apex and radius equal to the inclined length in elevation. A similar method can be used for the cylinder, or the extent of the 'unrolled' area can be calculated by multiplying the diameter of the ends by π or $3 \cdot 141$.

Fig. 51 shows the method of finding the surface developments of the 'cloister' and 'cross' vault forms, pictorial views of which are given. The projection lines show how the diagonal sections are set up as well as how the developments are plotted.

Roof developments

Fig. 52 shows two examples of the graphical development of pitched roof surfaces, which are not represented in true proportion in ordinary orthographic projection, i.e. in plan and elevation. By following carefully the projection lines and noting the indexing, the way in which the developed, i.e. the actual, shapes of the surfaces are obtained will be understood. Pictorial views of the roofs are given to show their general appearance.

Similar exercises for various kinds of pitched roofs should be carried out as part of the study of geometrical drawing.

Spiral curves

Fig. 53 shows examples of the drawing of spiral curves.

1. A spiral about a cylinder or helix. This is the basis of the setting-out of a spiral staircase. The cylinder is shown in plan and elevation. The circumference on plan is divided into a number of equal parts, indexed 0–12 in

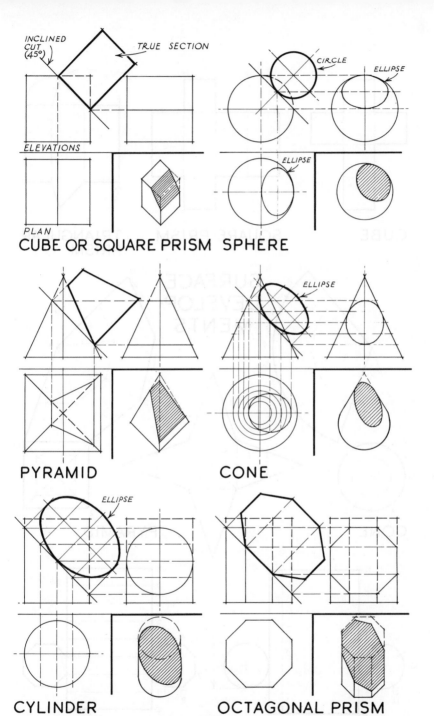

INCLINED CUTS AND TRUE SECTIONS

Fig. 49

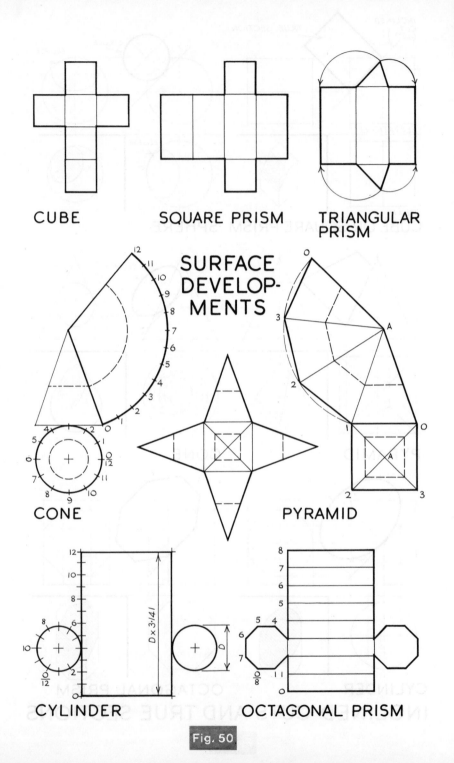

CUBE

SQUARE PRISM

TRIANGULAR PRISM

SURFACE DEVELOP-MENTS

CONE

PYRAMID

CYLINDER

$D \times 3 \cdot 141$

OCTAGONAL PRISM

Fig. 50

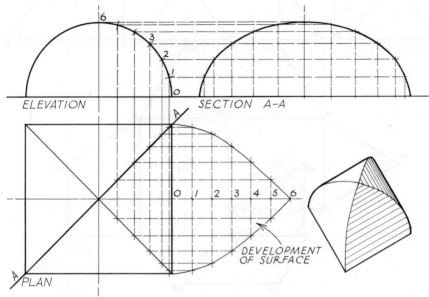

ELEVATION   SECTION A–A

6 3 2 1 0

A

O 1 2 3 4 5 6

DEVELOPMENT
OF SURFACE

A PLAN

'CLOISTER' VAULT FORM

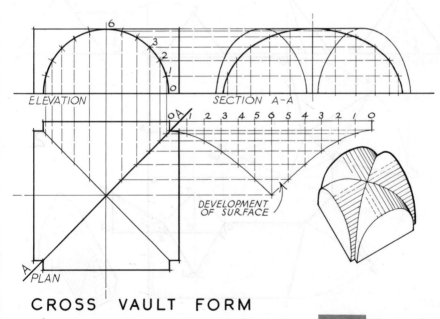

ELEVATION   SECTION A–A

6 3 2 1 0

O A 1 2 3 4 5 6 5 4 3 2 1 0

DEVELOPMENT
OF SURFACE

A PLAN

CROSS VAULT FORM

Fig. 51

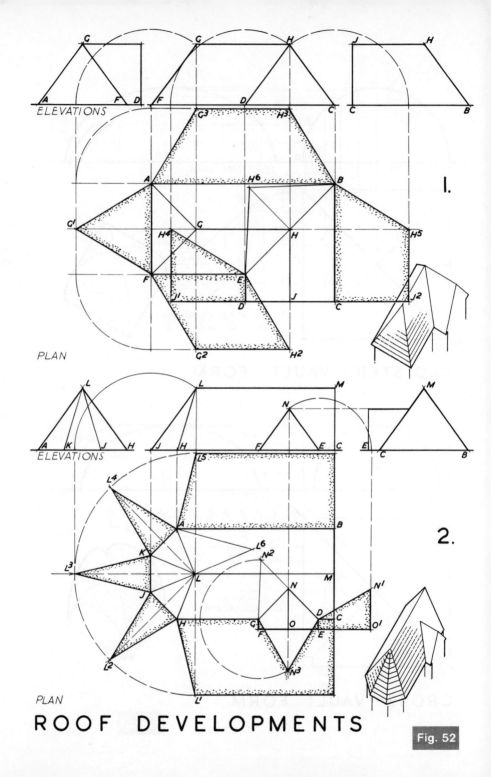

ELEVATIONS

I.

PLAN

ELEVATIONS

2.

PLAN

ROOF DEVELOPMENTS

Fig. 52

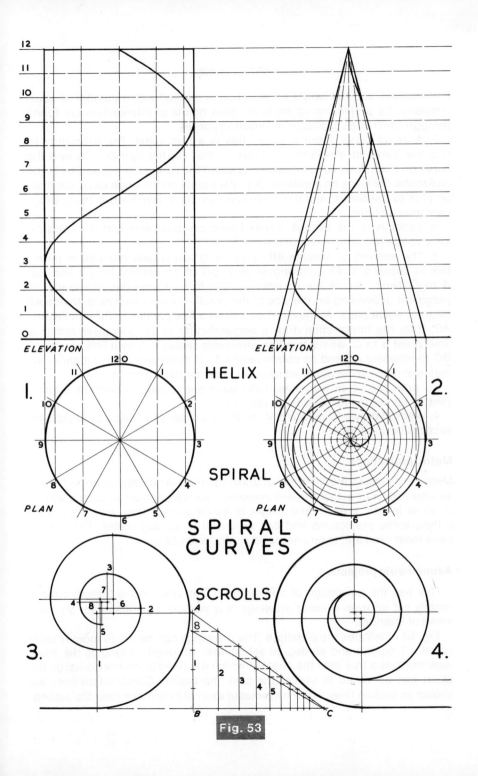

SPIRAL CURVES

HELIX

SPIRAL

SCROLLS

1.

2.

3.

4.

ELEVATION

ELEVATION

PLAN

PLAN

Fig. 53

the example, and the height on elevation is marked with a number of equal divisions. By projecting up from the plan points of intersection are found through which the spiral seen in elevation passes.

2. A spiral curve about a cone—this is a true spiral. The procedure to find the curve in elevation is similar to that for the cylinder. To find the curve on plan, draw concentric circles about the centre corresponding to the horizontal divisions on elevation. Join the points on the outer circumference on plan to the centre, and the curve can then be drawn through the appropriate intersections.

In addition to the various scrolls based on quadrants and the classical Ionic volute two other examples are:

3. The method is: Assume *AB* to be the greatest radii required or given; this is indexed 1. At right-angles draw *BC* of convenient length and join *A* to *C*. Next, decide the number of radii to be used—this is a matter of judgment depending on the size of the scroll—10 are taken here. Divide *AB* into ten equal parts. At the eight part draw a line parallel to *BC* intersecting *AC*, from the intersection draw a perpendicular to *BC*, this gives radius 2. Join point 8 to *C*, where this line intersects radius 2 draw a line parallel to *BC* to intersect *AC* and so obtain radius 3. By continuing in this manner the series of radii can be obtained reduced in geometrical progression.

To draw the scroll with these radii, each one is used to describe a quadrant, as shown in Fig. 53 as far as radius 8.

4. A scroll drawn from four centres at the corner of a square by describing successive quadrants.

Metric projections

Metric projections are methods of drawing buildings or objects so as to give an impression of actual three-dimensional appearance yet in such a way as to allow length, breadth and height to be measured. They are set up from orthographic projections and can be drawn to various scales. The projections most used are: axonometric, isometric and oblique.

Axonometric projection

This has the advantage of containing a true plan and is therefore more readily set up from existing drawings. It is particularly suitable for showing views of interiors.

Fig. 54 illustrates the principle. The drawings can be made most readily using a T-square and 45-degree set-square, although so long as the 'plan' view remains a true plan the angle at which it is tilted to the horizontal on the sheet can be varied to secure the best impression. Construction lines are shown as broken lines in the two smaller examples to make clear the setting-

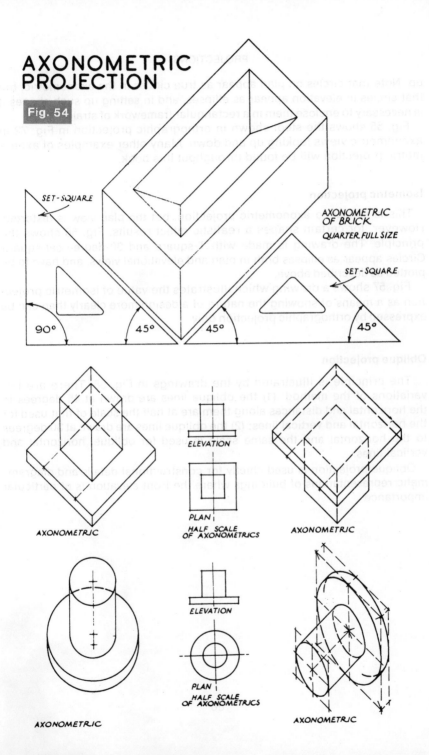

AXONOMETRIC PROJECTION

Fig. 54

SET-SQUARE

SET-SQUARE

AXONOMETRIC OF BRICK

QUARTER, FULL SIZE

90°   45°   45°   45°

AXONOMETRIC

ELEVATION

PLAN

HALF SCALE OF AXONOMETRICS

AXONOMETRIC

AXONOMETRIC

ELEVATION

PLAN

HALF SCALE OF AXONOMETRICS

AXONOMETRIC

AXONOMETRIC

up. Note that circles on plan appear as true circles in the axonometric, but that circles in elevation appear as ellipses, and in setting up such shapes it is necessary to enclose them in a rectangular framework of straight lines.

Fig. 55 shows the stool shown in orthographic projection in Fig. 72 in axonometric views looking up and down. Many other examples of axonometric projection will be found throughout this book.

Isometric projection

This is similar to axonometric projection, but the plan view is distorted. However, for certain shapes a realistic effect results. Fig. 56 shows the principle. The drawing is made with T-square and 30-degree set-square. Circles appear as ellipses both in plan and elevational views, and have to be plotted as described above.

Fig. 57 shows a drawing which illustrates the value of isometric projection as a means of showing the nature of a design more clearly than can be expressed by orthographic projection only.

Oblique projection

The principle is illustrated by the drawings in Fig. 58. There are two variations of the method: (1) the oblique lines are drawn at 45 degrees to the horizontal and distances along them are at half the scale of that used for the horizontal and vertical lines; (2) the oblique lines are drawn at 30 degrees to the horizontal and the same scale is used for oblique, horizontal and vertical lines.

Oblique projection is used chiefly for constructional details and diagrammatic representations of buildings where the front elevation is of particular importance.

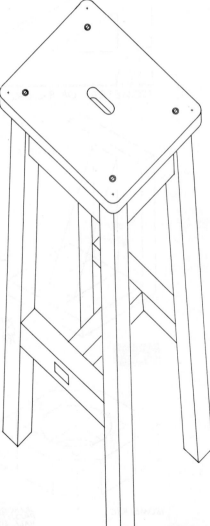

VIEW LOOKING DOWN

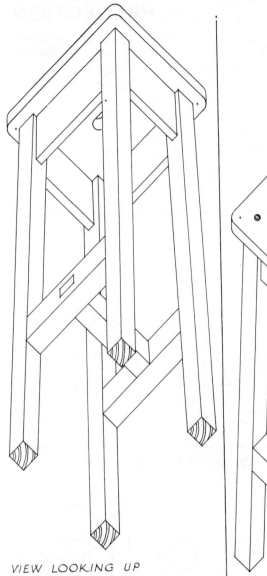

VIEW LOOKING UP

AXONOMETRIC
PROJECTIONS
OF A STOOL

Fig. 55

ISOMETRIC PROJECTION

Fig. 56

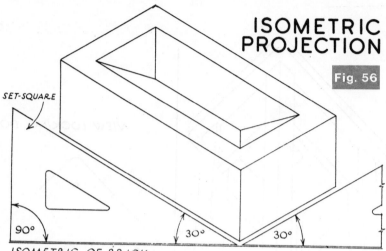

SET-SQUARE

90°   30°   30°

ISOMETRIC OF BRICK

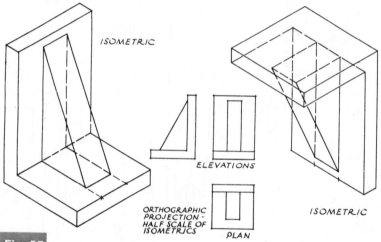

ISOMETRIC

ELEVATIONS

ORTHOGRAPHIC
PROJECTION -
HALF SCALE OF
ISOMETRICS

PLAN

ISOMETRIC

Fig. 57

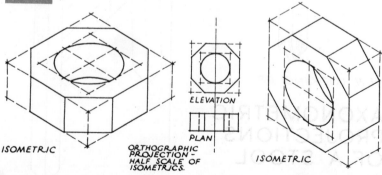

ISOMETRIC

ELEVATION

PLAN

ORTHOGRAPHIC
PROJECTION -
HALF SCALE OF
ISOMETRICS.

ISOMETRIC

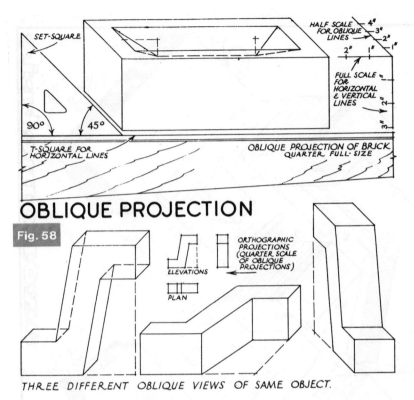

SET-SQUARE

HALF SCALE FOR OBLIQUE LINES 4" 3" 2" 1"

2" 1" 1"

FULL SCALE FOR HORIZONTAL & VERTICAL LINES 2"

90° 45°

T-SQUARE FOR HORIZONTAL LINES

3"

OBLIQUE PROJECTION OF BRICK
QUARTER FULL-SIZE

OBLIQUE PROJECTION

Fig. 58

ORTHOGRAPHIC PROJECTIONS (QUARTER SCALE OF OBLIQUE PROJECTIONS)

ELEVATIONS

PLAN

THREE DIFFERENT OBLIQUE VIEWS OF SAME OBJECT.

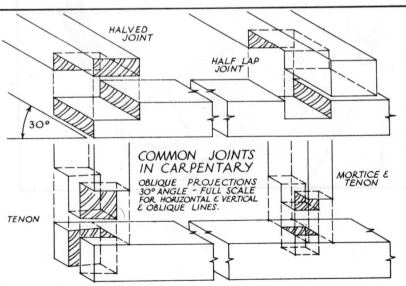

HALVED JOINT

HALF LAP JOINT

30°

TENON

COMMON JOINTS IN CARPENTARY

OBLIQUE PROJECTIONS
30° ANGLE – FULL SCALE
FOR HORIZONTAL & VERTICAL
& OBLIQUE LINES.

MORTICE &
TENON

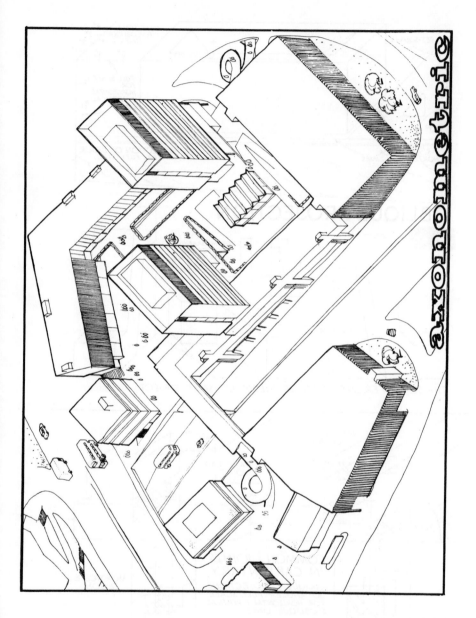

axonometric

Plate 6   Urban development. Student's axonometric drawing. Free-hand in ink over pencil projection.

I. G. Johns

4
Lettering

Little progress can be made in draughtsmanship without attention being paid to lettering.

Almost every drawing has to be titled and many of them, particularly production drawings, require descriptive words and notes in order that they can be clearly understood. It is important, therefore, for the draughtsman of whatever category to acquire as quickly as possible the habit of using good lettering on all his work. And as the study of lettering also affords excellent practice in drawing it is particularly suitable that it should be dealt with at an early stage in the training.

With all lettering, the first principle is that of *legibility*. Legibility depends on (1) shape or form of each individual letter, (2) spacing of letters and arrangement of words, and (3) the sizes and positions of the lettering according to relative importance. The second principle is that of suitability of shape to materials and method of execution; thus, lettering drawn in pencil on paper will differ in form to some extent from lettering incised in stone. Thirdly, the character of the lettering must be appropriate to its purpose. The type of letters and general composition of the wording should be expressive of the quality or use of the drawing, e.g. decorative lettering is completely out of place on a working drawing, just as crude stencil lettering would be on a highly finished perspective drawing.

English lettering is derived from that of the Romans, and the generally accepted standard is the lettering which was carved on Trajan's Column, Rome, in the second century A.D. This lettering was probably first 'painted' on the stone with a brush and then incised with a chisel, which procedure accounts to some extent for the forms and details, e.g. the thick and thin strokes from the brush-work, and the 'serifs', originally the chiselled terminations of parts of the letters. Nevertheless, the forms have now become familiar in printing types, and flat letters and the roman alphabet will always be the basis of good lettering.

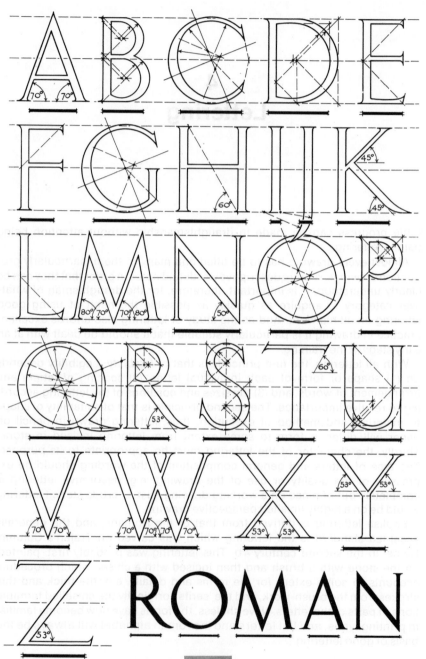

Fig. 59

The roman alphabet

There is, however, no absolute standard for roman lettering, and many of the variations are not suitable for ordinary draughting purposes. The one shown in Fig. 59 has been specially prepared for drawings, bearing in mind the need for preserving the essential shapes and for a simple setting-out. It is an alphabet which should be carefully studied, and the best way to study it is to draw it out, for the basic proportions. It can be used for the titling of important drawings.

The construction of each letter is shown and should be understood on examination. General points to be observed are: (1) all thin strokes are the same width, and all thick strokes—except the I and the J, which can be a little wider—are the same width. The thick strokes are about one-tenth the height of the letters; the thin strokes rather more than half the thick strokes; (2) the letters are all one height except the 'points' of A, M, N, V and W, which extend, as do C, G, O and Q, a little beyond the limits in order to make them appear the right size (do not exaggerate this subtlety); (3) the middle line between the top and bottom guide-lines determines the position of parts of several of the letters as well as centres for C, G. O and Q.

Individual points are:

A—both sides inclined at 70 degrees, the bottom of the cross-bar is midway between the middle and bottom guide lines.

B—explained by drawing; construction lines are at 45 degrees; centres of arcs are indicated by dots; arrows indicate radii.

C—outside curve is part of circle; inside curve is struck from centres indicated; axes at $22\frac{1}{2}$ degrees and $67\frac{1}{2}$ degrees to horizontal; widest parts rather wider than wide parts of thick strokes, same with G, O, and Q.

D—explained by drawing, note width of letter, about $\frac{3}{4}$ of height.

E—based on double square; note slight curve and slope of serif to top of lowest arm—same with L.

F—similar to upper part of E.

G—similar basis to C; note position of vertical stroke, determined by intersection of 45-degrees line from centre with outside curve—compare with C.

H—explained by drawing.

I—explained by drawing.

J—centres for arcs can be judged by eye; curve must be smooth and regular.

K—curve to lower leg is drawn freehand, points must not become 'hook'—same with R.

L—similar to lower part of E.

M—explained by drawing.

N—explained by drawing.

O—similar construction to C.

P—explained by drawing.

Q—similar construction to O; note positions along axis for centres of arcs for tail.

R—similar construction to P, but note junction of inner curve at top and junction between vertical stroke and leg; the leg should not be 'curly'.

S—explained by drawing; careful drawing necessary.

T—explained by drawing.

U—explained by drawing; foot can be omitted.

V, W, X, Y, Z—explained by drawing.

1.

2.

3.

Fig. 60

It is only possible to use the setting-out fully if the letters are drawn to a reasonably large size. For small letters, while the angles can be followed, some parts have to be drawn freehand by eye instead of with compasses.

'Serifs' must be neatly formed and smoothly joined up with the rest of the letter, and should be put in before the final lines are completed.

Fig. 60 shows the stages in setting up three letters: (1) The guide-lines and principal construction lines are drawn lightly, (2) the letters are lightly completed and the serifs drawn in freehand in the final line, (3) the letters are completed in the final line, curved lines being put in before straight lines in the case of B. *This procedure should be followed in general in making any drawing.*

The spacing of letter to form words can vary considerably within limits depending upon space available, purpose, and so on. Because the individual letters differ in shape the spacing has to be arranged to avoid crowding in some parts of words and too wide spacing in others. Until the eye becomes trained a useful guide to spacing is given by the thick black lines shown under each letter in Fig. 59. The line in each case can be taken as representing the 'value' of the letter according to its shape and size; the letters are then spaced so that the distances between these value lines are equal, as illustrated by the word ROMAN. This method need not be rigidly adhered to; some variations may have to be made at times to suit circumstances.

Titles of important drawings should always be set out on tracing paper to get the size and spacing right before being drawn on the final sheets.

Sans serif letters

In more recent times, letters without serifs, known as 'sans serif' alphabets, have been designed and are much used because of their simplicity, clarity and ease of execution. Fig. 61 shows the setting-out of such an alphabet[1] suitable for the titling of drawings, etc. The letters are formed of strokes all equal in thickness. One-tenth the height is an average thickness of the strokes, but it can be more or less according to the effect required. The thicker the stroke, the heavier or bolder the letter. The letters are all the same height. Suggested value lines for spacing are shown as in the case of the roman alphabet.

[1]Based on 'Gill Sans', a printing type designed by Eric Gill for the Monotype Corporation.

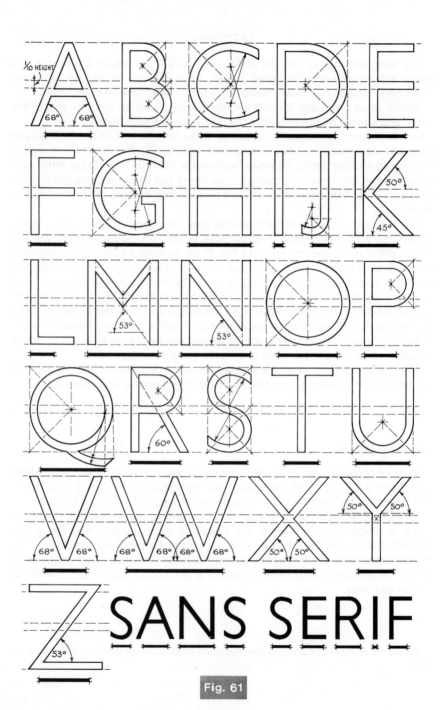

SANS SERIF

Fig. 61

Numerals

Fig. 62 shows the setting-out of roman and sans serif numerals. Regarding the former, the Roman did not, of course, use numerals of this kind, which are Arabic in origin, but the character of roman lettering is followed and the shapes are based on those in common use for many years.

Single-line lettering

For habitual rapid use in labelling and putting notes on drawings, a single-line alphabet is required. This should be based on the shapes and proportions of the 'Roman' letters, but without the use of serifs.

Fig. 63 shows such an alphabet and corresponding numerals. In order to illustrate the shapes and proportions, guide-lines dividing the height into eight equal parts and the centres of arcs are indicated. The lettering should, however, be drawn freehand at various sizes. It will be found, at first, that each letter has to be formed carefully and comparatively slowly to avoid distortion and wrong shapes. With practice, however, it is soon possible to letter quickly and accurately without conscious effort.

After a time certain individual characteristics will be acquired, but avoid the deliberate introduction of novel or fancy shapes in the mistaken idea that doing so imparts 'style'. Legibility and seemliness are far more important than individual idiosyncrasy.

Always rule faint guide-lines for freehand lettering and keep to them. Use a reasonably soft pencil.

Inclined lettering

Sometimes it is necessary to distinguish between two types of lettering, e.g. names of rooms on plan and notes regarding construction. While this might be effected by variations in size, it may be more convenient to use upright lettering for the one and inclined lettering for the other.

Fig. 64 shows inclined lettering similar in all respects otherwise to the single-line lettering above, but sloping uniformly at an angle of about 75 degrees. The slope should not be exaggerated. Many draughtsmen use inclined lettering for general use in preference to upright. It is a matter of personal choice.

Script lettering

Fig. 65 shows individually formed capitals, numerals and lower case letters which can be written in pencil or pen. If well executed it is an attractive way of labelling certain types of project presentation drawings.

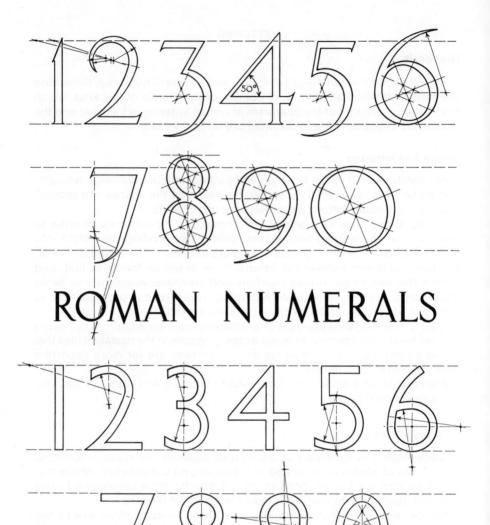

ROMAN NUMERALS

'SANS' NUMERALS

Fig. 62

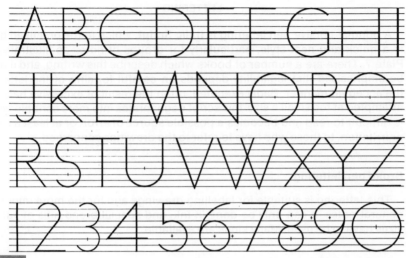

ABCDEFGHI
JKLMNOPQ
RSTUVWXYZ
1234567890
Fig. 63

ABCDEFGHIJKLMNOPQ
RSTUVWXYZ 1234567890
Fig. 64

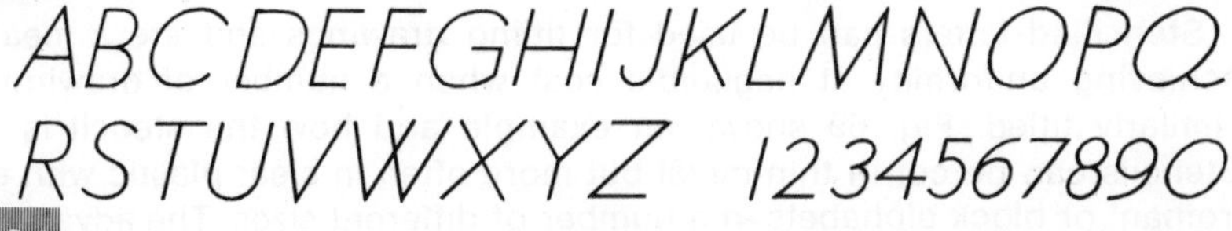

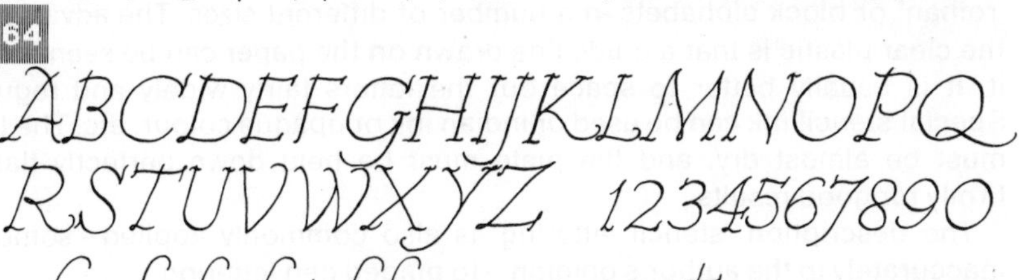

ABCDEFGHIJKLMNOPQ
RSTUVWXYZ 1234567890
abcdefghijklmnopqrstuvwxyz
Fig. 65

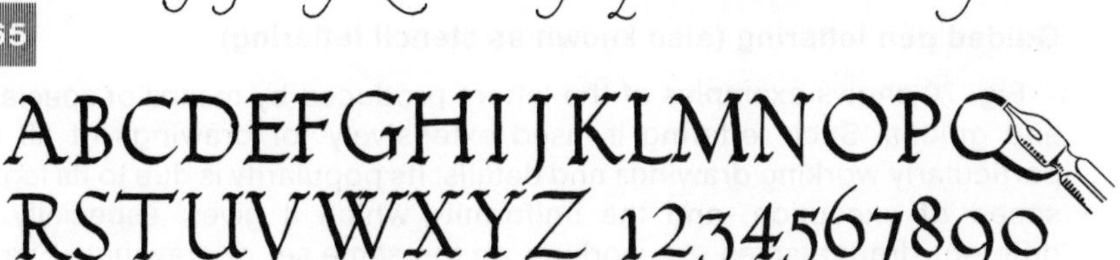

ABCDEFGHIJKLMNOPQ
RSTUVWXYZ 1234567890
abcdefghijklmnopqrstuvwxyz
Fig. 66

A popular cursive pen lettering is **Italic Script**, which to the practised hand is a quick and neat style, particularly for groups of notes as illustrated by Plate 7. There are a number of books which describe this writing, and it must be emphasised that legibility depends on careful forming of the letters in the accepted manner. Badly executed, often the result of excessive haste, or attempted at too small a size, this script degenerates into mere scribble which is difficult to read and becomes a possible source of error, or at least a cause or irritation, to those who have to refer to the drawings concerned.

Broad pen lettering

This lettering is suitable for labelling drawings and for the more important general notes. It can only be done in ink, and special broad nibs of various sizes have to be used. Many kinds are available.

Stencil lettering

Stencilled letters can be used for titling drawings and are a means of achieving uniformity at negligible cost when a number of drawings are similarly titled. Fig. 69 shows an example and how the stencil is used. Stencils can be cut in thin metal but more often in clear plastic with either 'roman' or block alphabets in a number of different sizes. The advantage of the clear plastic is that a guide line drawn on the paper can be seen through it. It is usually better to space out the letters fairly widely and regularly. Special stencil ink can be used or indian ink or opaque colour, etc. The brush must be almost dry, and the plate must be held down perfectly flat and firmly for good results.

The description 'stencil lettering' is also commonly applied — somewhat inaccurately in the author's opinion — to guided pen lettering:

Guided pen lettering (also known as stencil lettering)

Fig. 70 shows examples of the letters produced by means of special pens and guides. Such lettering is used extensively for drawings of all kinds, particularly working drawings and details. Its popularity is due to its legibility, speed of execution, and the uniformity which it gives, especially when different draughtsmen are working on the same set of drawings. Examples are also to be found in the illustrations used throughout this book.

Both upright and sloping guides are obtainable for capital, lower-case letters and numerals in a variety of sizes with corresponding pens. Drawing pens of the Rotring Variant type can also be used.

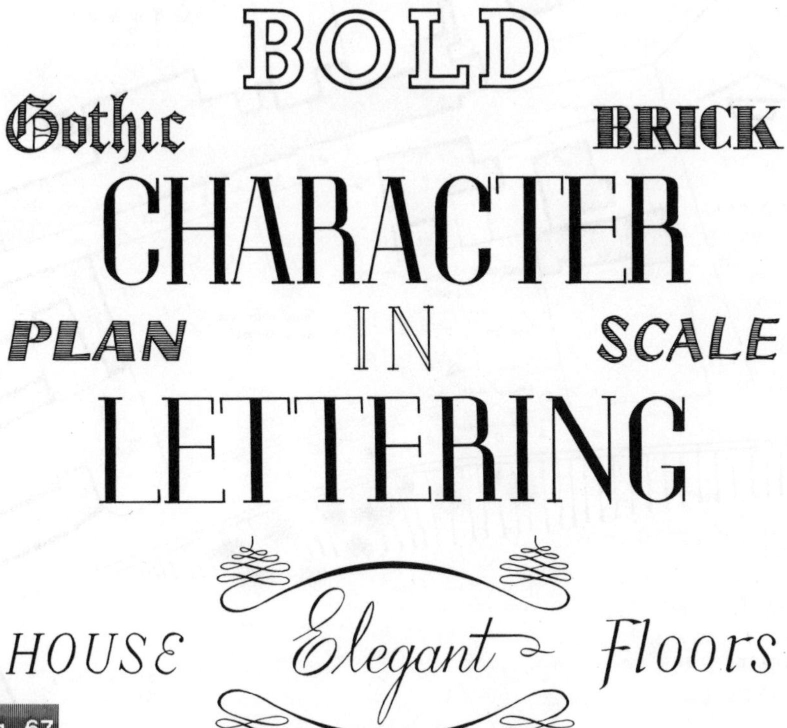

BOLD

Gothic   **BRICK**

CHARACTER

PLAN   IN   *SCALE*

LETTERING

HOUSE   *Elegant*   *Floors*

Fig. 67

UGLY

CRUDE   *and*   *tupid*

·unsuitable·

LETTERING

Fig. 68

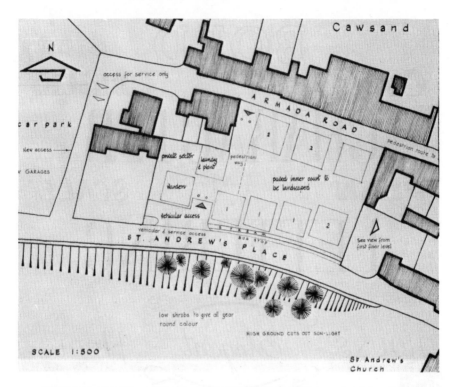

STAGE ONE DESIGN BRIEF
Disposition of dwelling types

CHARACTER AND USE OF MATERIALS:

The overall design of the old people's dwellings has taken into account the enclosed position of the site, with existing houses to the north, east and west. Detached units, rather than continuous development, gives the inner court an environment, which by way of the light being able to pass between the dwellings, brings the court into close proximity with the roads on both sides of the site. An existing, very overgrown orchard, will be removed and new planting of shrubs take place. The random rubble walls to the north and west of the new development will be retained as far as is possible, with pedestrian access limited to Armada Road and St. Andrew's Place in the west.

Although limestone walling was anticipated for the construction of the end walls of the units, this due to cost of labour and construction, has reverted to the use of a very rough textured brick (colour choice not yet established). A rough surfaced 'stonite' (white) will form the infill elevations between these end walls, giving a reflective surface to the otherwise unlit north facing walls. Slate hanging has been ruled out due to its tendency to crack when ball games are played in the vicinity. Roofing materials will be either very rough grey slate or similar tile. Window frames will be aluminium in painted or hardwood surrounds.

Plate 7 Part of student's drawing showing four types of freehand pen lettering, including italic.

Jonathan Lomas

ABCDEFGHIJKLM
NOPQRSTUVWXYZ
1234567890 Nº &

ABCDEFGHIJKLM
NOPQRSTUVWXYZ
1234567890 Nº &

ABCDEFGHIJKLMN
OPQRSTUVWXYZ
1234567890ONo/&

abcdefghijklm
nopqrstuvwxyz
1234567890No

Used carelessly, this lettering is as bad as the worst freehand and a certain amount of practice is necessary to obtain lettering which is pleasing in appearance as well as very legible.

A few hints are: (1) only a small quantity of ink should be put in the pen, (2) keep the pen perfectly upright in use, (3) wash the pen out immediately after use and see that the wire is pushed well home, (4) keep the guides clean, do not let the ink clog the letters. A special cleaning liquid can be obtained for pens and guides.

Always rule faint guide-lines for letters and consider the spacing before starting. Sometimes it may be advisable to make a trial setting-out.

Pressure-transfer lettering

This kind of lettering, also known as pressure sensitive, is extensively used on all kinds of architectural and planning drawings, particularly for titling and labelling. It is reasonably quick and most effective. It's only serious disadvantage is that it is rather expensive, especially as many letters of each sheet are never used.

The letters are printed on thin plastic sheets, usually 254 mm × 381 mm, although smaller sheets are available, in a variety of types of alphabets, numerals, punctuations, etc., and are protected by silicone-treated backing sheets. A typical example is illustrated by Plate 8. The characters can be applied to any smooth dry surface in any desired arrangement. Having decided on the type and size of letters to be used and estimated the placing on the drawing — this requires some experience — the technique of application is to remove the backing sheet and to position the first letter, on a previously ruled guide line if there are to be a series of letters, and then to 'shade' across the letter from top to bottom using a ball-point pen with moderate pressure. This action is continued until the letter appears lighter, which shows that it has been transferred to the surface of the paper. The lettering film is carefully peeled back until the letter is exposed; it is then moved to position the next letter and the transfer procedure is repeated. On completion of a word, or every few letters, even after each letter of the larger sizes, the backing sheet should be laid over and additional firm pressure applied by the finger or the edge of a scale in order to obtain maximum adhesion. When application is made to tracing paper or film from which dyeline prints are to be obtained it may be necessary to spray the letters with a matt fixative or they will be damaged in the printing process. As the spray will also 'fix' any parts of the drawing on which it may fall, it is advisable to confine the area by masking.

Points continually to be kept in mind are: avoid accidentally pressing any

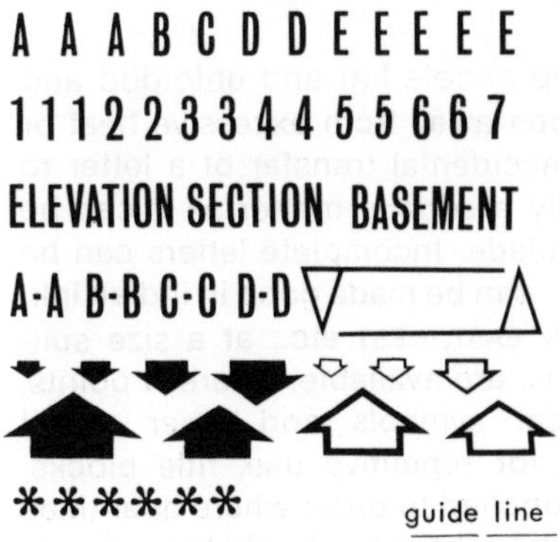
A A A B C D D E E E E E
1 1 1 2 2 3 3 4 4 5 5 6 6 7
ELEVATION SECTION BASEMENT
A-A B-B C-C D-D
******
guide line

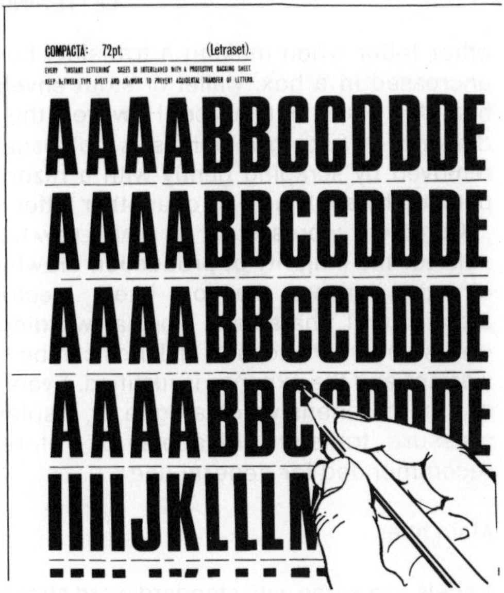
COMPACTA: 72pt. (Letraset).
EVERY "INSTANT LETTERING" SHEET IS INTERLEAVED WITH A PROTECTIVE BACKING SHEET.
KEEP BETWEEN TYPE SHEET AND ARTWORK TO PREVENT ACCIDENTAL TRANSFER OF LETTERS.
AAAABBCCDDDE
AAAABBCCDDDE
AAAABBCCDDDE
AAAABBCCDDDE
IIIIJKLLLM

Plate 8 Transfer lettering: alphabets, numerals, words and symbols. (Reproduced by permission of Letraset Ltd; arrangement by author.)

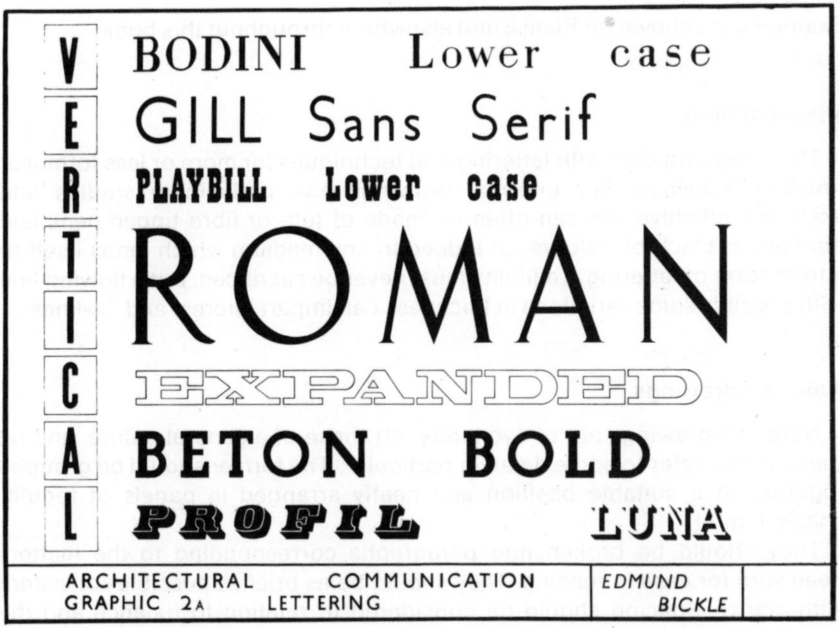
VERTICAL
BODINI Lower case
GILL Sans Serif
PLAYBILL Lower case
ROMAN
EXPANDED
BETON BOLD
PROFIL LUNA
ARCHITECTURAL COMMUNICATION
GRAPHIC 2A LETTERING
EDMUND BICKLE

Plate 9 Lettering drawn in indian ink. (Student's drawing.)

other letter when making a transfer; keep sheets flat and unfolded and uncreased in a box, wallet or stout envelope away from excessive heat or humidity when not in use. However, the accidental transfer of a letter to drawing or tracing materials is not usually a serious matter as it can be removed by scraping gently with a razor blade. Incomplete letters can be patched by applying part of another letter or can be made good in indian ink.

Complete words such as PLAN, ELEVATION, EAST, WEST, etc., at a size suitable for the majority of production drawings, are available, as are N points, direction arrows, section lines, electrical symbols and other useful architectural characters. Special wording for repetitive use, title blocks, crests and indications of all kinds can be supplied to order where quantities warrant and the expense is justified. Every draughtsman should have a copy of a comprehensive catalogue or display sheet of the various standard pressure transfer alphabets for reference. The following types are recommended for general use:

Main titles	— Compacta or Egyptienne expanded
Labels — to agree with standard word sheets	— Grotesque 7 (36 pt)
Names of rooms and grouped notes	— Grotesque 209 (10 pt)

Examples are shown on Plate 8 and elsewhere throughout this book.

Miscellaneous

The foregoing deal with lettering and techniques for more or less formal or finished drawings. For informal drawings and preliminary studies and sketches, effective use can often be made of felt- or fibre-tipped pens and markers in black or colours, or indeed in any medium which lends itself to a freer form of lettering. Legibility must never be sacrificed, but a flowing line with possibly some variations in thickness can impart interest and liveliness.

Notes on drawings

Notes on drawings are of two kinds: (1) those of a general nature, and (2) those which refer to some detail in particular. The former should be grouped together in a suitable position and neatly arranged in panels of regular shape, Fig. 71.

They should be broken into paragraphs corresponding to the matters dealt with for ease in reading. They should be as brief as possible consistent with clarity. Spacing should be considered in relation to balance and the

NOTES

GENERAL NOTES SHOULD NOT BE SCATTERED OVER THE DRAWING BUT SHOULD BE NEATLY ARRANGED IN PANELS OF REGULAR SHAPE

THEY SHOULD BE BROKEN INTO PARAGRAPHS FOR EASE IN READING.

THE LETTERS AND WORDS SHOULD NOT BE CRAMPED NOR SO W I D E L Y SPACED AS TO BECOME ILLEGIBLE

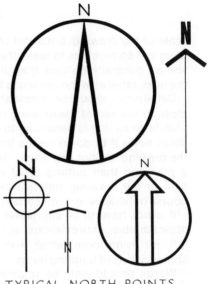

TYPICAL NORTH POINTS

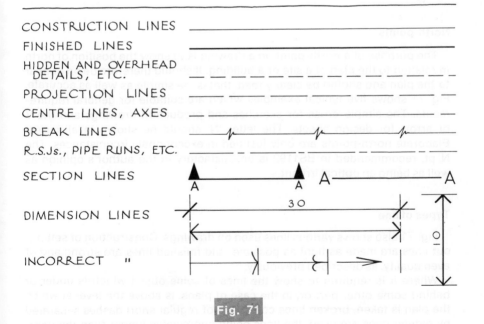

CONSTRUCTION LINES

FINISHED LINES

HIDDEN AND OVERHEAD DETAILS, ETC.

PROJECTION LINES

CENTRE LINES, AXES

BREAK LINES

R.S.Js., PIPE RUNS, ETC.

SECTION LINES

DIMENSION LINES

INCORRECT "

Fig. 71

scale of the drawing, but avoid cramping the letters and words or spreading them out so much as to make them illegible. The spaces between the letters should generally be less than the spaces between one line of notes and the next, otherwise the eye tends to read vertically, 'Chinese' fashion.

Detail notes should be reasonably small, 2–4 mm high, and neatly arranged close to the part of the drawing to which they refer. A short arrow as pointer should be all that is necessary to connect the note to the detail. Do not group detail notes if to do so means long 'snaky' arrows or lines to relate them to the drawing. Do not use 'keys', that is, for example, numbering the rooms on a plan and then putting a list explaining what the numbers mean at the side of the drawing, unless lack of space or other reason makes such a course imperative, e.g. for certain kinds of coded drawings.

If words have to be shortened, try to preserve clarity without resorting to objectionable abbreviations such as 'kitch.' for kitchen, 'kit.' is better; 'LR' for living-room rather than 'Liv. Rm.' See BS1192 12.1 for common abbreviations of building terms.

Words should only be underlined where special emphasis is required. Full-stops should not be used unless essential to the sense of the note.

North-points

The purpose of a north-point on a drawing is to show the position of north in relation to the plan of a site or a building. It should therefore be on or near to the plan and should be clearly read, that is, be simple as well as accurate. Fig. 71 shows five typical examples which are suitable for general requirements. The simple cross for sketches and production drawings and the V or arrow for design sheets. The letter 'N' should be shown in all cases. Elaborate north-points are only justified in exceptional circumstances. The N. pt. recommended in BS1192 is unsatisfactory in the author's opinion as well as being an optical irritant.

Types of line

Fig. 71 also shows various lines used on drawings. Construction or setting-out lines are made as light as possible, and finished lines are strong and of even quality, as described previously.

Where it is required to show the lines of some object which is under or behind some other part or, in the case of plans, is above the level at which the plan is taken, broken lines consisting of regular short dashes separated by regular gaps are used, the lines being appreciably longer than the gaps. 'Dotted' lines should not be used.

Projection lines should be light like construction lines, but broken by regular gaps.

Centre lines or axes (axial lines) are usually shown by comparatively light continuous lines with a short gap and short line at each end. An alternative line for this purpose recommended by the British Standards Institution is one consisting of alternate long and short lines separated by regular gaps, as shown in the figure for overhead RSJs, etc. Centre lines should project a short distance beyond the outlines of the part to which they refer.

Where it is intended to show that a drawing is incomplete, break lines consisting of ruled lines with short zig-zags at intervals are used.

Section lines, which indicate where a plan has been 'cut' (see Chapter 2) are commonly shown by either of the ways illustrated. The black triangles or the placing of the letters show the way the sectional view is taken.

Dimension lines (see also page 121) should be lighter or thinner than outlines and should be continuous, not broken for the insertion of dimension figures. They should be terminated by arrow-heads exactly touching the outlines or projection lines to which they relate, or the dimension lines can be continued past the outlines and projection lines and the points of intersection emphasised by a small stroke or dot. Dimension figures should be placed immediately above the corresponding dimension line, either near the centre or at the extreme left. The figures should always be disposed along the line and not at right-angles to it. Vertical dimension lines should have the figures on the left-hand side reading upwards.

Scales

When drawn scales are used — and it is the usual practice now not to do so unless the drawing is to be reproduced to a different size — they should be simple and easy to read. Three parallel horizontal lines with vertical sub-divisions and with the major units to the right and minor units to the left is a satisfactory arrangement for imperial drawings, and two horizontal lines with appropriate vertical sub-divisions and the words 'metres' and/or 'millimetres' for metric drawings.

5
Drawings

Scale drawings

Most technical drawings are *scale drawings*, that is, the land, buildings or objects shown on them are not represented at their true size, but are larger or, more often, smaller in some proportion.

Fig. 72 is a scale drawing of a stool in the proportion of 1:10, that is one-tenth fullsize. Note that the plan drawing consists of (1) a half-true plan looking down, and (2) a half-horizontal section through the legs. This method enables more details to be illustrated without repeating unnecessarily similar parts of the drawing. The sectional parts of the wood are defined more clearly by hatching between the outlines — see Chapter 6.

Fig. 73 shows a scale drawing of a small garage in orthographic projection consisting of plan, two elevations and two sections. The scale is 1:100. A pictorial drawing, not to the same scale, is included to show the general appearance of the garage. Note the representation of the brick walls on elevation by the horizontal lines of the courses, and of the vertical boarding of the doors. The conventional representation of certain other features, some of which occur here, are explained in the next chapter. As the drawing is not intended, however, as a working drawing, constructional details are omitted.

Normally, drawings such as those just discussed would be made using an appropriate boxwood or plastic scale for marking off the required distances. Only if it were necessary to work to some unusual proportion would a scale have to be drawn at the outset by dividing a line into whatever units and subdivisions were required.

Types of drawing

The following notes describe drawings for certain purposes in connection with building and land development. The techniques of draughtsmanship are in many respects common to all, but defined practice, including conven-

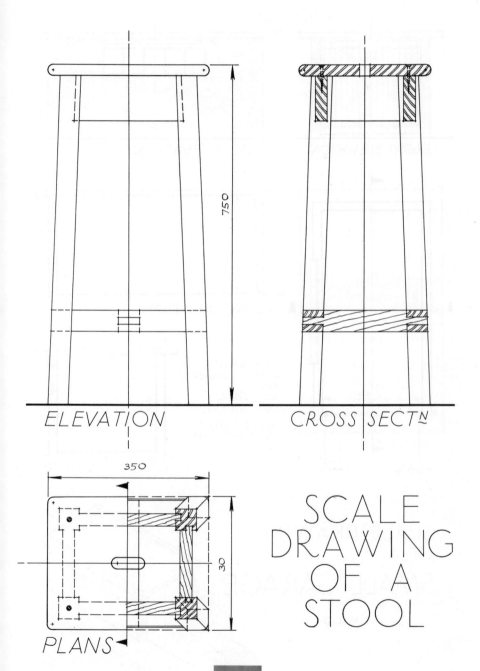

ELEVATION

750

CROSS SECTᴺ

350

30

PLANS

SCALE
DRAWING
OF A
STOOL

Fig. 72

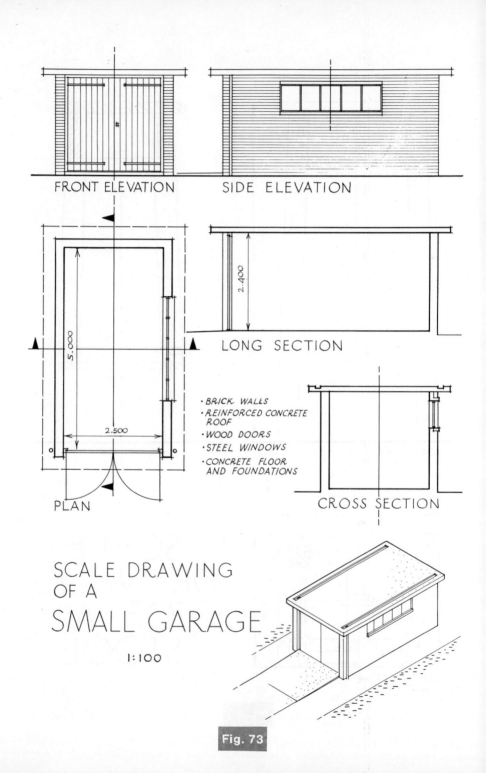

FRONT ELEVATION SIDE ELEVATION

PLAN

LONG SECTION

· BRICK WALLS
· REINFORCED CONCRETE ROOF
· WOOD DOORS
· STEEL WINDOWS
· CONCRETE FLOOR AND FOUNDATIONS

CROSS SECTION

5.000

2.500

2.400

SCALE DRAWING
OF A
SMALL GARAGE

1:100

Fig. 73

DRAWINGS

The following are recommended scales for use with the metric system

Use	Scale		Ratio
Maps	1 : 1 000 000		1 mm to 1000 m
	1 : 500 000		1 mm to 500 m
	1 : 200 000		1 mm to 200 m
	1 : 100 000		1 mm to 100 m
	1 : 50 000		1 mm to 50 m
Town surveys	1 : 50 000		1 mm to 50 m
	1 : 20 000		1 mm to 20 m
	1 : 10 000		1 mm to 10 m
	1 : 5000		1 mm to 5 m
		*1 : 2500	1 mm to 2.5 m
Survey and layouts		*1 : 2500	1 mm to 2.5 m
	1 : 2000		1 mm to 2 m
		*1 : 1250	1 mm to 1.25 m
	1 : 1000		1 mm to 1 m
	1 : 500		1 mm to 0.5 m
Site and key plans		*1 : 1250	1 mm to 1.25 m
	1 : 1000		1 mm to 1 m
	1 : 500		1 mm to 0.5 m
Sketch schemes, etc.	1 : 200		1 mm to 0.2 m
	1 : 100		1 mm to 0.1 m
Location drawings†	1 : 200		1 mm to 0.2 m
	1 : 100		1 mm to 0.1 m
	1 : 50		1 mm to 0.05 m
Component and	1 : 20		1 mm to 0.02 m
assembly detail	1 : 10		1 mm to 0.01 m
drawings	1 : 5		1 mm to 0.005 m
	1 : 1		Full size

*Scales so marked are included in recognition of the great problems that face Ordnance survey and map users in a changeover to ISO scales.

*The term 'location drawings' includes drawings of the sort that used to be called $\frac{1}{8}$th-scale working drawings.

Comparison of metric and and imperial (foot/inch)

Scales for use with metric system	Scales for use with foot/inch system	
1 : 1 000 000	1 : 1 000 000	$\frac{1}{16}$ in to 1 mile approx.
1 : 500 000	1 : 625 000	$\frac{1}{10}$ in to 1 mile approx.
1 : 200 000	1 : 250 000	$\frac{1}{4}$ in to 1 mile approx.
1 : 100 000	1 : 126 720	$\frac{1}{2}$ in to 1 mile
1 : 50 000	1 : 63 360	1 in to 1 mile
1 : 20 000	1 : 25 000	$2\frac{1}{2}$ in to 1 mile approx.
1 : 10 000	1 : 10 560	6 in to 1 mile
1 : 5000		
1 : 2000	1 : 2500	1 in to 208.33 ft
1 : 1000	1 : 1250	1 in to 104.17 ft
1 : 500	1 : 500	1 in to 41.6 ft
	1 : 384	$\frac{1}{32}$ in to 1 ft
1 : 200	1 : 192	$\frac{1}{16}$ in to 1 ft
1 : 100	1 : 96	$\frac{1}{8}$ in to 1 ft
1 : 50	1 : 48	$\frac{1}{4}$ in to 1 ft
1 : 20	1 : 24	$\frac{1}{2}$ in to 1 ft
1 : 10	1 : 12	1 in to 1 ft
1 : 5	1 : 4	3 in to 1 ft

tional representations and indications, vary for each profession, and reference should be made to current accepted standards and methods, and to specimens and examples of contemporary work.

Planning drawings

In this category are survey maps and diagrams made to show existing topography, buildings, communications, etc., preliminary designs on broad lines to show proposed new development, statutory scheme maps, detailed layouts and townscape studies. Many planning drawings are prepared on or over Ordnance sheets, some of which may have to be brought up-to-date. As the scales are often small, minor slips can be serious and great care should be taken with such drawings. Draughtsmanship must be precise.

Particulars of standard notations and representations for official survey and development plan maps in Britain are given in circulars and other publications of the Department of the Environment, which incorporates the former Ministry of Housing and Local Government (previously Ministry of Town and Country Planning). These directives and guides * have been prepared not only to achieve uniformity and clarity but also with regard to ease and economy in the reproduction of plans, many

*In particular *Development Plans: A Manual of Form and Content*, HMSO, 1970

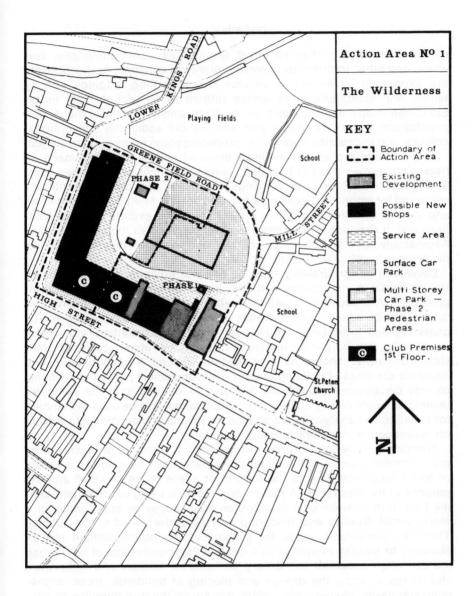

Plate 10 Example of drawing of part of town plan showing proposed redevelopment indicated by various edgings, hatchings, letters, etc. (Reproduced by permission of Hertfordshire County Planning Officer, Laurence C. Kitching, M.B.E., M.T.P.I., M.I.Min.E.)

copies of which are often required. Boundaries, communications, services, and other information covering planning concepts and proposals are expressed by means of various cross-hatching, edgings and by letters and combinations of letters related to an alphabetical index. Specimen maps are included to illustrate these representations and annotations to various scales with and without additional conventional colours, and to describe methods of preparing plans for printing in stages.

In the design process, preliminary planning studies are often made on tracing paper over maps in freehand, using soft pencils or felt-nibbed pens. Strong black outlines and shadings are used, and distinctive colours employed for emphasis. Lettering is free and flowing whether in ink or pencil, and various 'shorthand' symbols project ideas and explore possible solutions and, if required, convey them to other members of the planning team. Alternatively, similar but more diagrammatic sketches may be made on detail paper in coloured chalks.

Developed design drawings may be more carefully made over maps on tracing media in ink outlines with rules hatchings and transfer lettering for photoprint reproduction to which mechanical tones and conventional colours can be added. Such drawings will show, according to scale, appropriate detailed indication of buildings, roads, trees, planting, etc. Trees, incidentally, may be put on negatives or prints by rubber stamps or from standard transfer sheets as described in Chapter 9. Axonometric and isometric drawings of building masses may supplement plans and sections, as may perspectives individually prepared or derived from the computer technique mentioned in Chapter 8. Computers can also be used in Planning for collating and analysing data and for the storing of mappable information for subsequent retrieval and graphic presentation.

Townscape drawings in further explanation of planning proposals or as part of environmental architectural presentation can be made in a variety of techniques according to the subject or scene to be depicted and the purpose of the illustration. A reasonable free style using pencil or pen-and-ink lines with monochrome or coloured washes may be appropriate, or a more formal drawing and rendering may be better suited to the subject. There is considerable scope for imaginative expression without loss of accuracy or realism. People of all kinds and the impedimenta of daily urban life are often essential but dreary caricatures, human and otherwise, should not obscure the design and placing of buildings, trees, signs, lamp standards, pavings, etc., which it is surely the true intention to portray. The imitation of strongly individualistic styles should be avoided.

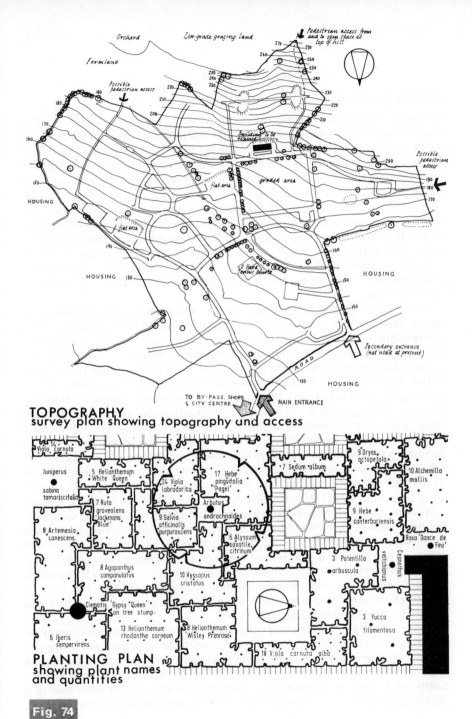

TOPOGRAPHY
survey plan showing topography and access

PLANTING PLAN
showing plant names
and quantities

Fig. 74

Fig. 74 Examples of landscape drawings reproduced from *Techniques of Landscape Architecture* by permission of the Institute of Landscape Architects.

Landscape drawings

Landscaping covers a wide range of work in connection with outdoor environment, from the conservation and management of regional areas to the laying out and planting of small spaces between buildings. Drawings of various kinds are employed. Broadly classified, they fall into three groups corresponding to general procedure, i.e. site analysis and preliminary, main report, and working drawings.

In the first category there are drawings made over existing maps, new survey drawings showing contours and topographical details, and sketches of the terrain and its surroundings, followed by drawings, freehand in the main, to illustrate preliminary outline proposals. Any appropriate technique may be used, and coloured pencils and felt-tipped pens with simple hatchings and basic indications can quickly produce 'think' drawings and help develop ideas.

Drawings to accompany a main report, which are communications between designer and client, require to be of a more finished nature, using conventional and easily-understood representations and techniques. The drawings should be fully annotated with cross-references as necessary. Plans should be to scale. There is an advantage in making them to the same scales as subsequent working drawings, but to do so may involve more drafting time and detail work than justified at this stage. Generally, drawings need be no bigger nor more in number than adequate to show the intended work. Elaborate drawings will not compensate for weak or undeveloped designs, although scruffy drawings may obscure good ideas. Sections may be required to show changes in ground levels, sight lines, etc., and perspective sketches will help in conveying the character of the completed design or the effect of various proposals. Use can be made of bold arrows, broken lines, lines of different thicknesses, shading and colour to clarify the design.

Working drawings may be less exact than building or planning drawings, but nevertheless they should be set out with reasonable accuracy from maps or surveys. For very large sites, drawing techniques may well follow civil engineering practice, e.g. in regard to major earthworks, drainage schemes, etc. For even more extensive areas, standard map notations may be adopted, perhaps with a key master plan related to detail drawings. For general construction purposes, drawings should be made in accordance with the current British Standard Specification.

Trees are usually represented by plain or serrated circles, which may be drawn by compasses but more quickly through a template, unless of special significance, when a more literal representation may be used. Diameters should be approximately to scale and the trees accurately placed in their positions. Letters or numerals are commonly used to relate each tree to a legend giving the botanical name, which is usually too long to be repeated,

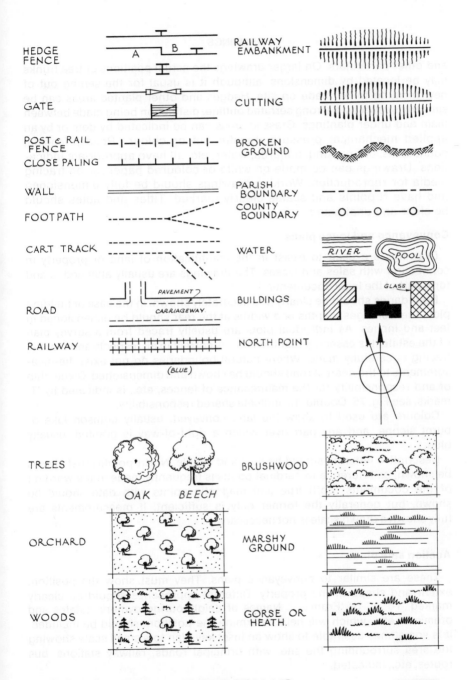

CONVENTIONAL INDICATIONS
FOR SURVEY DRAWINGS

Fig. 75

and other particulars. On larger drawings the actual positions of tree trunks may be located by dimensions, although it is usual for the setting out of new planting to be made on site. Hedges and other planted areas can be similarly shown by a strong serrated outline, distinction being made between main and under plantings. Grassed areas can be indicated by dots or by an applied mechanical pressure transfer tint or colour. Roads, fencing, boundaries, car parking, bollards, water, etc. all have appropriate indications. Drawings can be made on white or coloured paper, or on tracing media for reproduction. Working drawings should be fully dimensioned and have N-points and scales clearly marked. Titles and notes should be clear and unaffected.

Conveyance and lease plans

Drawings are used to assist in the identification of land or property in connection with sales and leases. The drawings are usually attached to and form part of the legal documents.

Boundaries should be clearly and accurately shown. In the case of building plots the frontages, depths and widths at the rear should be dimensioned in feet and inches. As individual plots are usually traced from a survey plan of the estate it is essential that the latter is correct in all respects and that the tracing is carefully made. Where natural boundaries do not exist, tie-measurements to the nearest road should be shown and dimensioned. Ownership of and responsibility for the maintenance of fences, etc., is indicated by 'T' marks, see Fig. 75. Double 'Ts' indicate shared responsibility.

Colours are used to show the land conveyed, usually crimson lake or burnt sienna, and any part over which a right-of-way is granted, usually blue.

Descriptive lettering should be neat and legible. North-points must always be shown, as reference to cardinal points is frequently made in the wording of the documents. Both true and magnetic points with date should be shown, but generally the former only is sufficient. If measurements are fully shown a drawn scale is not necessary.

Auction sale plans

These are similar to conveyance plans. They must show the position, extent and shape of the property. Different approaches should be clearly marked 'To ...' or 'From ...'. Names of neighbouring owners, estates and premises, etc., which will help determine the position, should be included. It is sometimes desirable to show an inset key plan to a small scale showing the area surrounding the site, with principal roads, railway stations, bus routes, etc., indicated.

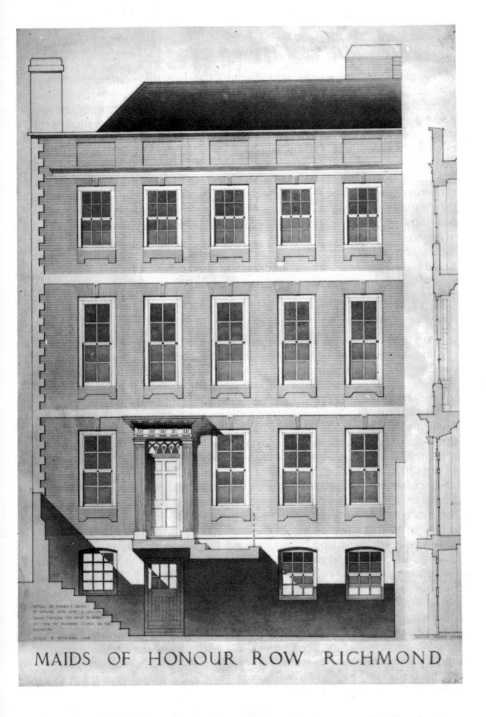

MAIDS OF HONOUR ROW RICHMOND

Plate 11 Student's measured drawing of building of historic interest. Pencil and water colour wash with conventional shadows.

The plans are frequently reproduced or traced from Ordnance Survey maps; 1/500 scale is often used for urban districts.

It is not essential that such plans should be extremely accurate and any misunderstanding in this connection can be avoided by a note added to the drawing as follows: 'This plan is for identification purposes only and although believed to be correct is not guaranteed and shall not be deemed part of any contract.'

A north-point is essential and a scale should be drawn as well as stated. It may also be necessary to show dimension lines and figured dimensions for frontages and depths, positions of building lines, if existing, approximate positions and directions of flows of any sewers, and the positions and kinds of any trees.

Lettering should be placed where it can be easily read and, so far as possible, should 'read' in one direction.

Measured drawings

These scale drawings are made from carefully taken measurements of existing buildings of historic interest and architectural merit as part of students' training in design and to an increasing extent, for purposes of recording such works (especially in connection with preservation and conservation under Town Planning legislation) and also any building to which alterations, additions or restorations are to be made. The drawings may illustrate a whole building or part of a building and may range from small-scale plans and elevations to full-size details. Space here does not allow a full description of the various types of subject and their presentation. Sometimes, form or decoration is the chief interest; in other cases constructional features are of most importance. Technique must vary accordingly, but elaborate rendering is generally unnecessary. The more direct the exposition the better, with special care being taken in regard to freehand detail, titles and lettering. Accuracy, of course, a first essential, should be of the highest. Drawings mainly in pencil with outlines of plans and sections in ink and perhaps with openings and conventional shadows in wash are usually satisfactory. Part plans and sections are often superimposed over corresponding details shown in elevation. The scale and north-point should always be shown prominently and descriptive notes should be well arranged.

In making the survey of a building, the first step is to make a series of diagrammatic sketches (see Chapter 10) on which the necessary measurements can be marked. The importance of these sketches cannot be over-emphasised. They should be made in suitable stiff-backed sketch-books or on clipboards on thin but tough plain paper, preferably not less than A3 size. Complicated work is best plotted to a small scale as the measuring proceeds.

Sketch measured drawings are carefully made sketches, often in perspective and sometimes with approximate scale details added, on which overall main measurements are shown by lines and arrows.

Architectural drawings

The range of architectural drawings is considerable, and despite efforts at standardisation there are widely differing techniques and styles used in their preparation. The following is a broad classification of the main types:

1. *Preliminary*. This includes graphic interpretation of sites and site conditions, feasibility studies, i.e. investigation and analysis of the building's requirements (brief), and the working out of main lines of possible design solutions. Such drawings are generally 'short life' drawings, sometimes little more than diagrams, and are usually made freehand, often on gridded paper or over gridded boards or backing sheets, although where appropriate they may be set up to small scales using T-square and set-square. Simple perspectives may also be made at this stage, and for environmental studies, or discussions with clients and others, surroundings and shadows can be indicated.

Sketch designs which are part of architectural training are somewhat similar to the above but, as well as planning exercises, they include a large proportion of design problems of a more imaginative kind, calling for the rapid and effective presentation of solutions usually in perspective. Usually not more than six hours are allowed for the preparation of such drawings and the presentation must therefore be on broad lines without overmuch attention to detail, the suggestion of the essential qualities of the design, construction and general character being all that is required. Freedom of technique is imperative and the opportunities should be taken for experiments in appropriate media, such as soft pencil, crayon, charcoal, pastel, poster colour, etc., and in the using of various papers, including coloured and textured papers.

2. *Design*. This includes drawings made for the development of designs, which in certain cases require the collaboration of consultants and specialists such as structural and mechanical engineers; draft constructional details; and complete design drawings which may be highly finished. Development drawings can vary greatly in techniques and scales according to the purposes for which they are prepared, e.g. for the putting down of the designers' thoughts (thinking drawings) and conversely for graphic representation to stimulate new ideas, to help forward stage by stage the

logical process of designing and to provide a means of communication between members of the design team. Depending upon the size and type of a particular project, there may be many such drawings, most of which are made on tracing paper and have a relatively short life.

Finished design drawings show a minimum of constructional detail, although the construction must be fully worked out before they can be properly completed. In practice it often happens that after agreement has been reached on a preliminary sketch design, the next step is the preparation of production drawings with such modifications as may be necessary, and finished design drawings are not made until later, if at all. The designs of students, however, are usually required to be shown fully on well-finished presentation drawings.

In all cases the drawings may be orthographic projections, metric projections, or perspectives accurately drawn and effectively rendered. The lay-out of the sheets is important, and care must be taken to avoid crowded and unbalanced arrangements. Dimensions should not normally be shown, nor should notes of materials—except as footnotes—nor structural details on plan and section unless required for some special purpose.

Conventional shadows should be shown (see page 180) in order to explain the forms, etc., and appropriate surroundings can be included. The degree of formality or freedom of the presentation will depend upon the character of the subject and the use to which the drawing will be put. Lettering in particular must be carefully arranged and executed in a suitable alphabet. It will be confined in the main to the title, labelling of plans, elevations and sections, names of rooms, etc., and possibly some brief general notes.

Colour design drawings are usually orthographic or axonometric projections of the interiors of rooms and serve both to show the design and to guide the execution of the actual work. Colours should therefore be as near as possible to those to be used. Flat opaque hues should be used for painted areas. Designers' colours, poster colours or ordinary water-colours added to a base of Chinese white is the medium to adopt. Other materials should be naturally represented.

3. *Production*—Formerly described as 'working drawings', production drawings are made for the purpose of conveying precise constructional information, e.g. for the use of quantity surveyors; in combination with other documents, for obtaining planning and building regulations approvals, for obtaining tenders or negotiating contracts, and for instructing contractors and other members of the building team. They are invariably drawn in final form on good-quality tracing paper or film, usually in pencil with some ink work and applied lettering, but sometimes wholly in ink, for reproduction by photoprinting processes. The negatives are valuable documents to be handled and stored with care.

Plate 12 Perspective drawing of offices. (Architects: main building—D. B. and J. S. Coombe, A/ARIBA, AA. Dip., interior and additions—Fraser Reekie and Associates.)

F. A. Evans

DRAWINGS

The drawings are generally orthographic projections to scale—an appropriate ratio being used according to size and purpose—although metric projections may also be included to explain detail construction. Arrangement of each sheet should be well organised, and for each job drawings should be standard in size, and uniform in technique, annotation, dimensioning, references, etc.

The typical set of traditional production drawings, which are still extensively used particularly for smaller buildings, comprises complete plans, elevations and sections drawn to a scale of 1:100 or 1:50 ($\frac{1}{8}''$ or $\frac{1}{4}''$ to 1'0'') and details to larger scales ranging from 1:20 ($\frac{1}{2}''$ to 1'0'') to full-size, on which more or less total construction is shown. Negative prints are sometimes made of the basic plans and on these are added services such as electrical, sanitary, and heating and ventilating layouts. The drawings are supplemented by door and window schedules, etc. The method has the advantage of conveying information by comparatively few drawings of a kind better understood by the less sophisticated building firms; both in the drawing stage and on the site the relationships between adjoining and interconnecting elements can be more readily grasped. However, with the increasing complexity of construction, multiplicity of lines and lettering can cause confusion and error, a situation worsened if changes are made during the progress of the works.

To overcome this problem, where larger projects are concerned, drawings can be made on an operational or elemental basis. Master skeleton layouts, e.g. structural grids, are prepared, and on negative prints thereof the work of one trade or one sub-contractor only is shown on each drawing. This enables operational information to be quickly and clearly conveyed and facilitates job information. Disadvantages are the greatly increased number of drawings required for each job, and the tendency for omissions and lack of co-ordination to occur unless particular care is exercised, as of course it should be, in making and checking the drawings.

No shadows or shading other than the indication of materials, and no extraneous details not relevant to the construction should be shown. A 'busy' working drawing in which every detail is drawn elaborately and repeated unnecessarily has no advantages and may be illegible. Lettering must be clear and tidily arranged, particularly as it may constitute half the drawing. Nevertheless, it must be kept as brief as possible and any general notes should not be expanded to long clauses belonging properly to the specification.

A useful reference is Working Drawings in Use by C. D. Daltry and D. T. Crawshaw, published by the Building Research Establishment of the Department of the Environment.

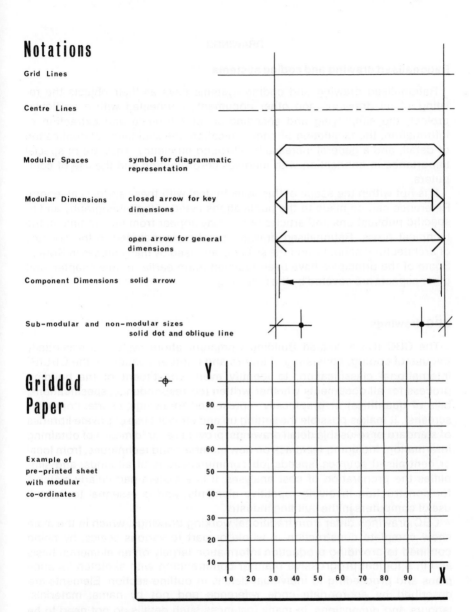

Notations

Grid Lines

Centre Lines

Modular Spaces   symbol for diagrammatic representation

Modular Dimensions   closed arrow for key dimensions

     open arrow for general dimensions

Component Dimensions   solid arrow

Sub-modular and non-modular sizes
     solid dot and oblique line

Gridded Paper

Example of
pre-printed sheet
with modular
co-ordinates

Modular Drawing

Plate 13 Standard notations, and example of gridded paper used in the preparation of drawings for modular co-ordination.

Rationalised drawing and coding systems

Rationalised drawing and coding systems have as their objects the re-lating of all drawings and other documents connected with a particular project, the simplifying and speeding-up of reference and extraction of information, the facilitating of communication, the avoidance of duplication of detail, and a general increase in all-round efficiency. They are of special importance in connection with modular co-ordination and the use of computers.

It is not within the scope of this book to deal with these systems at length. Reference can be made to the publications listed in the bibliography and to specific publications and articles which may appear from time to time in the technical press. Rationalised drawing practice is included in the courses of architectural schools, and the systems are used by many offices in Britain. Some of the principles have been touched upon earlier in this chapter, and other aspects are covered by the following:

CBC drawings

The CBC (Co-ordinated Building Communication) system is essentially the use of coding, consisting of letters and numbers based on the CI/SfB[1] international classification, to identify every constituent of the building process for all documents whether written (correspondence, specifications, bills of quantities) or graphically represented (drawings, charts, computer screens). It makes possible the setting up and efficient use of private libraries of standard or re-usable detail drawings, provides a rapid means of obtaining information, including feedback on new materials and techniques, from local or centralised sources, speeds job communications of all kinds, and simplifies the preparation of cost analyses. It is a system particularly suitable for construction involving repetitive elements, and is essential to the full use of computers in the building industry.

CBC drawings differ from traditional working drawings, which in the main show complete construction in whole or part to various scales, by being confined to providing production information largely on an elemental basis and in a logical progressive manner commencing with skeleton location plans and proceeding to individual details in outline section. Elements are described by appropriate code reference and not by name, materials, labours and dimensions. In many instances such details do not need to be drawn accurately to scale, although, as with all drawings, it is a wise precau-

---

[1]Construction Index/Samarbetskommitten för Byggnadsfragnor derived from a Swedish system of classifying technical information.

tion to do so to prevent confusion and misinterpretation. Many more draw-ings are required for the CBC system but as maximum use is made of nega-tive prints of basic layouts and of standard details, production of drawings is greatly expedited, especially as they are much simpler and easier to make. There is a sharp distinction between design and production draw-ings. Design drawings may be made in any of the ways previously men-tioned or in any other way which may be satisfactory, but the knowledge that the CBC system will be subsequently used for production drawings will affect their preparation to some degree. Design drawings must be complete before production drawings are commenced. In the event of revisions being necessary, drawings are not altered but new drawings bearing new numbers are made.

CBC drawings are coded in accordance with their respective categories. Sizes of drawings can conform with previously recommended standard sizes for folding to fit together for binding with other documents. The preparation of CBC drawings is part of the work of building technicians.

References: *CI/SfB Project Manual* by Alan Ray-Jones and Wilfred McCann, Architectural Press, London, and *Redland Guide to the Construction Industry,* annual published by Redland Ltd., Reigate, England.

Drawings for modular co-ordination

The basic technique differs little from that for traditional or conventional drawings, and modular drawings are usually simpler because they can be prepared over grids — the lines of which correspond with the module size — which not only makes measuring by scale unnecessary, but also eliminates the need for many dimension lines, descriptive notes, etc.
Apart from the site plan there are four main types of drawings:

Location and key drawings. These give the overall layout of the design and general location of the main elements and components in relation to the reference lines of the planning grid. They do not describe the compo-nents nor the methods of assembly. The drawings are usually to a small scale, i.e. 1:100, 1:50, and include plans, elevations and sections.

Assembly drawings. These show the condition of assembly of components in relation to the basic modular (M) grid. Usually to a large scale, i.e. 1:5, 1:2 and FS.

Component range drawings. These show sets of components, such as doors, windows, panels, etc., with their modular sizes and with reference numbers so that they can be related to other drawings. Usually small scale, i.e. 1·50, 1:20.

Component detail drawings. These are in effect manufacturers's drawings and provide the information needed for the production of a component.

They may also indicate fixing methods. Dimensions show both work sizes and permitted tolerances, usually to fairly large scales.

Typical examples of these drawings are shown in BS1192 1969, and a recommended standard system of notation is shown in Plate 13. It is important that there is a clear distinction between the system of reference, the modular sizes and the work sizes.

General. Broadly speaking, traditional drawing practice is best for traditional building methods, whereas rationalised and coded systems are best for industrialised, modular and similar kinds of construction. The latter may gradually become accepted for most projects, but traditional practice is being continually modified and a lengthy period of change and adjustment throughout the industry still lies ahead. The draughtsman must be aware of developments and be responsive to new ideas.

Computers and drawings

Considerable advances have been and are being made in the use of computers as aids in architecture and building. Apart from the rapid carrying out of complex calculations for which they were primarily designed and the preparation of perspective projections described in Chapter 8, they now make possible the retrieval of previously stored coded drawings, the making of amendments thereto, and the reproduction of them on paper at selected scales.

From experience gained from measurements and performance evaluations of particular types of buildings, e.g. schools, hospitals and airports, integrated suites of computer programs can be developed relevant to the outline proposal stage of design, comprising analyses of accommodation, generation of layouts, and appraisals in economic, functional and environmental terms. Much of these can be graphically expressed by diagrams and drawings produced on normal tracing and detail paper, using conventional drawing pens and ink, and in most respects they are analogous to corresponding manually produced graphic representations.

At town planning level, appropriate programs have been devised for the purpose of aggregating population maps and optimally to locate such central facilities as schools and shops, as well as for the study of land use possibilities, e.g. the provision of residential, recreational and other major areas.

For reinforced concrete structural engineering, which is well suited to computerisation, program libraries produced by qualified engineers experienced in computer techniques include analyses of various types of structures together with general arrangement drawings, details of columns, beams, foundations, walls and slabs, etc.

General lay-out of drawings

These notes apply to all types of drawings, but are made with special reference to architectural drawings.

Sizes of working drawings and site plans should conform to the standard dimensions referred to previously, page 25, but architectural design drawings and students' exercise drawings need not necessarily be standardised. Fig. 76 shows a suitable lay-out for the last-named, providing spaces for title, student's name, and date, mark, etc. Some such lay-out is advisable for early geometry, construction and similar sheets.

Fig. 77 shows the lay-out of design drawings. Titles are usually best placed towards the bottom of the sheet and should be symmetrically disposed if the arrangement as a whole is otherwise symmetrical, but the title must always be included as part of the composition of the drawing, and it may therefore be advisable to place the title in some other position. The title must never be 'mean' or out of keeping with the character of the subject. The name of the designer(s) and draughtsman should appear in the bottom right-hand corner unless forming part of the title. Borders should be simple and neatly drawn, consisting of two or three ruled lines with perhaps a band of colour. They are helpful in pulling together a loosely composed sheet, but are not essential.

Fig. 78 shows a type of lay-out for contract and production drawings which is becoming standard practice. Such a standard arrangement makes easier the reading of drawings, makes it possible for essential references to be located without trouble — an important point when drawings are prepared in several offices for one job, and reduces the likelihood of essential information being omitted. The placing of general and revision notes in a panel immediately above the name-panel makes them readily seen if the drawings or prints are bound together or folded.

Fig. 79 shows a detail of a revision panel and name block, which may be drawn, stamped, pre-printed or applied.

Titles of jobs and descriptions of drawings should be as brief as possible. The title should not be varied on different drawings relating to the same work, nor during the progress of the contract. If the drawings or prints are to be bound together, as shown in Fig. 80, it is probably better to have the title and sheet number in the top right-hand corner; if the sheets are to be kept loose in the drawers of a plan chest, the title, etc., is more readily seen if put along the bottom.

Fig. 81 shows the arrangement of a typical 1 : 100 ($\frac{1}{8}''$) scale working drawing of a small house on a standard sheet laid out as shown in Fig. 78. Further details of the plans, elevation, sections, etc., are given in Figs. 110–112.

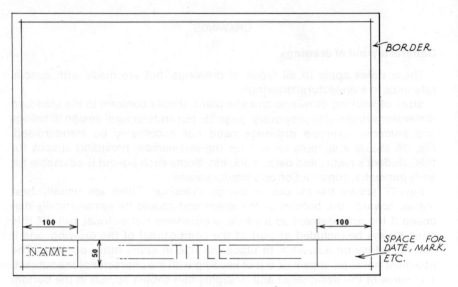

GENERAL LAY-OUT OF STUDENT'S EXERCISE
DRAWING   NORMAL DRAWING PAPER SIZES.

Fig. 76

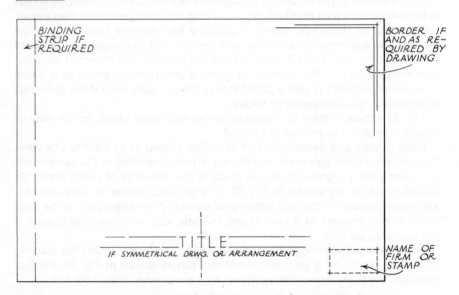

GENERAL LAY-OUT OF DESIGN DRAWINGS
NORMAL DRAWING PAPER SIZES

Fig. 77

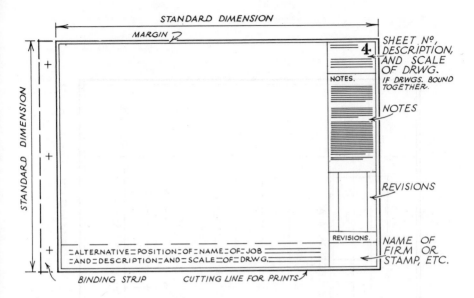

GENERAL LAY-OUT OF WORKING DRAWINGS

Fig. 78

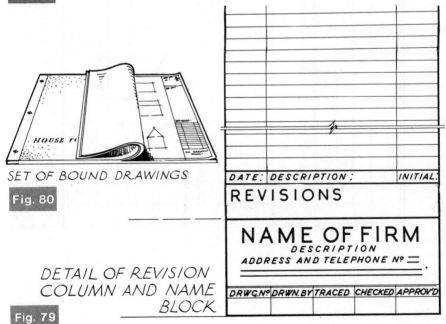

SET OF BOUND DRAWINGS

Fig. 80

DETAIL OF REVISION
COLUMN AND NAME
BLOCK

Fig. 79

DATE:	DESCRIPTION :	INITIAL:

REVISIONS

NAME OF FIRM
DESCRIPTION
ADDRESS AND TELEPHONE Nº

DRWG.Nº	DRWN.BY	TRACED	CHECKED	APPROV'D

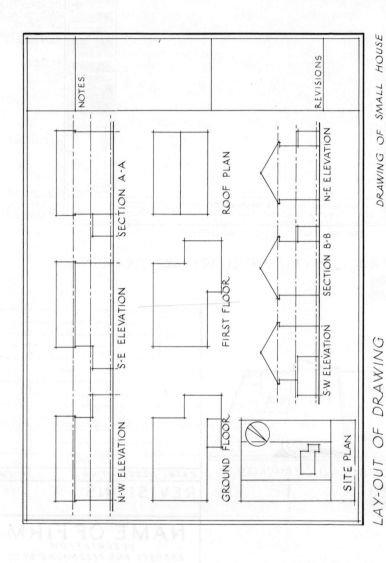

LAY-OUT OF DRAWING

DRAWING OF SMALL HOUSE

Fig. 81

View A

3   Deemed-to-satisfy' examples

These examples show imaginary projects that conform to these standards. They do not show preferred solutions. Their purpose is to illustrate to developers the type of housing environment which they might create using these standards, and to show the potential within the constraints.

Diagram 3.1 is part of an estate with a collector road coming off the local distributor. Varying numbers of houses are grouped around access ways with a secondary footway system which would link play spaces, shops, bus stops, etc. These footways and back boundaries are suitable places for planting forest trees.

Plate 14 Black and white drawings from design guide. Freehand drawing above with interesting tree delineation and texture tone for roadway. Plan to right uses transfer tone for minor access roads, transfer trees, and dots indicating footways. Reproduced from *Planning Standards: Residential Roads*, Cheshire County Planning Department 1973, with permission of the Department.

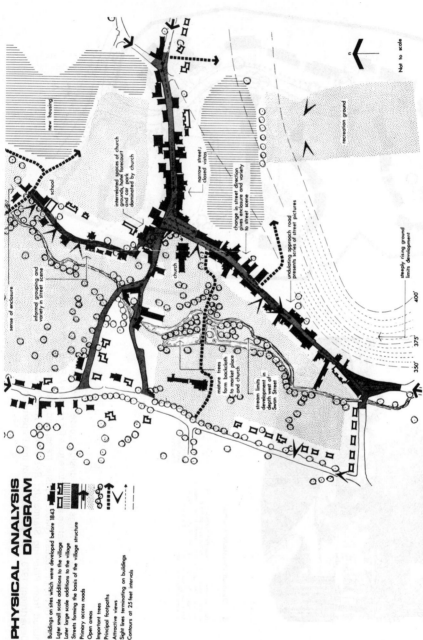

Plate 15 Example of physical analysis diagram. Note use of transfer tones to indicate different areas of use, and lines and conventional symbols for various purposes. Reproduced from *Planning Villages* by permission of the author, Andrew Thorburn BSc FRTPI, County Planning Officer, East Sussex County Council.

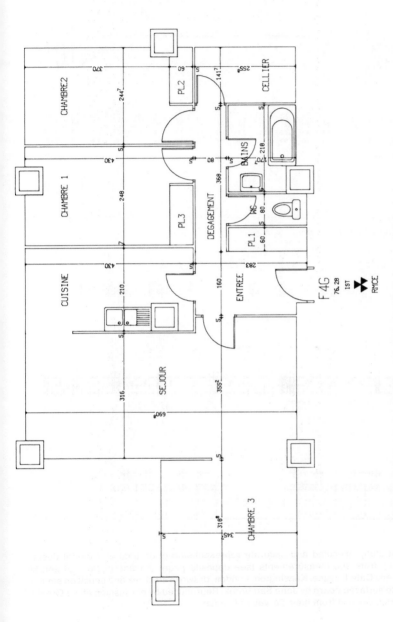

Plate 16 Computer produced plan, one of a number of general arrangement drawings and related structural details for a design in reinforced concrete. Note that the indication follows conventional representation. Reproduced by permission of Building Computer Services Ltd.

58   56

Plate 17 A carefully executed and accurate representation of original elevational design set up from site measurements (see opposite page). Facade of Nos. 56 and 58 Queens Gate Terrace, Kensington, London, drawn in black ink and pencil on smooth white surfaced board by John Sambrook. Reproduced by permission of the Greater London Council from their *Survey of London*.

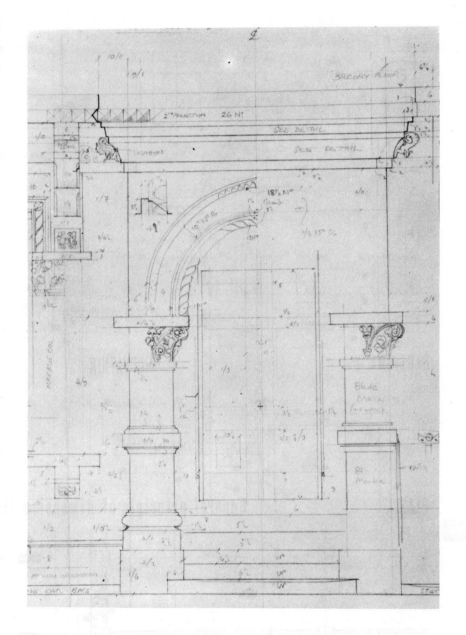

Plate 18 One of the on-site plottings made during the measuring of Nos. 56 and 58 Queens Gate Terrace (see opposite page). Measured and drawn by John Sambrook.

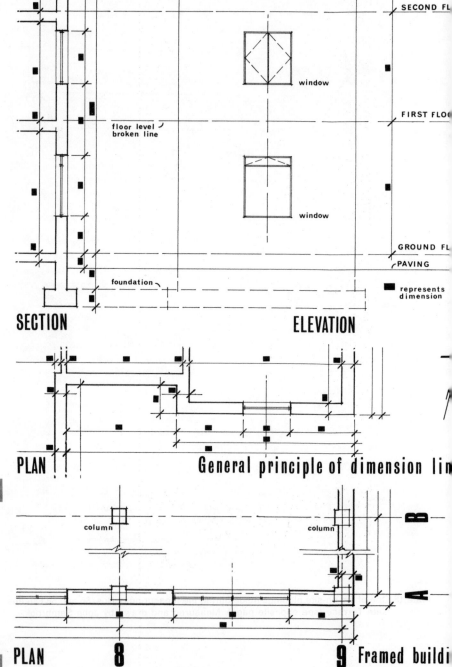

SECOND FL

window

FIRST FLO

floor level
broken line

window

GROUND FL

PAVING

foundation

represents
dimension

SECTION   ELEVATION

PLAN   General principle of dimension lin

Fig. 82

column   column

PLAN   **8**   **9** Framed buildi

Fig. 83

6

Conventional Indications and Representation on Drawings

The following notes deal with various conventional methods of indicating details and representing materials on architectural drawings, with particular reference to production drawings.

Indication of dimensions

Traditional Drawings – Reference has previously been made to the drawing of dimension lines. Fig. 82 shows portions of the plan, elevation and section of a building of solid construction, and illustrates how the dimension lines are arranged. Horizontal dimensions are shown on plan so far as possible. Generally, two lines are necessary running parallel to and a short distance away from the outside walls. From every 'break' or change of direction of the wall and from every 'rough' opening in it, short perpendicular lines are taken to cut the inner dimension lines, and the dimensions of each horizontal part of the wall can then be figured between them. The outer dimension lines are used for the over-all lengths of walls and are terminated by lines brought out at the ends of the building. Where the wall is long and divided up by pronounced breaks, these lengths may be indicated in addition to the over-all length. Care must be taken that there is agreement between the inner and outer dimensions.

Dimension lines are also drawn inside the enclosing walls of the building a short distance from the inner faces. They are extended to cut the enclosing walls at right-angles, and are dimensioned to show thicknesses of walls and partitions as well as lengths and widths of rooms between unfinished wall surfaces. It is usually impossible to put the dimension figures for wall thickness within the outlines of the walls, and they should therefore be put a little to one side with a link line to show to what they refer. Where it is necessary to show the height of a room on plan, the dimension should be enclosed in a circle.

Vertical dimensions are shown on section. Two vertical lines are drawn a little away from the outside walls, the inner one to show positions of openings in relation to floor levels and the outer one to show floor to floor heights. Sometimes a dimension line is put inside the building to show floor to ceiling heights or floor to inside sill heights, but generally this is not necessary. Overall heights except where they have special meaning are also unnecessary. Heights should not be taken from ground level, which is of course variable, but from some datum, usually a suitable point on the ground-floor level, although the required level of outside paving can be shown.

Horizontal broken lines should be drawn across elevations and sections at the various floor levels (see Fig. 82), and should be lettered: 'Basement', 'Ground Floor', 'First Floor', and so on. The floor levels can be shown at the ends of these lines in relation to a datum, those above the datum being prefixed by a + sign, and those below by a − sign, although if possible a suitable fixed point should be taken as job datum so that all other levels are positive. The figures should be enclosed in semi-circles or rectangular 'boxes'. Levels should be given in metres to three decimal places, i.e. in millimetres, (or in feet and decimals of a foot). For large jobs it is usual to relate the job datum to the Ordnance Survey datum in Britain, or to an equivalent datum elsewhere. Exact positions of levels on plan should be marked by crosses, and the figures left unenclosed for existing levels or enclosed in 'boxes' or circles for intended levels. See BS1192 for examples.

In addition to the main dimension lines referred to above, other dimension lines may be necessary in order that the position of no part of the building is in doubt. All dimensions necessary for the carrying out of the work must be given. It should not be necessary to scale a drawing for this purpose other than a full-size detail. Dimensions which are not to scale, however, should be indicated by the addition of the letters 'NTS'.

Framed Structures — Where the structure is framed, dimensions should be related to the column or stanchion centres, as shown in Fig. 83. This usually necessitates three outside dimension lines — the innermost one for 'breaks' and openings and stanchion centres, the middle one for stanchion centres only, and the outermost one for over-all measurements — and the extension of column centre lines to reference numbers and letters. Centre lines in one direction are usually marked 1, 2, 3, etc. and in the other direction, A, B, C, etc., starting from the top left corner of the drawing. The system is applicable to both regular and irregular plan shapes and the framing lines do not necessarily have to be straight or at right-angles to one another. Columns can be described by reference to the intersection of lines, e.g. B3 at the intersection of lines B and 3. Fig. 97 illustrates the basic principle.

Representation of Materials

Fig. 84 shows the conventional line indications of materials in general use.[1] All diagonal lines are at 45 degrees. The spacing of the lines should be varied, of course, according to the scale of the drawing, but the general proportions shown here should be adhered to. A common error is to space the hatching for brickwork either too widely apart or too close together. Modifications according to the scale are suggested in regard to certain indications. Where large areas of hatching need to be indicated, and especially for such materials as plaster and concrete, only a portion near the edge or ends should be shown, the hatching gradually 'fading' towards the middle, as shown in the examples.

The elevational indications are for materials which are otherwise difficult to distinguish. The indication for glass should not be used for windows.

Where confusion is likely to occur in the interpretation of the indications a legend or key should be added to the drawing.

Indication of materials by colour is less used than formerly, but the following is a list recommended for standard practice.

For elevations, colouring should be in lighter washes of the above for working drawings, but reasonable liberties are permissible to avoid a garish effect so long as misinterpretations are not likely to arise.

Material	Colour	Material	Colour
Brick	Vermilion	Cast iron	Payne's grey
Concrete	Hooker's green No. 1	Wrought iron	Prussian blue
Earth	Sepia	Granite, marble other natural stones	Cobalt blue
Hardcore or dry fill	Chrome yellow medium	Steel	Purple
Plaster	Terra verde	Cast or reconstructed stone	Viridian
Special plaster, acoustic, fibrous etc.	Mauve	Unwrought timber	Raw sienna
Asbestos cement	Neutral tint	Wrought timber	Burnt sienna (Vandyke brown for hardwood if to be distinguished from softwood)
Faience, tiles, etc.	Chrome orange		
Cement screed	Payne's grey	Glass	Pale blue wash

Other materials at the discretion of the draughtsman.

[1]Reference should also be made to the current British Standard BS1192.

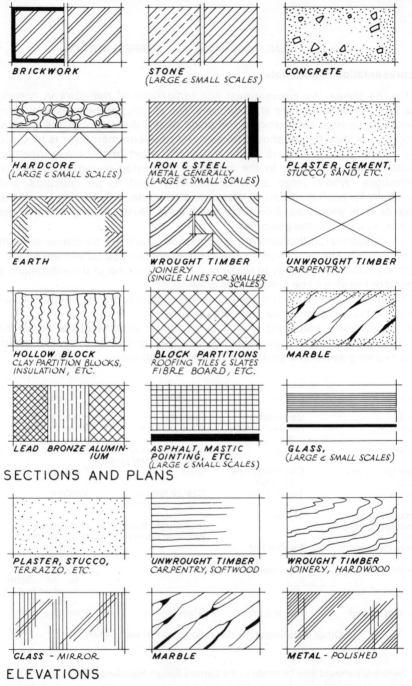

BRICKWORK

STONE
(LARGE & SMALL SCALES)

CONCRETE

HARDCORE
(LARGE & SMALL SCALES)

IRON & STEEL
METAL GENERALLY
(LARGE & SMALL SCALES)

PLASTER, CEMENT,
STUCCO, SAND, ETC.

EARTH

WROUGHT TIMBER
JOINERY
(SINGLE LINES FOR SMALLER
SCALES)

UNWROUGHT TIMBER
CARPENTRY

HOLLOW BLOCK
CLAY PARTITION BLOCKS,
INSULATION, ETC.

BLOCK PARTITIONS
ROOFING TILES & SLATES
FIBRE BOARD, ETC.

MARBLE

LEAD BRONZE ALUMIN-
IUM

ASPHALT, MASTIC
POINTING, ETC.
(LARGE & SMALL SCALES)

GLASS,
(LARGE & SMALL SCALES)

SECTIONS AND PLANS

PLASTER, STUCCO,
TERRAZZO, ETC.

UNWROUGHT TIMBER
CARPENTRY, SOFTWOOD

WROUGHT TIMBER
JOINERY, HARDWOOD

GLASS - MIRROR

MARBLE

METAL - POLISHED

ELEVATIONS

CONVENTIONAL INDICATION OF MATERIALS

Fig. 84

CONVENTIONAL INDICATIONS AND REPRESENTATION

Colours and coloured lines should not, of course, be used on tracings or drawings from which photo-print reproductions may be required, but may in some cases be replaced by transferred mechanical tone.

Abbreviations

The following is a list of abbreviations of words commonly used on drawings. The list includes Imperial units that will eventually become obsolescent but are still likely to be seen on some drawings.

Primary Units

Centimetre	cm	Chain	ch.
Cubic centimetre	cm³	Cubic foot	ft³ or cu ft
Cubic metre	m³	Cubic inch	in³ or cu in
Cubic millimetre	mm³	Cubic yard	yd³ or cu yd
Gramme	g	Dozen	doz.
Kilogramme	kg	Hundredweight	cwt
Metre	m	Inch	in
Millimetre	mm	Ounce	oz
Square centimetre	cm²	Pound	lb
Square metre	m²	Square foot	ft² or sq ft
Square millimetre	mm²	Square inch	in² or sq in
Tonne	t	Square yard	yd² or sq yd
Volt	V	Ton	ton
		Yard	yd

Materials and General Terms

Aggregate	Agg.	Invert	inv.
Air brick	AB	Lavatory Basin	LB
Approved	appd	Left hand	LH
Approximate	approx.	Macadam	Mac.
Asbestos	Asb.	Manhole	MH
Asphalt	Asph.	Mild steel	MS
Bench mark	BM	Not to scale	NTS
Birmingham gauge	BG	Number	No.
Bitumen	Bitn	Petrol interceptor	PI
Brickwork	Bwk or B	Radius	rad.
British Standard	BS	Rain-water pipe	RWP
Cast iron	CI	Reinforced concrete	RC
Cement	Cem.	Right hand	RH
Centre line	CL or C	Rising main	RM
Centre to centre	c/c	Rain-water outlet	RWO
Checked	ckd	Round	rd
Chemical closet	CC	Sink waste	SW
Clearing eye	CE	Sink	S
Concrete	Conc.	Sketch	sk.
Corrugated	Corr.	Sluice or stop valve	SV
Diameter	dia.	Soil and vent pipe	S&VP
Drawing	Dwg	Soil pipe	SP
Drinking fountain	DF	Specification	Spec.
Earth closet	EC	Spigot and socket	S&S
Figure	Fig.	Square	sq.
Fire hydrant	FH	Standard Wire Gauge	SWG

Materials and General Terms (cont.)

Flushing cistern	FC	Stand pipe	St. P
Fresh air inlet	FAI	Street gully	SG
Galvanised	Galv.	Tongued and grooved	T&G
Glazed-ware pipe	GWP	Traced	Tcd
Grease trap	GT	Urinal	U
Ground level	GL	Vent pipe	VP
Gully	G	Volume	vol.
Height	ht	Waste pipe	WP
Hose bib	HB	Waste and vent pipe	W&VP
Inspection chamber	IC	Water closet	WC
Insulated *or* insulation	insul.	Weight	Wt
Intercepting trap	IT	Yard gully	YG
Internal	int.		

Other abbreviations are given in lists prepared by BSI, Regional Hospital Boards, Professional Engineering Bodies, and Modular & Industrial Building Organisations, etc. In general, units of measurement are given in lower case letters, and abbreviations of materials or names when represented by several letters have a capital for the first letter with the remainder in lower case letters.

Drawing and indication of constructional materials

I. *Brickwork*—On plan and section indicated by solid black at small scales and by conventional hatching at 1:100 ($\frac{1}{8}''$) scale and upwards (although some consider 1:100 ($\frac{1}{8}''$) scale too small for hatching). On detail drawings the horizontal course lines are sometimes shown in addition to or instead of hatching on section, especially where there is some particular relevance to the construction. Difficulties occur with hatching on curved walls on plan, but there seems to be no solution to the problem, nor to the optical illusions which the diagonal lines of the hatching tend to produce. The worst effects, however, can be avoided by carefully considering the placing of the lines.

Fig. 85 shows the indication of brickwork on elevation at various scales. It is better to set out the heights of the courses on a vertical line at the left-hand side of the sheet and to rule across from this with the T-square than to set out the courses actually on the elevation, where the markings tend to become confused and are difficult to rub out. The courses can also be numbered and provide a means of checking other settings-out.

The courses are not usually shown at less than 1:100 ($\frac{1}{8}''$) scale, except in pencil on some careful design drawings. At 1:100 ($\frac{1}{8}''$) scale single lines are shown, individual bricks being indicated only for flat arches and similar features. At 1:50 ($\frac{1}{4}''$) scale vertical joints can be indicated also if necessary, but are not essential. At 1:20 ($\frac{1}{2}''$) scale and larger it is possible to show double lines to indicate the thicknesses of joints. In general, joint lines should be thinner than outlines whether in ink or pencil. They should extend over the whole area of the material or be confined to regular areas which will be

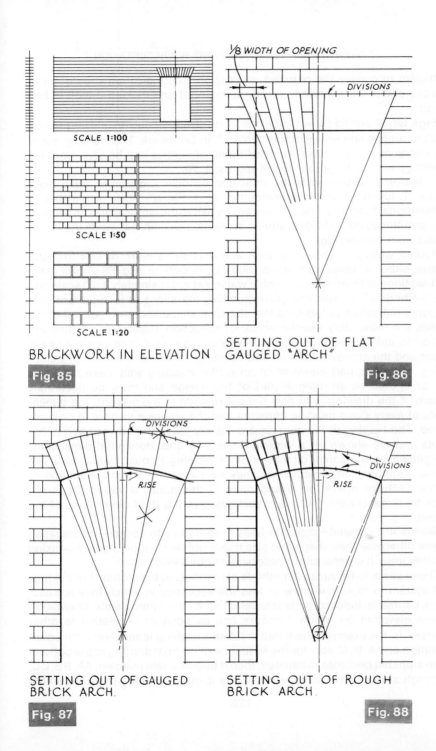

SCALE 1:100

SCALE 1:50

SCALE 1:20

BRICKWORK IN ELEVATION

Fig. 85

⅛ WIDTH OF OPENING

DIVISIONS

SETTING OUT OF FLAT
GAUGED "ARCH"

Fig. 86

DIVISIONS

RISE

SETTING OUT OF GAUGED
BRICK ARCH.

Fig. 87

DIVISIONS

RISE

SETTING OUT OF ROUGH
BRICK ARCH.

Fig. 88

sufficient to convey the required impression. The indication should not be spotted about the elevation, so camouflaging it and making it look in bad repair.

Figs. 86, 87 and 88 show typical methods of setting out flat and segmental gauged arches and segmental rough arch in brickwork. The marking-out of the positions of the bricks and the finding of centres can be seen from the drawings, which are reproduced at approx. 1:20.

2. *Masonry*—Stone walls are indicated on plan and section solid black under 1:100 ($\frac{1}{8}''$) scale and sometimes at 1:100 ($\frac{1}{8}''$) scale, otherwise by conventional hatching. The courses are shown to the larger scales on section, and sometimes the individual stones are shown on plan, e.g. when the facing differs from the backing.

Rubble walling is shown on plan and section as more or less irregular stones either in black with white joints or in outline. Fig. 89 shows plans and sections of three types of rubble walling at approximately 1:20 scale and the methods of drawing the corresponding elevations. It is important with masonry indication of this kind that the size, shape and arrangement of the stones are reasonably like the actual construction. Haphazard scribble will not do to indicate rubble, nor will careful drawing if long vertical joints occur and the stones at angles and openings are impossible in practice.

Fig. 90 shows part elevation of an ashlar masonry wall. Here the joints are or should be an integral part of the design and must be accurately shown. If the drawing is to give full information to the masons, the dimensions of every stone must be apparent and the stones may have to be numbered. The heights of the courses are usually taken from bed to bed of the joints and are shown on a vertical dimension line. Horizontal dimensions are shown on horizontal dimension lines passing through typical courses. Some additional dimension lines may be necessary around openings or similar features where the arrangement of the stones is varied. Openings must be dimensioned. Plans and sections give the third dimensions of the stones.

Stones are crossed—diagonal lines from corner to corner—on elevation where otherwise their shape and size might not be clear owing to dimension or other lines. It is generally unnecessary to cross every stone.

There seem to be various methods of numbering the stones, but the logical system is to follow more or less the sequence in which they are laid. Each course is indexed by letters referring to the approximate orientation of the elevation on which it occurs and its position in relation to other courses. In the example illustrated the distinguishing letters are: S for south elevation and A, B, C, etc., for the sequence of cources starting at the bottom. If the alphabet becomes exhausted, then it begins again doubled, AA, BB, CC, although some abbreviation is necessary if the building is of considerable

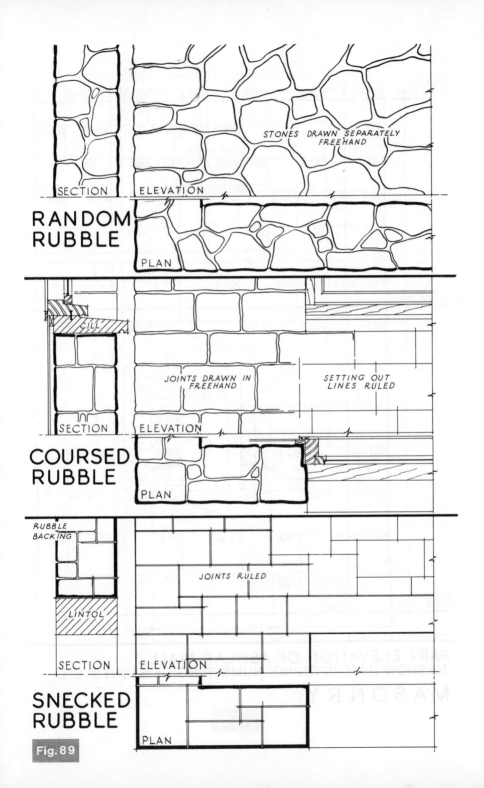

STONES DRAWN SEPARATELY FREEHAND

SECTION ELEVATION

RANDOM RUBBLE

PLAN

CILL

JOINTS DRAWN IN FREEHAND

SETTING OUT LINES RULED

SECTION ELEVATION

COURSED RUBBLE

PLAN

RUBBLE BACKING

JOINTS RULED

LINTOL

SECTION ELEVATION

SNECKED RUBBLE

PLAN

Fig. 89

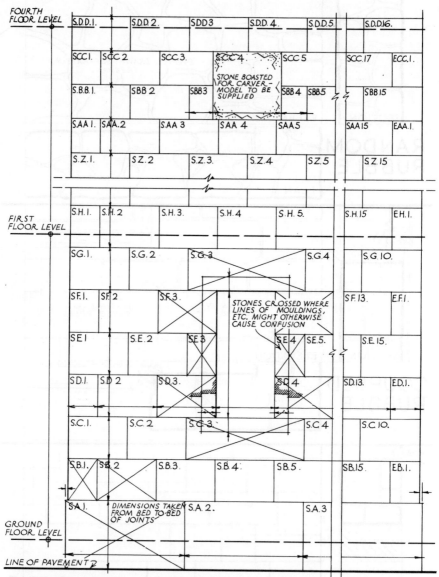

PART ELEVATION OF ASHLAR WALL
TO SHOW DIMENSIONING, NUMBERING OF STONES, ETC.

MASONRY

height. The stones take the indexing of their course and are numbered from left to right. Note that where there is a return elevation the stones which appear on two elevations take their numbers from the elevation on which the larger faces show. No stone can have two numbers. The numbers are put in the top left-hand corners of the stones on the drawing.

3. *Timber* — On plan and section timber frame construction is shown either as a solid black wall of appropriate thickness at small scales or in outline with solid black studs or framing. At 1:50 ($\frac{1}{4}''$) scale and larger it is possible to show the outer and inner facings and to cross the studs, etc., in the conventional manner for unwrought timber. Fig. 91 shows part plan, section and elevation of a small timber building.

On elevation, continuous thin lines are drawn to represent vertical or horizontal boarding as the case may be. Cross joints are not usually shown. Edges which are intentionally irregular can be drawn freehand over ruled construction lines.

4. *Steelwork* — Fig. 92 shows the drawing and conventional indication of typical details and sections of structural steelwork.

Steel sections when adjacent and shown solid black to a small scale should have a thin white space — the thickness of a line — left between them.

Fig. 94 shows part of a steel framing plan, the type of drawing, usually at 1:100 ($\frac{1}{8}''$) scale, prepared to show details of the beams at each floor level for a steel frame building. The conventional indication for such a plan is also shown. Fig. 97 shows an alternative method of annotating the grid lines of a steel-framed building.

Note that steelwork on, say, the third-floor framing plan is the steel carrying the third floor, and the stanchions are the ones running from second to third floor.

A typical column or stanchion schedule, sometimes shown on the drawings, is also shown in Fig. 94. Stanchions usually run through two floors and are spliced a short distance above floor level.

When the drawings of a building are to be used by a structural engineer, who sometimes prepares the framing plan as a tracing over the architect's drawings, they should show: the nature and thicknesses of all walls; the nature and thickness or the weights of all floor finishes; maximum possible depths for all beams; positions and weights of any heavy loads, such as tanks, machinery and lifts.

5. *Reinforced concrete* — Fig. 95 shows related details of various kinds and at various scales to show the drawing of reinforced concrete construction for general indications. For structural engineering practice reference should be made to the technical report *The Detailing of Reinforced Concrete*, published by The Concrete Society and the Institution of Structural Engineers, from which illustration, Fig. 96, is reproduced.

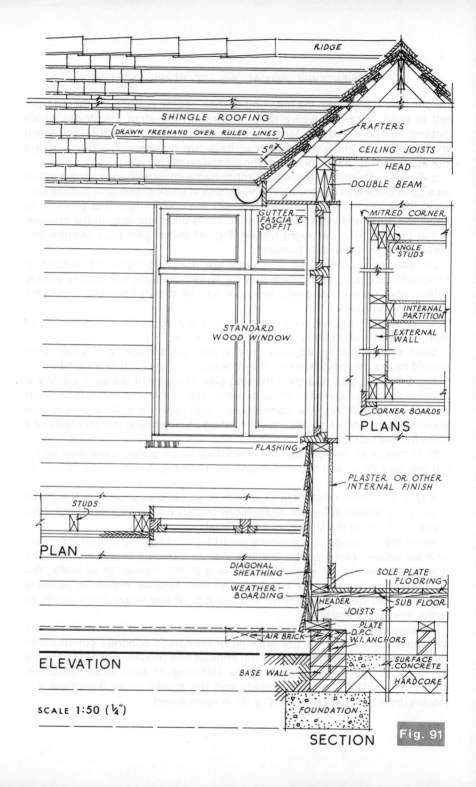

RIDGE

SHINGLE ROOFING
(DRAWN FREEHAND OVER RULED LINES)

RAFTERS

CEILING JOISTS

5"

HEAD

DOUBLE BEAM

GUTTER
FASCIA &
SOFFIT

MITRED CORNER

ANGLE
STUDS

INTERNAL
PARTITION

EXTERNAL
WALL

STANDARD
WOOD WINDOW

CORNER BOARDS

PLANS

FLASHING

PLASTER OR OTHER
INTERNAL FINISH

STUDS

PLAN

DIAGONAL
SHEATHING

WEATHER-
BOARDING

SOLE PLATE
FLOORING

SUB FLOOR

HEADER

JOISTS

AIR BRICK

PLATE
D.P.C.
W.I. ANCHORS

ELEVATION

BASE WALL

SURFACE
CONCRETE

HARDCORE

SCALE 1:50 (¼")

FOUNDATION

SECTION

Fig. 91

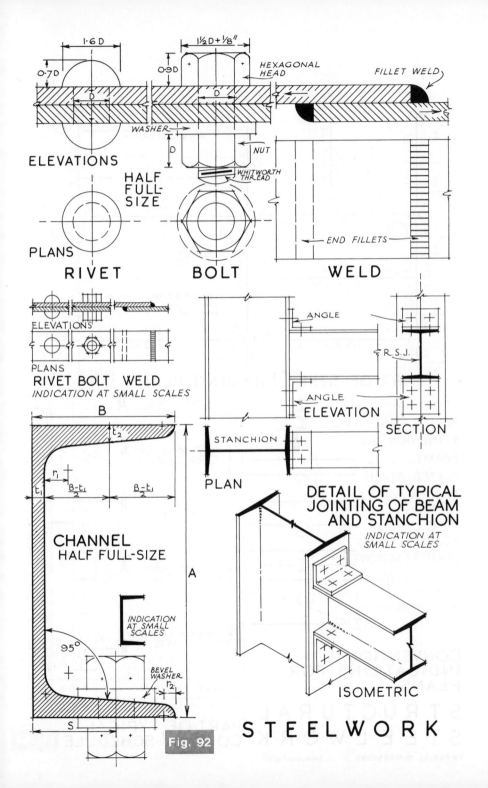

ELEVATIONS

1·6 D

0·7 D

D

PLANS

RIVET

HALF
FULL-
SIZE

1½D + ⅛"

0·9 D

D

HEXAGONAL
HEAD

WASHER

NUT

WHITWORTH
THREAD

D

BOLT

FILLET WELD

WELD

END FILLETS

ELEVATIONS

PLANS

RIVET BOLT WELD
INDICATION AT SMALL SCALES

ANGLE

R.S.J.

ANGLE

ELEVATION

SECTION

STANCHION

PLAN

DETAIL OF TYPICAL
JOINTING OF BEAM
AND STANCHION
*INDICATION AT
SMALL SCALES*

B

t_2

r_1

t_1

$\dfrac{B - t_1}{2}$

$\dfrac{B - t_1}{2}$

CHANNEL
HALF FULL-SIZE

A

*INDICATION
AT SMALL
SCALES*

95°

BEVEL
WASHER

r_2

S

ISOMETRIC

STEELWORK

Fig. 92

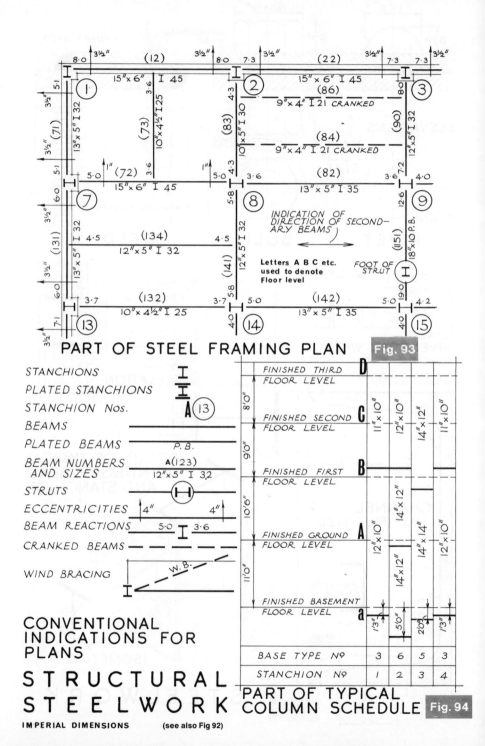

PART OF STEEL FRAMING PLAN

Fig. 93

CONVENTIONAL INDICATIONS FOR PLANS

STANCHIONS	I
PLATED STANCHIONS	
STANCHION Nos.	A (13)
BEAMS	
PLATED BEAMS	P. B.
BEAM NUMBERS AND SIZES	A(123) 12"×5" I 32
STRUTS	(H)
ECCENTRICITIES	4" 4"
BEAM REACTIONS	5·0 I 3·6
CRANKED BEAMS	— — —
WIND BRACING	W.B.

STRUCTURAL STEELWORK

IMPERIAL DIMENSIONS   (see also Fig 92)

PART OF TYPICAL COLUMN SCHEDULE

Fig. 94

	STANCHION Nº	1	2	3	4
	BASE TYPE Nº	3	6	5	3

Notes within schedule:
- FINISHED THIRD FLOOR LEVEL — D
- FINISHED SECOND FLOOR LEVEL — C
- FINISHED FIRST FLOOR LEVEL — B
- FINISHED GROUND FLOOR LEVEL — A
- FINISHED BASEMENT FLOOR LEVEL — a

Heights: 8'0", 9'0", 10'6", 11'0"

Member sizes: 11"×10", 12"×10", 14"×12", 11"×10", 12"×10", 14"×12", 14"×14", 12"×10", 14"×12"

INDICATION OF DIRECTION OF SECONDARY BEAMS

Letters A B C etc. used to denote Floor level

FOOT OF STRUT

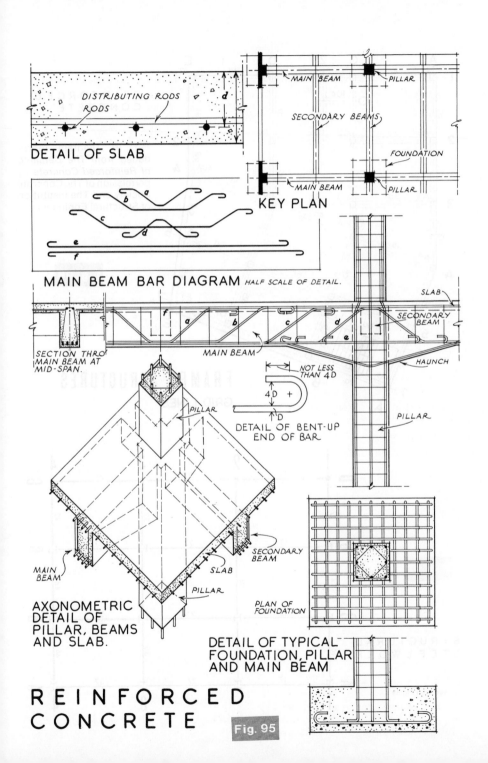

DISTRIBUTING RODS
RODS

d

DETAIL OF SLAB

MAIN BEAM

PILLAR

SECONDARY BEAMS

FOUNDATION

MAIN BEAM

PILLAR

KEY PLAN

a
b
c
d
e
f

MAIN BEAM BAR DIAGRAM *HALF SCALE OF DETAIL.*

SLAB

SECONDARY BEAM

HAUNCH

f *a* *b* *c* *d*
e

SECTION THRO'
MAIN BEAM AT
MID-SPAN

MAIN BEAM

PILLAR

NOT LESS
THAN 4D

4D +

D

DETAIL OF BENT-UP
END OF BAR

PILLAR

PILLAR

MAIN
BEAM

SECONDARY
BEAM

SLAB

PILLAR

AXONOMETRIC
DETAIL OF
PILLAR, BEAMS
AND SLAB.

PLAN OF
FOUNDATION

DETAIL OF TYPICAL
FOUNDATION, PILLAR
AND MAIN BEAM

REINFORCED
CONCRETE

Fig. 95

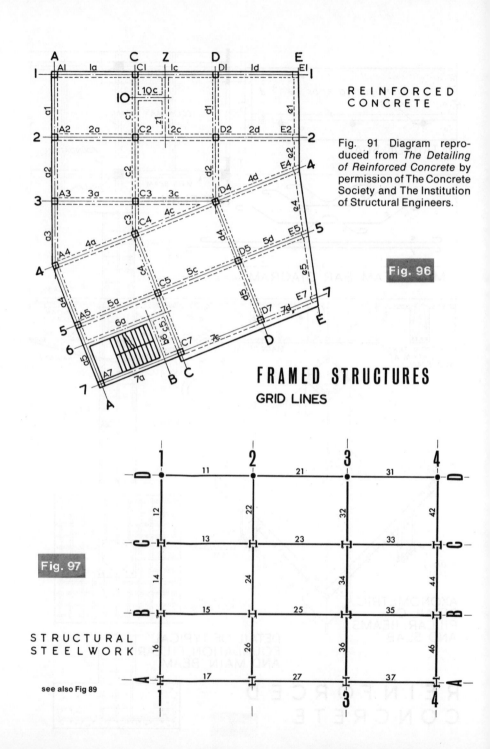

Fig. 96

FRAMED STRUCTURES
GRID LINES

Fig. 97

STRUCTURAL
STEELWORK

see also Fig 89

Representation and plan indication of details and fittings

Doors — Fig. 98 shows an example of the drawing of a door and frame at various scales. This indicates the amount of detail which can be reasonably included in each case. It is a common mistake to attempt to show too much at the smaller scales. No hard and fast rules can be laid down, however, and it may be permissible to show more in a carefully executed design drawing than in a working drawing. Fig. 99 shows typical conventional plan indications of doors at small scale. The door is indicated by a single line at right-angles to the wall and the swing of its opening edge by a quadrant or semi-circle. Note that the centre of the arc must be where the pin of the hinge is. Where the door lines at right-angles to the wall might be confused with other lines on the drawing, they can be shown at a lesser angle provided the indication is consistent throughout the drawing. An alternative indication is the use of a straight line at 45 degrees instead of the quadrant curve. This method saves time as such lines can be drawn by pen or pencil and set square quicker and easier than can curves by compasses. However, it is less expressive and can cause confusion to those unfamiliar with the convention.

Wood Windows — Fig. 100 shows an example of the drawing of a typical wood casement window at various scales. Double-hung sashes should be denoted at small scales by the letters 'DHS' on plan and elevation.

Metal Windows — Fig. 101 shows the representation at various scales of a typical metal window. Note particularly the indication of the metal sections, which cannot be drawn satisfactorily in full at less than 1 : 10. As metal windows are standard products they are not usually detailed except in relation to other construction, and the indication of the opening parts in elevation is therefore all the more necessary. It used to be the general practice to cross the opening parts, but the conventional indication shown in Fig. 102, which denotes the hinged side or pivot of the opening, is becoming general.

Domestic kitchen equipment — Fig. 103 shows the conventional indication on plan and elevation at 1 : 100 ($\frac{1}{8}''$) scale of various equipment and fittings.

Sanitary fittings — Fig. 104 shows the conventional indication on plan and elevation at 1 : 100 ($\frac{1}{8}''$) scale of various sanitary fittings. The centres of arcs are shown in some cases, although these would not appear in the drawing. Alternatives are given in the cases of baths, bidets, and W.C.'s. Clear plastic templates are available for drawing these and other symbols.

Furniture, etc. — Fig. 105 shows a common conventional indications of domestic furniture at 1 : 100 ($\frac{1}{8}''$) scale. These articles, with the possible exception of beds, are not shown on working drawings unless forming parts of the permanent structure. If known, the sizes can be made to conform to those

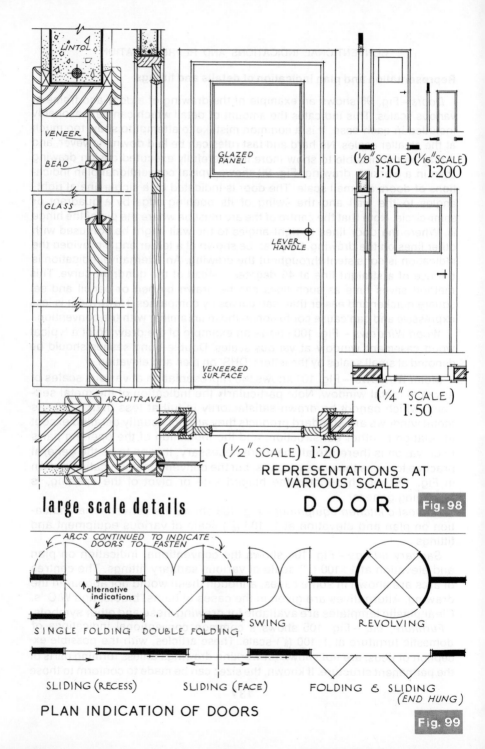

LINTOL

VENEER

BEAD

GLASS

GLAZED
PANEL

LEVER
HANDLE

VENEERED
SURFACE

ARCHITRAVE

large scale details

(½" SCALE) 1:20

(⅛"SCALE) (1/16"SCALE)
1:10   1:200

(¼" SCALE)
1:50

REPRESENTATIONS AT
VARIOUS SCALES

D O O R   Fig. 98

ARCS CONTINUED TO INDICATE
DOORS TO FASTEN

alternative
indications

SINGLE FOLDING DOUBLE FOLDING   SWING   REVOLVING

SLIDING (RECESS)   SLIDING (FACE)   FOLDING & SLIDING
(END HUNG)

PLAN INDICATION OF DOORS

Fig. 99

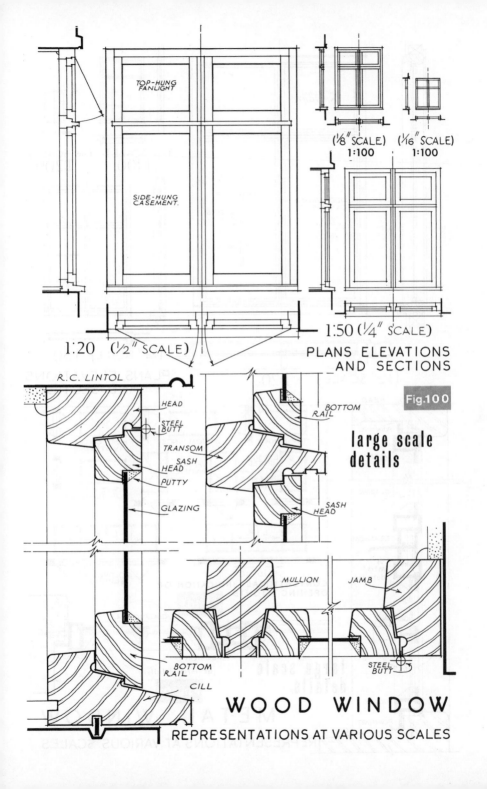

TOP-HUNG FANLIGHT

SIDE-HUNG CASEMENT.

(⅛″ SCALE) 1:100   (1/16″ SCALE) 1:100

1:50 (¼″ SCALE)

1:20 (½″ SCALE)

PLANS ELEVATIONS AND SECTIONS

R.C. LINTOL

HEAD
STEEL BUTT
TRANSOM
SASH HEAD
PUTTY
GLAZING

BOTTOM RAIL

SASH HEAD

Fig.100

large scale details

MULLION   JAMB

BOTTOM RAIL

CILL

STEEL BUTT

WOOD WINDOW

REPRESENTATIONS AT VARIOUS SCALES

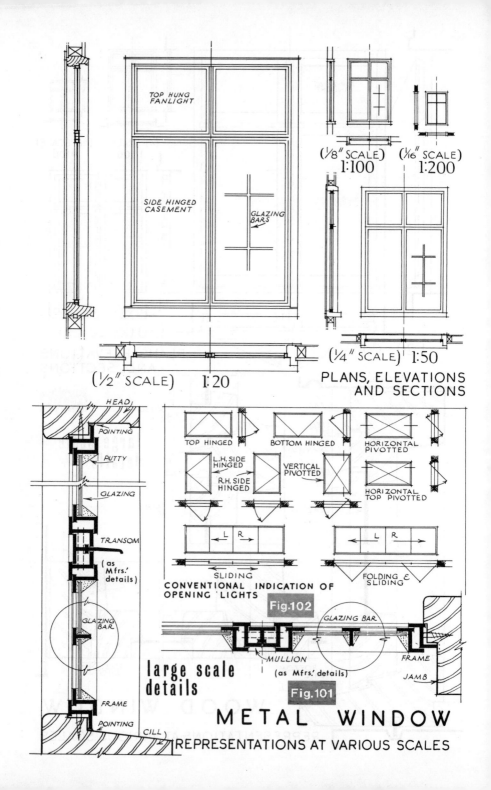

TOP HUNG
FANLIGHT

SIDE HINGED
CASEMENT

GLAZING
BARS

(⅛" SCALE) (⅟₁₆" SCALE)
1:100 1:200

(¼" SCALE) 1:50

(½" SCALE) 1:20

PLANS, ELEVATIONS
AND SECTIONS

HEAD

POINTING

PUTTY

GLAZING

TRANSOM

(as
Mfrs.'
details)

GLAZING
BAR

FRAME

POINTING

CILL

TOP HINGED   BOTTOM HINGED   HORIZONTAL
PIVOTTED

L.H. SIDE
HINGED
              VERTICAL
              PIVOTTED
R.H. SIDE
HINGED
HORIZONTAL
TOP PIVOTTED

L R   L R

SLIDING   FOLDING &
                   SLIDING

CONVENTIONAL INDICATION OF
OPENING LIGHTS   Fig.102

GLAZING BAR

large scale
details

MULLION
(as Mfrs.' details)

Fig.101

FRAME

JAMB

METAL WINDOW
REPRESENTATIONS AT VARIOUS SCALES

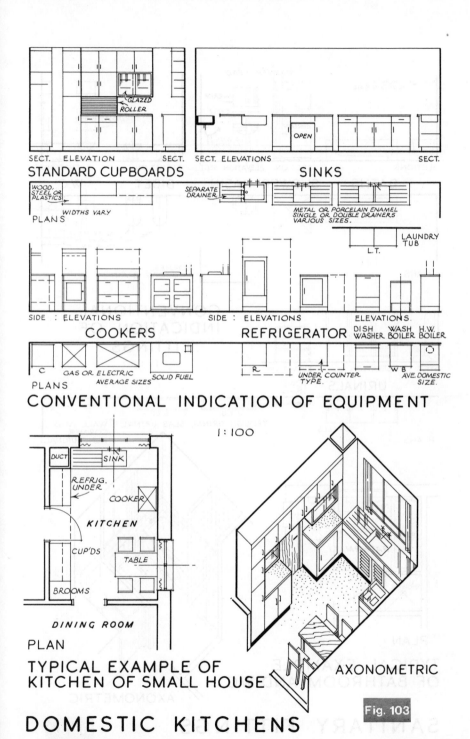

SECT. ELEVATION   SECT.   SECT. ELEVATIONS   SECT.

STANDARD CUPBOARDS   SINKS

WOOD,
STEEL OR
PLASTICS

WIDTHS VARY

PLANS

SEPARATE
DRAINER

METAL OR PORCELAIN ENAMEL
SINGLE OR DOUBLE DRAINERS
VARIOUS SIZES.

LAUNDRY
TUB

L.T.

SIDE : ELEVATIONS   SIDE : ELEVATIONS   ELEVATIONS.

COOKERS   REFRIGERATOR   DISH WASH H.W.
WASHER BOILER BOILER

C

GAS OR ELECTRIC
AVERAGE SIZES   SOLID FUEL

R

UNDER COUNTER
TYPE.

W B

AVE. DOMESTIC
SIZE.

PLANS

CONVENTIONAL INDICATION OF EQUIPMENT

1:100

DUCT   SINK

REFRIG.
UNDER

COOKER

KITCHEN

CUP'DS

TABLE

BROOMS

DINING ROOM

PLAN

TYPICAL EXAMPLE OF
KITCHEN OF SMALL HOUSE   AXONOMETRIC

Fig. 103

DOMESTIC KITCHENS

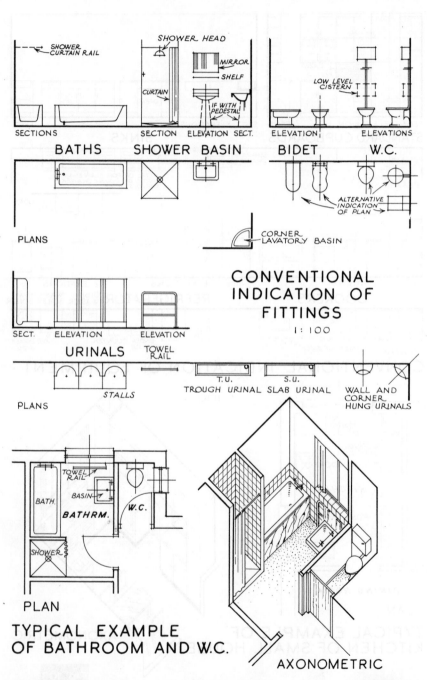

SECTIONS   SECTION   ELEVATION SECT.   ELEVATION   ELEVATIONS

BATHS   SHOWER BASIN   BIDET   W.C.

SHOWER CURTAIN RAIL

SHOWER HEAD

MIRROR

SHELF

CURTAIN

IF WITH PEDESTAL

LOW LEVEL CISTERN

PLANS

ALTERNATIVE INDICATION OF PLAN

CORNER LAVATORY BASIN

CONVENTIONAL INDICATION OF FITTINGS
1:100

SECT.   ELEVATION   ELEVATION

URINALS   TOWEL RAIL

STALLS

PLANS

T.U.   S.U.
TROUGH URINAL SLAB URINAL

WALL AND CORNER HUNG URINALS

TOWEL RAIL

BATH.

BASIN

W.C.

BATHRM.

SHOWER

PLAN
TYPICAL EXAMPLE OF BATHROOM AND W.C.

AXONOMETRIC

SANITARY FITTINGS   Fig. 104

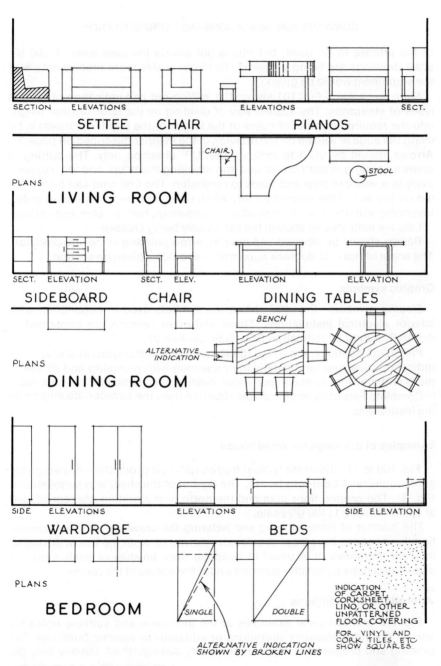

SECTION ELEVATIONS   ELEVATIONS   SECT.
SETTEE   CHAIR   PIANOS

CHAIR
STOOL

PLANS

LIVING ROOM

SECT. ELEVATION   SECT. ELEV.   ELEVATION   ELEVATION
SIDEBOARD   CHAIR   DINING TABLES

BENCH

ALTERNATIVE
INDICATION

PLANS

DINING ROOM

SIDE ELEVATIONS   ELEVATIONS   SIDE ELEVATION
WARDROBE   BEDS

PLANS

BEDROOM

SINGLE   DOUBLE

INDICATION
OF CARPET,
CORKSHEET,
LINO, OR OTHER
UNPATTERNED
FLOOR COVERING

FOR VINYL AND
CORK TILES, ETC
SHOW SQUARES.

ALTERNATIVE INDICATION
SHOWN BY BROKEN LINES

FURNITURE   1:100

Fig. 105

of the articles to be used, but this is not always the case when 1 : 100 ($\frac{1}{8}''$) scale drawings are being prepared. To larger scales more precise details of the equipment would be given.

Staircases, etc. — Fig. 101 shows the setting-out and indication of various types of staircases. The easiest way of dividing up the floor-to-floor height into the required number of risers or the length of the flight into treads is by using the edge of a scale on the drawing in the manner described on page 37. Arrows should be used to indicate the 'UP' direction only. The putting of arrows pointing in both directions and labelling them 'up' and 'dn' respectively is a waste of time and leads to confusion. The first riser can be indicated on the line of the arrow by a dot. All risers should be numbered in order, beginning with the lowest, on production drawings, both on plan and section.

Lifts are indicated as shown; the car usually being crossed.

Ramps should be labelled and have an arrow pointing in the 'up' direction. The angle of rise — 15 degrees maximum — should be given on section.

Graphic symbols

Electric symbols — Fig. 107 shows the symbols used in connection with interior electrical installations. These and other symbols are contained in British Standard Specification B.S. 3939, section 27.

Plumbing, drainage, etc — Fig. 108 shows some of the symbols and ways of indicating pipe runs and details in connection with plumbing and drainage plans and drawings to show gas, water, heating and ventilation lay-outs, etc.

Complete lists of symbols can be obtained from the appropriate engineering institutions.

Examples of drawings for small house

Fig. 109 to 111 illustrate typical traditional-type production drawings for an economical 4-bedroom house. The lay-out of the sheet was suggested in Fig. 81. The ground floor plan and the north-east elevation are reproduced at approximately 1 : 100 ($\frac{1}{8}''$) scale.

The manner of dimensioning and lettering the drawings and the conventional indications have been previously referred to. Note the use of arrows to indicate entrances. It is usual to describe floor finishes of each room on plan; this is done by smaller lettering under the names of the rooms.

Alterations and additions

Fig. 112 shows typical examples of the indication and suitable notes for use on drawings showing alterations or additions to existing buildings. The existing and proposed work must be clearly distinguished. Usually only the

144

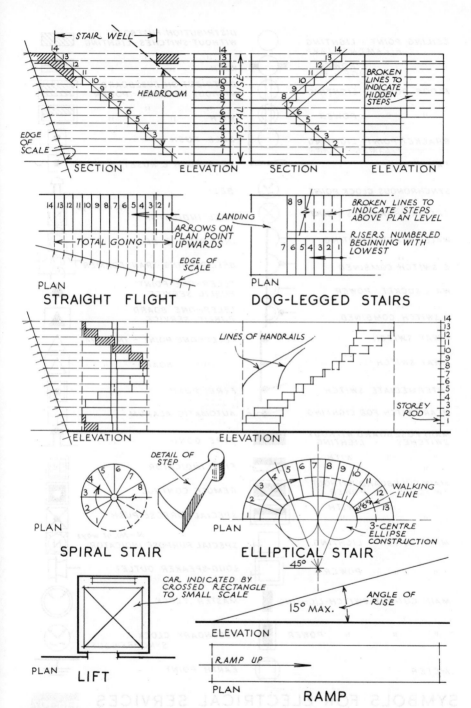

STAIRS ETC. INDICATION AND SETTING OUT

Fig. 106

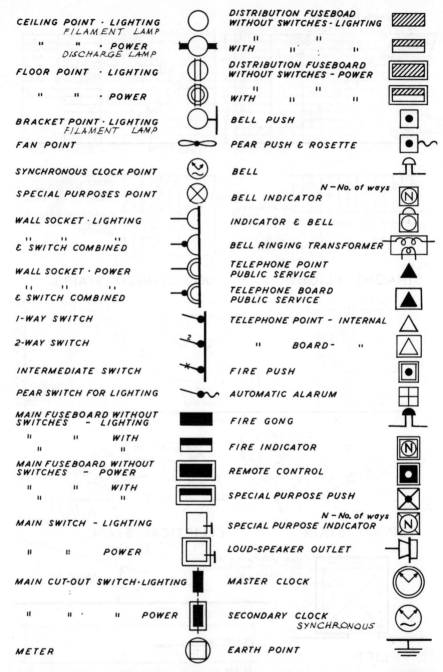

CEILING POINT · LIGHTING *FILAMENT LAMP*		DISTRIBUTION FUSEBOAD WITHOUT SWITCHES - LIGHTING	
" " · POWER *DISCHARGE LAMP*		WITH " : "	
FLOOR POINT · LIGHTING		DISTRIBUTION FUSEBOARD WITHOUT SWITCHES - POWER	
" " · POWER		WITH " "	
BRACKET POINT · LIGHTING *FILAMENT LAMP*		BELL PUSH	
FAN POINT		PEAR PUSH & ROSETTE	
SYNCHRONOUS CLOCK POINT		BELL	
SPECIAL PURPOSES POINT		BELL INDICATOR *N – No. of ways*	
WALL SOCKET · LIGHTING		INDICATOR & BELL	
& SWITCH COMBINED		BELL RINGING TRANSFORMER	
WALL SOCKET · POWER		TELEPHONE POINT PUBLIC SERVICE	
& SWITCH COMBINED		TELEPHONE BOARD PUBLIC SERVICE	
1-WAY SWITCH		TELEPHONE POINT - INTERNAL	
2-WAY SWITCH		" BOARD - "	
INTERMEDIATE SWITCH		FIRE PUSH	
PEAR SWITCH FOR LIGHTING		AUTOMATIC ALARUM	
MAIN FUSEBOARD WITHOUT SWITCHES - LIGHTING		FIRE GONG	
" " WITH " "		FIRE INDICATOR	
MAIN FUSEBOARD WITHOUT SWITCHES - POWER		REMOTE CONTROL	
" " WITH " "		SPECIAL PURPOSE PUSH	
MAIN SWITCH - LIGHTING		SPECIAL PURPOSE INDICATOR *N – No. of ways*	
" " POWER		LOUD-SPEAKER OUTLET	
MAIN CUT-OUT SWITCH·LIGHTING		MASTER CLOCK	
" " " POWER		SECONDARY CLOCK SYNCHRONOUS	
METER		EARTH POINT	

SYMBOLS FOR ELECTRICAL SERVICES   Fig. 107

FOR OTHER SYMBOLS SEE BRIT

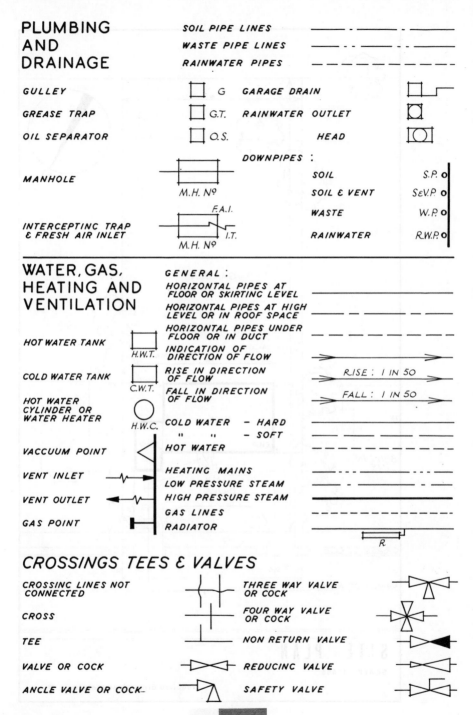

PLUMBING AND DRAINAGE

	SOIL PIPE LINES	—— · —— ·
	WASTE PIPE LINES	—— · · —— · ·
	RAINWATER PIPES	— — — — —

GULLEY — ☐ G — GARAGE DRAIN

GREASE TRAP — ☐ G.T. — RAINWATER OUTLET

OIL SEPARATOR — ☐ O.S. — HEAD

DOWNPIPES :

MANHOLE — M.H. Nº

SOIL — S.P. o

SOIL & VENT — S&V.P. o

F.A.I.

WASTE — W.P. o

INTERCEPTING TRAP & FRESH AIR INLET — I.T. — M.H. Nº

RAINWATER — R.W.P. o

WATER, GAS, HEATING AND VENTILATION

GENERAL :

HOT WATER TANK — H.W.T.

HORIZONTAL PIPES AT FLOOR OR SKIRTING LEVEL

COLD WATER TANK — C.W.T.

HORIZONTAL PIPES AT HIGH LEVEL OR IN ROOF SPACE

HORIZONTAL PIPES UNDER FLOOR OR IN DUCT

HOT WATER CYLINDER OR WATER HEATER — H.W.C.

INDICATION OF DIRECTION OF FLOW

RISE IN DIRECTION OF FLOW — RISE : 1 IN 50

FALL IN DIRECTION OF FLOW — FALL : 1 IN 50

VACCUUM POINT

COLD WATER — HARD
    "   "   — SOFT

HOT WATER

VENT INLET

HEATING MAINS
LOW PRESSURE STEAM

VENT OUTLET

HIGH PRESSURE STEAM

GAS LINES

GAS POINT

RADIATOR — R.

CROSSINGS TEES & VALVES

CROSSING LINES NOT CONNECTED

THREE WAY VALVE OR COCK

CROSS

FOUR WAY VALVE OR COCK

TEE

NON RETURN VALVE

VALVE OR COCK

REDUCING VALVE

ANGLE VALVE OR COCK

SAFETY VALVE

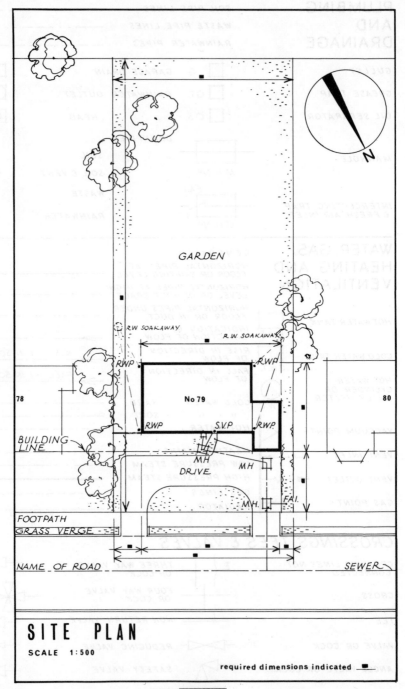

GARDEN

R.W. SOAKAWAY

R.W. SOAKAWAY

RWP

RWP

78

No 79

80

RWP

S.V.P.

RWP

BUILDING
LINE

MH

MH

DRIVE

M.H.

F.A.I.

FOOTPATH

GRASS VERGE

NAME OF ROAD

SEWER

SITE PLAN

SCALE 1:500

required dimensions indicated ▪

Fig.109

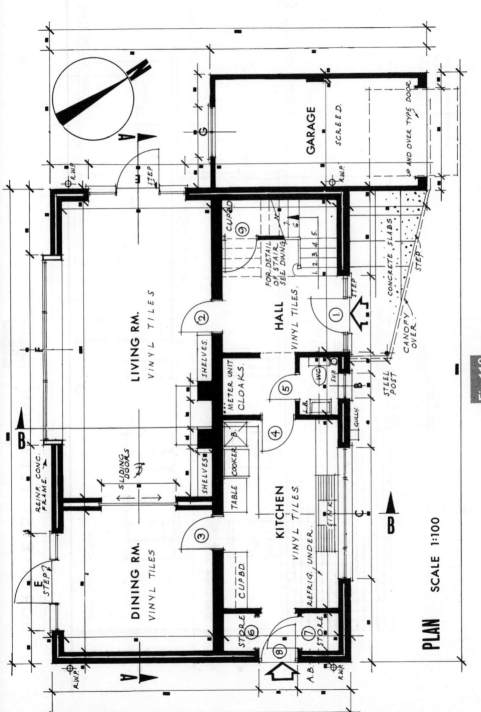

PLAN SCALE 1:100

Fig.110

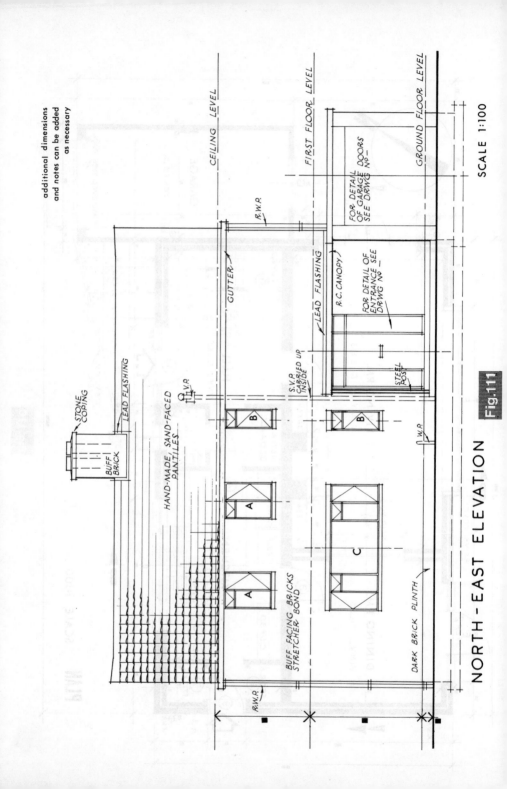

additional dimensions
and notes can be added
as necessary

CEILING LEVEL

FIRST FLOOR LEVEL

GROUND FLOOR LEVEL

SCALE 1:100

R.W.P.

FOR DETAIL OF GARAGE DOORS SEE DRWG No —

GUTTER

LEAD FLASHING

R.C. CANOPY

FOR DETAIL OF ENTRANCE SEE DRWG No —

S.V.P. CARRIED UP INSIDE

STEEL POST

STONE CORING

LEAD FLASHING

BUFF BRICK

HAND-MADE, SAND-FACED PANTILES

S.V.P.

B

B

A

A

C

BUFF FACING BRICKS STRETCHER BOND

R.W.P.

DARK BRICK PLINTH

R.W.P.

NORTH-EAST ELEVATION

Fig.111

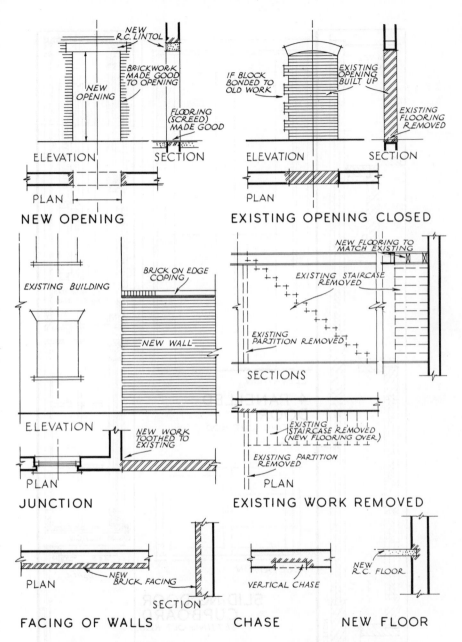

ALTERATIONS AND ADDITIONS
TYPICAL EXAMPLES OF INDICATION

Fig 112

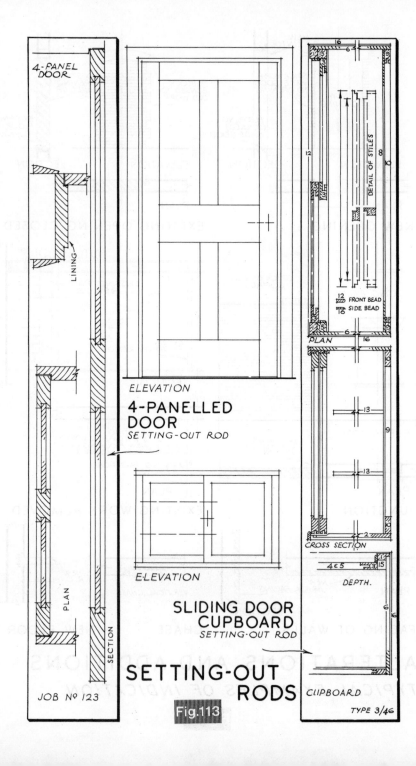

4-PANEL DOOR

LINING

PLAN

SECTION

JOB Nº 123

ELEVATION

4-PANELLED DOOR
SETTING-OUT ROD

E·LEVATION

SLIDING DOOR CUPBOARD
SETTING·OUT ROD

DETAIL OF STILES

12 FRONT BEAD
18 SIDE BEAD

PLAN

CROSS SECTION

DEPTH.

CUPBOARD

TYPE 3/46

SETTING-OUT RODS

Fig.113

minimum essential outlines of the former are drawn (see 'junction'), the new work being indicated in the normal manner. Existing walls are usually outlined in a heavy black line or blacked in solid. When drawings are coloured the colouring is confined to the new work.

Full-size details

These are drawings to show details of construction or, less often, designs which cannot be shown sufficiently clearly on small-scale drawings for the setting-out of workshop drawings. They are usually made for carpenters', joiners' and masons' work. They are drawn on tracing or detail paper and are largely sectional in type. All members are shown to exact finished shape and size.

The drawing is made in strong pencil line and the sections of each member are outlined with coloured pencils or pens or by an $\frac{1}{8}''$ band of water-colour in the conventional colours. Lengthy sections are often divided up for convenience, although sometimes they are drawn on a continuous roll of paper.

Workshop drawings

These further working drawings, nearly always to full size, are usually made by foremen or special 'setters-out' in the workshops of the various trades, etc., from the architect's scale drawings and full-size details. Sometimes, however, architects prefer to make the workshop drawings themselves.

From these workship drawings the working lines are transferred to the material or templates. They are made on thick cartridge paper or on specially prepared boards of straight-grained timber or sheets of plywood about 8' 0" long. The boards are termed 'rod'. Their surfaces are glass-papered and covered with a thin coating of whitewash and size or are chalked over, and the drawing is done with a strong pencil line. Coloured pencils are sometimes used to emphasise sections.

Fig. 113 shows two setting-out rods, one for a four-panelled door, the other for a cupboard with sliding door. The boards bear job numbers and sometimes the various members of the work are given reference numbers.

Check list for production drawings

The following refers to some of the main points to be dealt with in making traditional production drawings. All of them may not apply to every job, and other items can be added to the list according to individual ideas. Such a list does, however, help to avoid omissions.

CONVENTIONAL INDICATIONS AND REPRESENTATION

General

1. Careful arrangements of sheets and drawings for maximum legibility and help to users.
2. Use of standard signs, hatching and symbols.
3. Compliance with Building Regulations, Planning Authorities' requirements, etc.
4. Dimension lines and dimensions; agreement of total lengths, etc.
5. All necessary notes, labelling, titles, north-point, scale, etc.
6. Indication of entrances.
7. Direction of stairs, numbering of risers.
8. Numbering of doors, windows and other plan units.
9. Door swings.
10. Floor finishes.
11. Direction of ramps.
12. Sanitary fittings. Only fittings made or ordered by contractor to be shown.
13. Positions of artificial light points, etc.
14. Positions of radiators.
15. Positions of service points.
16. Levels in relation to ordnance or other datum.

Basement Plan

1. Foundations of structural walls.
2. Steppings in site and foundation concrete.
3. Tanking.
4. Casing of steelwork, numbering of stanchions, etc.
5. Thickness of heating chamber walls, fire-clay lining to flues.
6. Positions of boilers, etc.
7. Finished level of heating chamber floor and surface concrete.
8. Electrical intake and switch room.
9. Boiler room sump.
10. Drainage of areas.
11. Ducts for pipes.
12. Gullies.
13. Drainage pipe lines, manholes, invert levels and arrows to show direction of fall, interceptor and f.a.i.

Ground and Upper Floors

1. Site lay-out.
2. Numbering of stanchions, etc., steel beams, sizes, weights, levels.
3. Sleeper walls dotted.
4. Directions of floor spans.
5. Ducts. Flues.
6. Drainage lines, manholes, etc.; rainwater, soil, vent pipes, etc.
7. Fuel chute.
8. Railings to areas.

Roof Plan

1. Direction of falls.
2. Positions of rainwater pipes, vent pipes, etc., cesspools, rainwater heads.
3. Tanks and circulation.
4. Stacks.
5. Type of covering.
6. Directions of spans.
7. Access to roof.

CONVENTIONAL INDICATIONS AND REPRESENTATION

Elevations and Sections

1. Levels of floors, etc. in relation to datum.
2. Dimensions of heights of windows, etc.
3. Joint lines.
4. Stonework blocks crossed where necessary.
5. Joints of all unit materials.
6. Types, numbers and openings of windows.
7. Exposed pipes, gullies, etc., to be shown.
8. Air-bricks, to rooms and timber ground floors, etc.
9. Foundations and steepings – show by broken line on all elevations.
10. Steps, ramps, railings, etc.
11. Existing ground line, finished paving line.
12. DPCs Tanking.
13. Stacks.

7
Tracings and Reproduction of Drawings

Tracings are made for the purpose of copying or developing existing drawings, whether on drawing paper or tracing paper, and are used either as finished drawings in themselves or, more often, as negatives for reproduction by photoprinting.

Tracing media are briefly described in Chapter 1. Any appropriate drawing method can be used, but usually lines are drawn in pencil or in indian ink or a combination of both, e.g. plans, elevations, etc. in pencil with dimensions and lettering in ink. Transfer lettering, tones and figures can also be used. Pencil work is best carried out using a fairly hard lead—selected in accordance with prevailing humidity—of a type specially made to give a dense yet crisp line free from grittiness, dust and smearing. Firm, even pressure is needed, but not so great as to 'bite' into the paper, or any subsequent erasures may result in 'ghosting'. Ink lines are best drawn using one of the drawing pens previously described which overcome most of the inconsistencies of thickness, risks of smudging, and general inconvenience associated with the old-style ruling pen. Nevertheless, the beginner may have difficulty with wayward and ragged lines until practice perfects control. A piece of paper for trying out the pen and a lint-free cloth for keeping the nib or point clean should be handy. The general sequence of drawing should be as recommended for inking-in on page 36. Ink lines should be of thicknesses according to their purposes, and should not be unduly fine or they may fail to be reproduced in the printing process. Main outlines can be thickened for clearer definition. In ink drawings, details which are not to be given prominence in the printing can be drawn in a hard pencil, e.g. brick courses, hatching, shading, etc.

With all drawing on tracing media it is essential that the surface is worked over or touched by hand as little as possible. If not to be traced over an existing drawing or grid, the general arrangement should be pre-established and main lines should be set up on a preliminary sheet over which the final drawing is made. Unless the final drawing is to be completed in one operation, it is as well to divide it into sections to be completed in turn. This procedure will also minimise trouble arising from movement of the paper due to overnight stretching or shrinkage in conditions of variable humidity, sections of the drawing not being worked on always being kept covered by strips of tracing paper for protection.

Drawing on tracing cloth can be done in pencil, for which a specially prepared quality of the material is obtainable, but most drawing is done in indian ink on the dull or matt side, not the glossy. A little powdered chalk should be rubbed gently over the surface to remove any grease and to assist the flow of the ink. More than one application of powder may be necessary during the course of work. Before using, tracing cloth (and, for that matter, tracing paper), a large sheet should be allowed to adjust itself to the atmosphere where it is to be used; the material is affected by moisture in the air when taken straight from the roll or packet. The sheet may be hung up, after removal of the selvedges, by two drawing pins, or may be left lying flat and free in some convenient place for a few hours.

Care must be taken in making corrections on tracing media. If the surface is damaged, marks will show on the copies. Erasures can be made most easily on paper and cloth by means of a razor blade. Unwanted pencil lines and dirt can be removed from tracing cloth by wiping lightly with a piece of cotton wool dipped in petrol, lighter fuel or similar spirit.

Finished drawings on tracing paper can be coloured by dry techniques. Coloured cloth tracings are sometimes required for attaching to title-deeds or other purposes. Colouring is done on the glossy side in gouache or water colour, which appear satisfactorily on the other side.

Reproduction of drawings

The following are the main types of photocopying processes for making copies of drawings. Copies are usually referred to as 'prints'.

1. *Dyeline*. This semi-dry process requires a transparent or translucent negative, e.g. a drawing on tracing media. This is passed, in contact with diazo paper sensitive to ultra-violet light, through a machine in which it moves around a special tubular lamp emitting such light. Good ink negatives give a dark-brown almost black line on a white background. Pencil negatives, according to the strength of line and the efficiency of the printing, show some background tint. If this tint or tone is reasonably even it is not detrimental and can be advantageous if the print is to be coloured or otherwise rendered. Most machines can be adjusted to give the desired background. Dyeline prints can be made on airmail paper, which is very flimsy and difficult to handle, on medium paper, which is normal and suitable for general use,

on stout paper, which is best for mounting, colouring and presentation, and on cotton-backed paper. Master copies or new negatives, from which further copies can be made, can also be produced on tracing paper, lacquered tracing paper, tracing cloth and polyester-based materials. The last two are for heavy use, polyester materials being dimensionally stable. Such copies are used for the adding of specialist information, as a basis for the preparation of operational drawings, and for supplying remote and overseas sites with the means of obtaining local reproductions.

Dyeline prints are suitable for most purposes and as they are relatively cheap and easy to produce, dyeline machines of which there are many kinds, are used by commercial printers and in most offices and schools. Another kind of dyeline print is dry-developed by ammonia gas. Results are similar, but the lines are bluish. All dyeline prints tend to fade on long exposure to daylight.

2. *True-to-scale.* Known as TTS, this method of printing from ink tracings gives a dense black line of the same size as the original negative on medium or stout white cartridge paper, mounted paper, opaque and transparent tracing cloths, and polyester-based materials. As the lines are in printer's ink they do not fade and can be regarded as permanent. Additions made in indian ink match the printed line. It is possible for portions of the original tracing to be omitted and for portions of other tracings to be added, and for unwanted marks and dirt to be cleaned up during the process. Prints can also be made in coloured inks. The standard paper takes colouring of any kind very well. The method is expensive but well worthwhile for drawings of special importance.

3. *Photostats.* This is a normal photographic process using a camera for making copies of any kind of drawing or document. It is a two-stage process. A true negative is first made, i.e. white lines on a black background, from which positive prints of the same size as the original, or proportionately larger or smaller, can be made on a variety of papers as best suited to the subject. If prints are subsequently to be coloured they should have a matt surface. Copies on translucent materials can be made, thus enabling them to be reproduced by dyeline process without need for intermediate tracing.

Mention may be made here of the microfilming of drawings, a photographic process by which miniature transparencies are made for convenience of safe storage and retrieval. Also of the various kinds of ordinary office copiers: thermographic, electrographic and diffusion transfer, which, although developed primarily for the copying of typed or printed documents, are excellent for the rapid copying of small drawings — or larger drawings in parts which can be subsequently joined. Larger models, up to A1 size, are capable of making master copies of drawings for reproduction by the dyeline process.

8
Perspective Drawing

Perspective projection

Perspective drawings are amongst the most important of design drawings as they convey more or less the actual appearance of the building or object, and are therefore of considerable value in enabling laymen to appreciate points of design which are not easily understood by them from orthographic projections. There are a number of ways of setting up perspectives and the underlying theories are complex and can only be described in words at great length. The best way to learn to make perspectives, however, is to study the essential principles from examples and then to practise their application.

What is probably the most satisfactory method for general use is illustrated in Figs. 114 to 118. Fig. 114 shows in orthographic projection the plan and two adjacent elevations of a rectangular prism or block, and how it is set up in perspective to give a view such as would be obtained by looking obliquely at the block from a level slightly above it.

The first step is to draw the plan of the block. Then the position of 'eye' of the spectator, point S, in relation to the plan according to the view required must be decided. The position is a matter of judgement in the light of experience, but a little imagination will help the beginner to get it somewhere near where it is wanted. Assuming for simplification that the spectator is looking directly at the near corner of the block, a line is drawn from S through this corner. This line is the *direct line of vision* and somewhere along its length another line to represent the *picture plane* is drawn at right-angles. The picture plane is an imaginary vertical plane on to which is projected the required view – see axonometric diagram in Chapter 3. Through the remaining corners of the block on plan further lines are drawn from S to the picture plane to locate these points in the perspective. Lines are also drawn from S parallel to the sides of the block to the picture plane. These points, VP1 and VP2, locate the positions of the vanishing points along the eye-level to which in the perspective the outlines of the sides

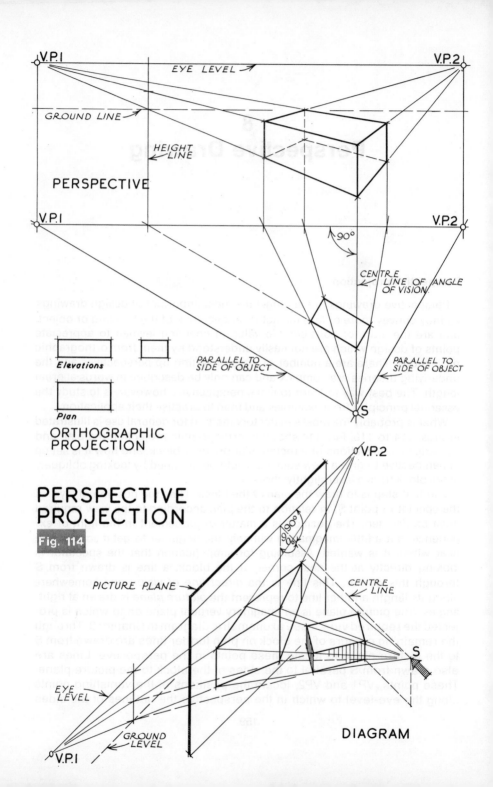

V.P.1

EYE LEVEL →

GROUND LINE →

HEIGHT LINE ←

PERSPECTIVE

V.P.2

V.P.1

90°

V.P.2

CENTRE LINE OF ANGLE OF VISION

Elevations

Plan

ORTHOGRAPHIC PROJECTION

PARALLEL TO SIDE OF OBJECT

PARALLEL TO SIDE OF OBJECT

S

PERSPECTIVE PROJECTION

Fig. 114

V.P.2

90° 90°

PICTURE PLANE →

CENTRE LINE

S

EYE LEVEL

GROUND LEVEL

V.P.1

DIAGRAM

of the block will converge. Another line is also drawn on plan in continuation of one or other side of the block to the picture plane; this line – shown broken in the figure – gives a point on the picture for the position of a *height line*.

The next step is to draw the 'elevation', as it were, of the picture plane, which, although shown bounded in the diagram, is actually not defined in extent. At some reasonable distance above the plan, therefore, a horizontal line is drawn; this line represents the *eye-level* of the spectator, and to it are projected perpendiculars from the picture plane on plan from VP1 and VP2 and the point for the height line. As the view required is one looking down on the block, then a point must be marked down the height line from the eye-level equal to the estimated position of the eye above the 'ground' or horizontal plane on which the block rests. Through this point a horizontal line is drawn and is called the *ground line.* Up the height line from the ground line is measured the height of the block taken from the elevation, i.e. at the same scale as the plan of the block. Through the point obtained and from the intersection of ground line and height line, lines are drawn from VP1 to contact the direct line of vision continued from the plan. From the points of contact lines are drawn to VP2, and then by projecting up from the picture plane on plan it will be seen how the outline of the block in perspective is obtained.

Fig. 115 shows the application of the same method to the making of a perspective of the small garage shown in orthographic projection in Fig. 73. Most of the construction lines are shown. In drawing the plan of the garage it is only necessary to show in detail the outside lines of the two sides which will appear in the perspective, but care must always be taken that every salient feature is indicated. Note the broken line representing the projecting eaves of the roof.

The direct line of vision should preferably not pass through the near corner of the building and never so as to bisect it or the effect will be spoiled. A good way of fixing its position is to draw lines from S to the limits of the building, or wider if it is proposed to include much of the surroundings in the picture; the angle formed by these lines, which is termed the *angle of vision* and which should be between 40 and 60 degrees to correspond to the normal range, is then bisected to find the direct line of vision.

The picture plane must always be at right-angles to the line of vision, and the angle between the lines drawn to locate the vanishing points must also be a right-angle.

In the perspective of the garage the eye-level has been taken at a height of 1 metre (33″) above ground level. 'Normal' eye-level can be regarded as about 1,600 mm (5′3″) above ground level, but somewhat lower than this is better for small buildings.

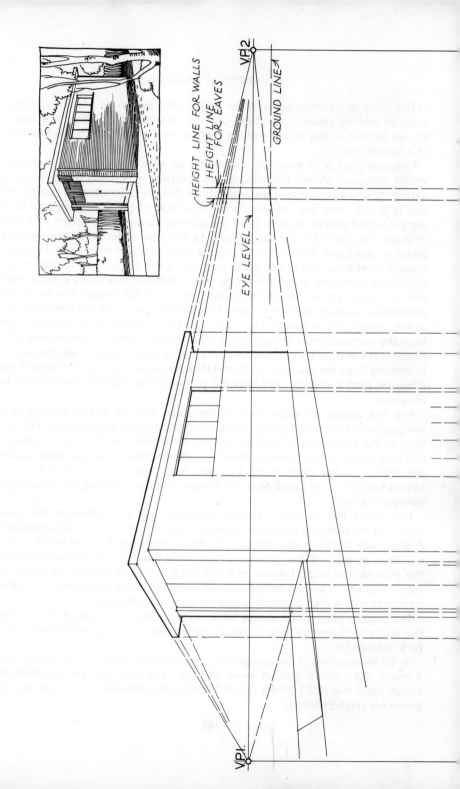

HEIGHT LINE FOR WALLS

HEIGHT LINE FOR EAVES

GROUND LINE

EYE LEVEL

VP2.

VP1.

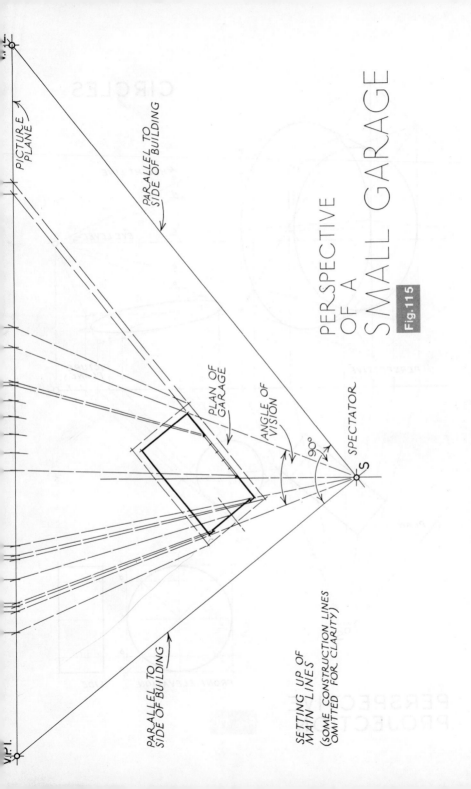

PICTURE PLANE

PARALLEL TO SIDE OF BUILDING

PLAN OF GARAGE

ANGLE OF VISION

90°

SPECTATOR

S

PARALLEL TO SIDE OF BUILDING

SETTING UP OF MAIN LINES
(SOME CONSTRUCTION LINES OMITTED FOR CLARITY)

PERSPECTIVE OF A SMALL GARAGE

Fig. 115

CIRCLES

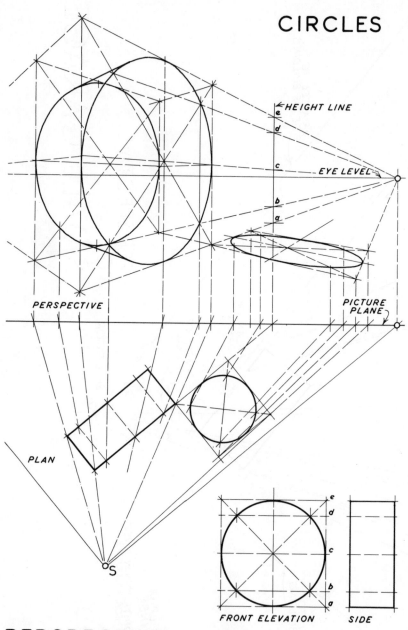

HEIGHT LINE

EYE LEVEL

e
d
c
b
a

PERSPECTIVE

PICTURE PLANE

PLAN

S

FRONT ELEVATION

SIDE

e
d
c
b
a

PERSPECTIVE PROJECTION

Fig. 116

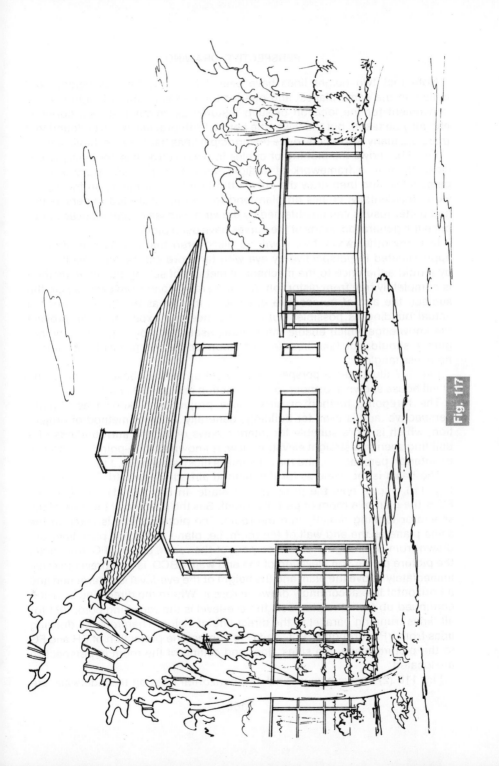

Fig. 117

Note that two height lines have been taken, one for wall heights and details in the same planes, and one for the eaves. As many height lines as convenient for the location of such features as chimney stacks, dormers, etc. may be taken, but the fewer the better. With practice it will be found that there are many 'short cuts' once the principal lines have been established.

Fig. 116 shows the plotting of circles in perspective. It is necessary to enclose them in a framework of straight lines, to set up the framework in perspective and then draw the curves through located points on the framework. Incidentally, circles on plan tend to become distorted in perspective and better results can be obtained by drawing ellipses or part ellipses by eye once the general positions of the curves have been plotted.

In many other ways, too, it will be discovered that details can often be approximated in perspective by eye with far more satisfactory results than by a rigid adherence to the mechanical method of setting-up, as no method is completely free from distortion. And generally, apart from exercises in the subject, the aim of perspective drawing is to give as true a picture of the actual building as possible. But only practice and experience can provide the knowledge which enable these improvisations to be made, and the beginner should not take liberties too soon or he will probably get into a hopeless tangle.

Fig. 117 illustrates a perspective view set up by the above method of the small house shown in orthographic projection in Figs. 110 and 111.

The foregoing method of perspective projection is known as '2-point perspective' and is used for buildings generally. Another method of projection, which is more suitable for interior views or for the surroundings of a building seen in a straight elevation view, is known as 'one-point' or 'parallel' or 'interior' perspective, and the principle is illustrated in Fig. 118.

The basis is the same as for the method already described. The diagram, Fig. 118, shows how the projection is made. In Fig. 118 (1), AD, BC, EH, FG is the plan of a room or part of a room; S is the position of the 'eye' of the spectator looking directly into the room. The picture plane is taken in the same plane as the end wall of the room, i.e. plane ABCD. On plan, lines are drawn from S through the near corners of the room, EH and FG, to contact the picture plane. The elevation of the end wall, ABCD, is now drawn to scale immediately above the plan, and the height of the eye-level is determined and a horizontal line accordingly drawn across it. Where the direct line of vision continued up from the plan cuts the eye-level is the vanishing point VP1 for all 'lines' running parallel to the direct line of vision. Therefore, by drawing lines from VP1 through A, B, C and D to contact the projection of EH and FG to the picture plane, the sides, floor and ceiling of the room in perspective are located.

Fig. 118 (2) shows how vertical and horizontal lines on the side walls are drawn. On plan, points L and M represent vertical 'lines' on the left-hand wall of the room, e.g. mullions, panelling, etc. By drawing through these points from S and projecting perpendiculars upwards, the lines can be drawn in the correct positions on the side wall in perspective. KJ is a horizontal 'line' on the same wall; the height of it above the floor or the distance below the ceiling is known and is marked to scale along the corner of the room, AD, on the picture plane, and the line can then be drawn in perspective from VP1.

Fig. 118 (3) shows the location of two points, O and P, on the floor and ceiling respectively. Their positions are marked on the plan and lines are drawn from them at 45 degrees to the picture plane (for convenience one is taken to the left and one to the right). By reference to Fig. 118 (1) it will be seen how vanishing points, VP2 and VP3, are obtained for lines running at 45 degrees across the plan. From the point where the line on plan from O cuts the picture plane a perpendicular is projected upwards to cut the bottom line of the end wall extended; through this intersection a line is drawn from VP2 to contact a line from VP1 through the point where a perpendicular from O on plan cuts the end wall floor line, thus locating O in the perspective. Point P is found in a similar manner, the line of the ceiling level of the end wall being used in the construction.

Fig. 118 (4) shows a further stage illustrating in a similar manner the construction of, say, a book-case, QW, RU, SV, TX, projecting at right-angles from the side wall.

The main lines or salient points of any pattern or object within the room can be plotted by the above methods in perspective.

In all perspective drawing the construction lines should be very light, but clearly and accurately drawn. The slightest error can easily become greatly exaggerated and upset the whole working. It is sometimes advisable to index points and lines on plan with letters or figures when they are numerous or close together in order to keep track of them. Always set up the main lines of the building or object first and work progressively from large to small details.

Perspective grids

Provided there is a clear understanding of the foregoing principles of perspective projections, which can only result from experiment and practice with various shapes and forms, much time and inconvenience can be saved in the initial setting out by tracing over pre-drawn grids. Fig. 119 shows such a grid for external 2-point perspective projections made by the author some years ago and since used for many drawings including that illustrated by Plate 9.

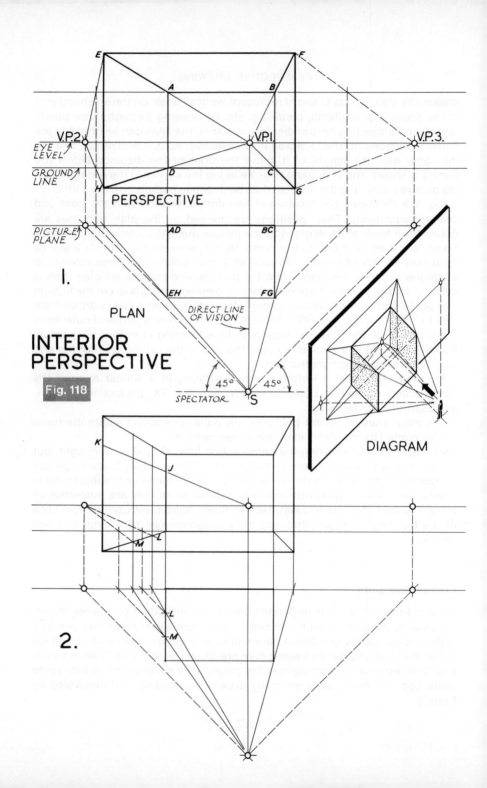

V.P.2

EYE
LEVEL

GROUND
LINE

PICTURE
PLANE

PERSPECTIVE

V.P.1

V.P.3.

I.

PLAN

DIRECT LINE
OF VISION

INTERIOR
PERSPECTIVE

Fig. 118

45° 45°

SPECTATOR S

DIAGRAM

K

J

M L

L

M

2.

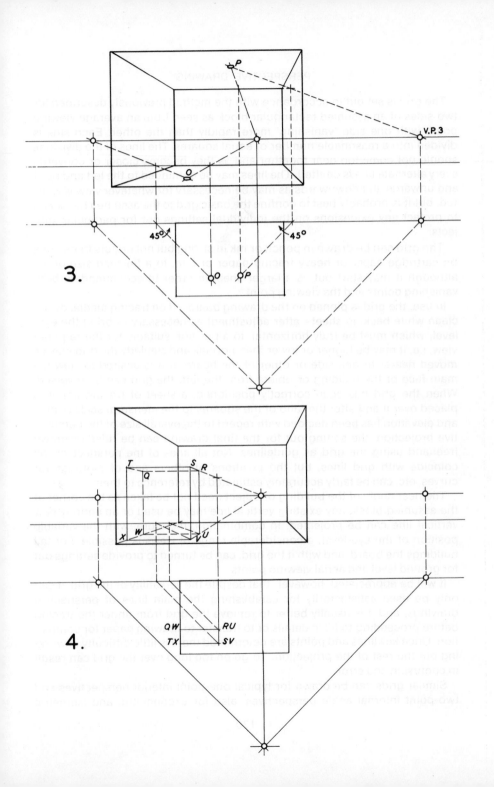

3.

4.

PERSPECTIVE DRAWING

The grid is set out in accordance with the method previously described for two sides of an assumed rectangular block as seen from an average viewing point, with one side 'vanishing' more rapidly than the other. Each side is divided into a reasonable number of equal squares. The lines of the divisions should not come too near together and as they become closer or converge every alternate line is omitted. The lines may be continued to the left and right and upwards and downwards as may be necessary for whatever view is wanted, but it is probably best to confine the basic grid to the assumed block and to project any extensions on the individual settings out for particular subjects.

The grid can be drawn in pencil or ink in strong but not unduly thick lines on cartridge paper or heavy tracing paper or film, to a finished size of A1, although it may start out as a larger sheet in order to accommodate both vanishing points and the viewing point.

In use, the grid is pinned on the drawing board — if on tracing media, over a clean white backing sheet — after adjustment as necessary to bring the eye-level, which must be truly horizontal, to a position suitable for the required view, i.e. it may be higher or lower than normal, and similarly the grid may be moved nearer to one side or other of the board. If it is desired to view the main face of the building or object from the left, the grid can be reversed. When the grid has been correctly positioned, a sheet of tracing paper is placed over it and after the ratio of the squares to the mensural scale of plan and elevation has been decided with regard to the overall size of the perspective projection, the setting out for the final drawing can be ruled or drawn freehand using the grid as guidelines. Not all lines of the perspective will coincide with grid lines, but the positions of others and of plottings for curves, etc. can be fairly accurately estimated by reference to them.

The near angle of the building or object need not be taken as the corner of the assumed block: any existing vertical line may be used or an entirely new vertical line can be projected. In combination, therefore, with the variable position of the eye-level, a considerable range of views is possible. For tall buildings the board, and with it the grid, can be turned to provide settings out for ground level and aerial viewing points.

It will be appreciated, however, that despite the versatility of the grid, it can only be used satisfactorily for establishing the main lines of perspective drawings, and it is usually better to remove the grid from under the tracing before proceeding to fill in details or to transfer to drawing paper for completion. Once key lines and points are determined there is little difficulty in working out the rest of the projection. To go on too long over the grid can result in confusion and error.

Similar grids can be drawn for typical one-point interior perspectives and two-point internal angle perspectives, also for axonometric and isometric

Grid can be reversed or used vertically in either direction

lines can be extended as required

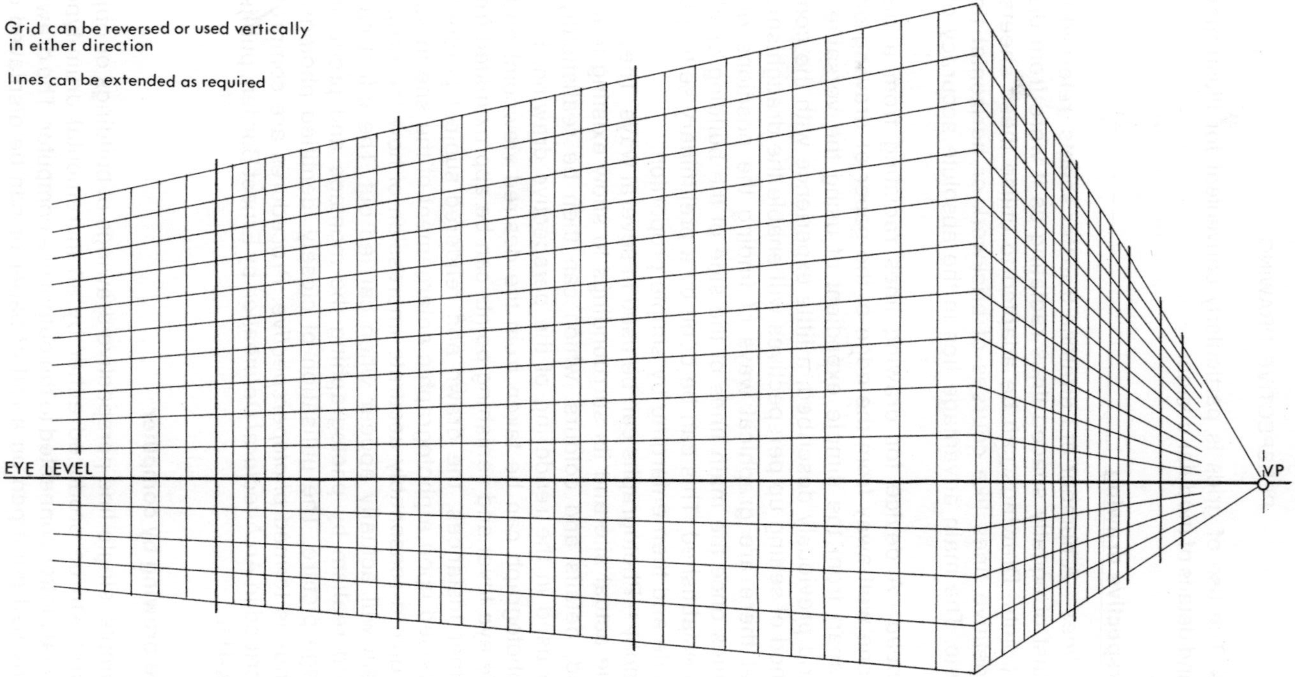

VP

EYE LEVEL

PERSPECTIVE GRID

ABOUT ONE-QUARTER ACTUAL SIZE

Fig. 119

projections. The use of grids is particularly convenient for illustrations of buildings and details of modular design.

Aids to perspective drawing

Transfer lines – A number of Letratone transfer sheets, referred to on p.223, consist of equally spaced lines radiating as it were from distant vanishing points. Drawings can be adapted to utilise these sheets, for use on repetitive lines like courses of brickwork or horizontal timber cladding, etc. The main advantage lies in the absolute accuracy of the spacing.

Centrolinead – A device for drawing lines radiating from a distant point, i.e. one well away from the edge of the paper or drawing board. However, apart from the simple expedient of using the versatile perspective grid previously described, a little experience with the conventional method of setting up perspectives will enable the draughtsman to realise that there are graphical ways of finding the positions of any required lines once the main lines of the side of the building or object have been established. This can be done by a preliminary setting up at a small scale and then enlarging by simple proportion.

Photography – Photographs can be used in several ways. They can be taken of the actual site and its surroundings to show existing features, background, details and colours, which can then be realistically but selectively used in the rendering of the perspective drawing. In some cases, a photograph can be taken from the desired viewpoint and the appropriate eye level and vanishing points can be approximated from a print. In other instances, the drawn and rendered subject perspective can be imposed upon a photographic enlargement of the site in such a way as to give a reasonably accurate impression of how the proposed development will actually appear when carried out. The effect can be given added realism by photographing the montage and producing a second stage picture. The utilisation of closely identified photographs and drawings is termed *photoperspective*. Procedures are comprehensively described in *Architectural Delineation* by Ernest Burden, published by McGraw-Hill.

Perspective drawing by computer

Small, simple, single-line perspective drawings of buildings or objects in block form can be produced either by an incremental drum-type or flat-bed digital plotter connected to the output of a computer. The drawings are made by ball-point pen on a roll of paper or can be displayed on a cathode-ray tube. The method is described in *Computers in Architectural Design* by D. G. Campion, published by the Elsevier Publishing Company Ltd. Typical drawings are shown in plates 21 and 22. It will be seen that they consist of straight or minutely serrated lines joining co-ordinates, i.e. the corners of a building or object, the positions of which are established in relation to a viewing point.

The position of the viewing point can be varied, and one of the main advantages of the method is the ease and speed with which different perspective views can be obtained. Additional detail and shadows can be added manually as desired, and completely new and larger drawings can be set up on the basis of the computer product. However, it would not normally be economic in time or cost to adopt the latter procedure if only a single pictorial perspective were required, as it could more easily be made by the methods described earlier in this chapter. Computer perspectives are most valuable where a number of views are needed in connection with massing studies, the relationship of a group of buildings, or for town planning and urban design purposes.

When using a visual display unit it is possible constantly to vary the viewing point and viewed point so as to give the effect of moving around the building or object.

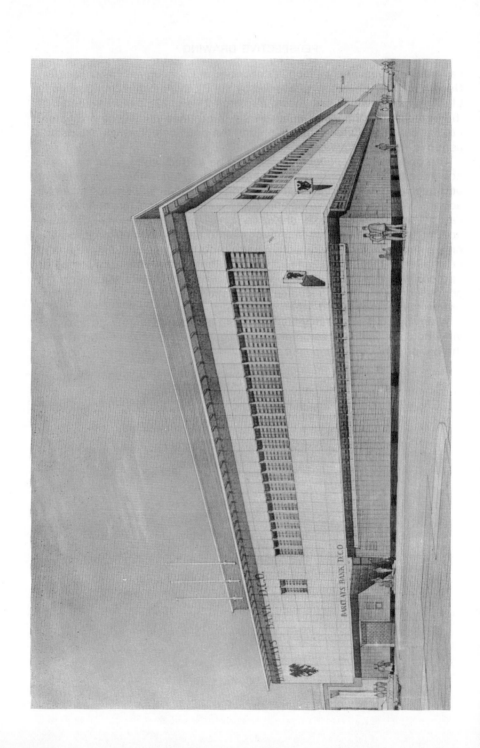

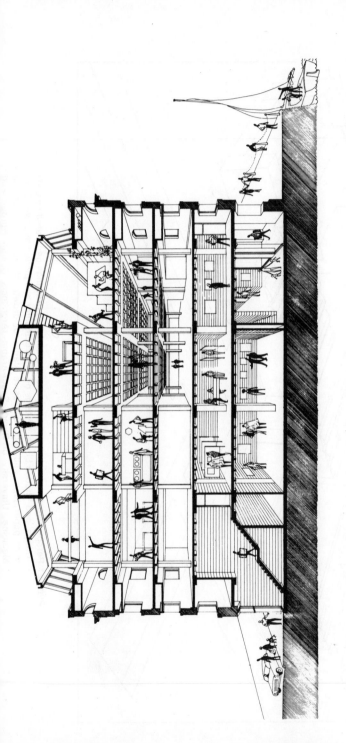

Plate 20 Example of ruled ink line drawing. Interior view of remodelled dock-side warehouse. True scale cross section in conjunction with one-point perspective. Note use of transfer figures to give scale and life. Bush Building, Bristol, England, reproduced by permission of J. T. Building Services Ltd., drawn by Michael Duckering.

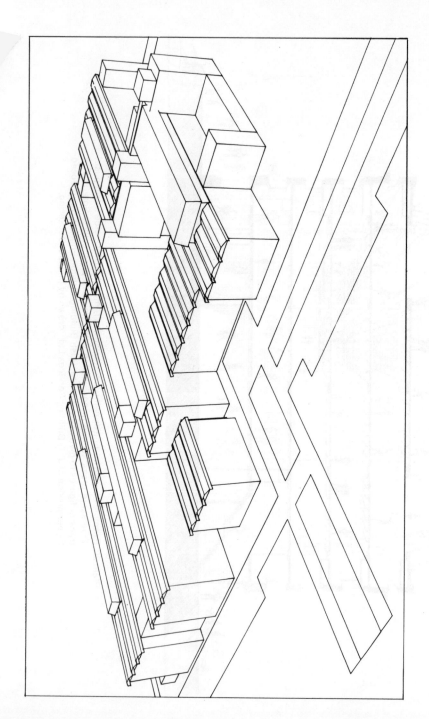

Plate 21 Perspective drawing by computer: one of a series of drawings generated by CAD 'Things' and 'Hidden Lines' systems on Atlas computer and plotted by Laser-Scan from paper tape, showing successive stages of growth of project: Faculty of Medicine, University of Riyad, Saudi-Arabia (Architects Cusdin Burden and

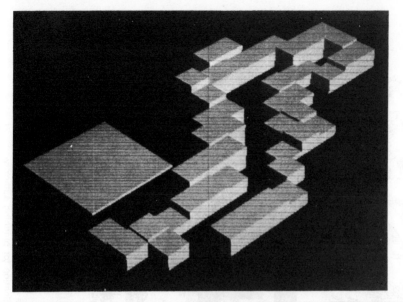

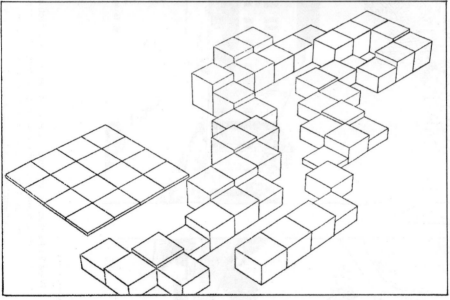

Plate 22 Computer perspective: greyscale image photographed from visual display unit, and corresponding line portrayal. One example of many different views for study of project: Hong Kong University Development Plan. (Architects Cusdin Burden and Howitt.) Acknowledgements to Computer-Aided Design Centre, Cambridge, England.

NORTH EAST ELEVATION

Plate 23 Psuedo-perspective drawing: a rapid and attractive way of showing a proposed development to the client or to accompany an application for planning authority approval. The building is in true elevation with foreground in perspective. The trees heighten the effect of depth of foreground without obscuring the view of the building. Council Offices, Tewkesbury, Building Partnership (Bristol) Ltd. Original

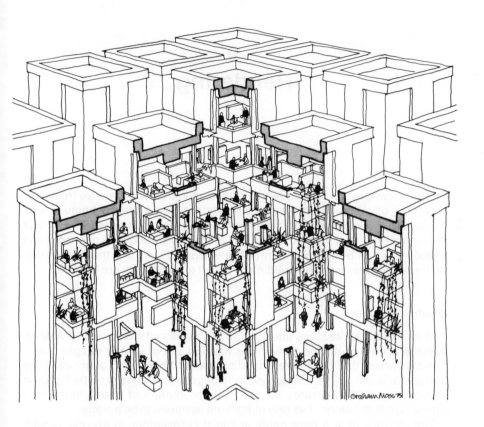

Plate 24 Example of freehand black ink lines made with 0.3 and 0.6 drawing pens on tracing
sheet over accurately set up cut-away interior perspective view of 'open plan'
office building. Sectional tone applied by pressure transfer. The simplicity of the
drawing technique was dictated in this instance by reproduction requirements.
The technique is well suited to dyeline printing. *Graham Moss*

9
Rendering

Design drawings can be 'rendered', that is, coloured or otherwise treated in a number of different ways employing various media and techniques with the object of explaining the design more clearly than is possible by a line drawing only. One of the first aids in this respect is the showing of shades and shadows, which bring out the three-dimensional forms and the relationship of the various planes of the building or object to which they are applied.

Shadow projection

In architectural drawings the addition of shades and shadows on buildings is made according to the convention that the sun or source of light illuminates downwards from the left-hand side at an angle of 45 degrees to the horizontal in elevation, and across at 45 degrees to the front of the building in plan. Fig. 120 illustrates the principle by means of axonometric and orthographic drawings. The rays of light are assumed to be parallel.

The convention is a reasonable one as it corresponds to average natural conditions, and has the advantages of (1) giving shadows the width and height of which are in most cases the same as the projection or recess causing them, and (2) making the plotting easy as it can be done entirely with T-square and 45-degree set-square. There is, however, no reason why the angle should not be varied, e.g. made 60 degrees, if this would avoid confusion with other lines on the drawing, although this problem seldom arises.

Usually the projection of shades and shadows is made from elevation and plan, but sometimes it is necessary to work from elevation and section or side elevation.

The following examples illustrate the application of the principle to various geometrical solids, which are analogous to building forms. It is only by working out such examples that the method can be really grasped.

Fig. 121 (1) shows the shadow cast by an upright square prism (post) on horizontal (ground) and vertical (wall) planes as seen in the axonometric.

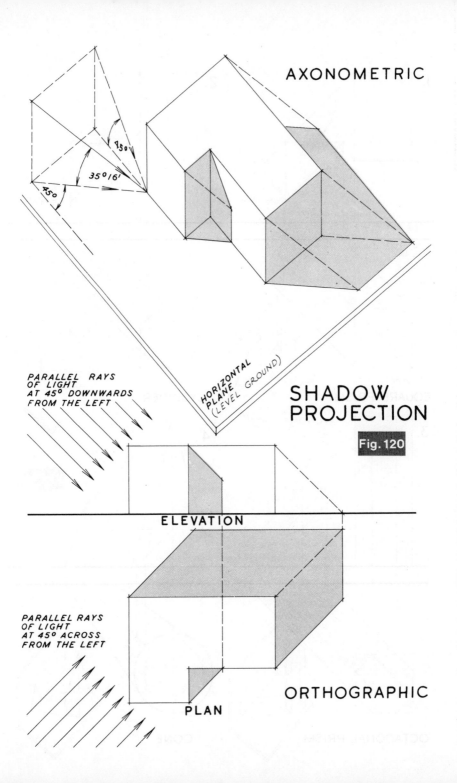

AXONOMETRIC

45°

35°16'

45°

PARALLEL RAYS
OF LIGHT
AT 45° DOWNWARDS
FROM THE LEFT

HORIZONTAL
PLANE
(LEVEL GROUND)

SHADOW
PROJECTION

Fig. 120

ELEVATION

PARALLEL RAYS
OF LIGHT
AT 45° ACROSS
FROM THE LEFT

ORTHOGRAPHIC

PLAN

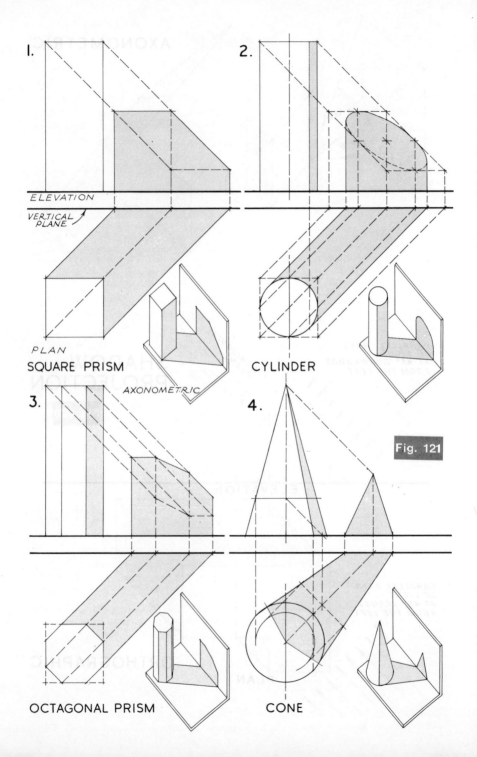

1.

ELEVATION

VERTICAL PLANE

PLAN

SQUARE PRISM

AXONOMETRIC

2.

CYLINDER

3.

OCTAGONAL PRISM

4.

Fig. 121

CONE

Lines at 45 degrees are drawn on elevation from the top corners of the prism in the direction of the light rays, and in a similar manner from the corners of the prism on plan. Where the lines on plan contact the vertical plane, perpendiculars are projected up to intersect the lines drawn on elevation and thus the outlines of the shadow are plotted. The various points are indexed on the drawing for clarity. If the prism has been far enough in front of the vertical plane its shadow would have fallen wholly on the horizontal plane. Its position would be found by projecting perpendiculars down from the points on the horizontal plane in elevation cut by the 45-degree lines from the top of the prism.

The sides of the prism away from the light source are in shade. The difference between shade and shadow is: *shade* occurs on a surface when because of its position in relation to the direction of the rays of light, it receives diminished light or no light at all; and *shadow* is that part of a surface receiving no direct light because some object comes between it and the source of light.

Fig. 121 (2) shows the casting of the shadow of an upright cylinder in a position similar to that of the prism. The shadow outline of the top has to be found by enclosing it in a square, by plotting the square in shadow and by then drawing through the common points of square and circle a smooth free-hand curve, actually an ellipse. Part of the shade of the cylinder appears in the elevation. This is found by projecting up from the tangent point where a 45-degree line touches the circle representing the cylinder on plan. Although shown as a straight line dividing surfaces of light and dark on elevation, there would be no such hard division but a gradual change from the lightest part of the cylinder to the darkest. On small scale drawings, however, it is usual to rule the line and darken to the right-hand side of it.

Fig. 121 (3) shows the shadow of an octagonal prism, and Fig. 121 (4) the shadow of a cone worked out on similar lines. In the case of the cone, note that the shadow position of the apex is first plotted on plan regardless of the vertical plane, and from the point so obtained lines, which define the shadow, are drawn to touch the base of the cone. From these points lines are drawn to the centre of the cone on plan to give the area of shade. Where the shadow lines meet the vertical plane project up to find the shadow on elevation.

Figs. 122 (1, 2 and 3) are examples of shadows cast by a square block on top of a square or rectangular prism, an octagonal prism and a cylinder. The construction lines are shown so that the plotting can be followed. Notice in regard to (1) that it is only necessary to draw down at 45 degrees from the bottom left-hand corner of the block to the left-hand side of the prism in elevation, and then to draw a horizontal line across the prism. For proof, any point, A, on the shadow-casting edge of the block can be plotted in shadow and it will be found to lie along the horizontal line. In (2) note the effect on

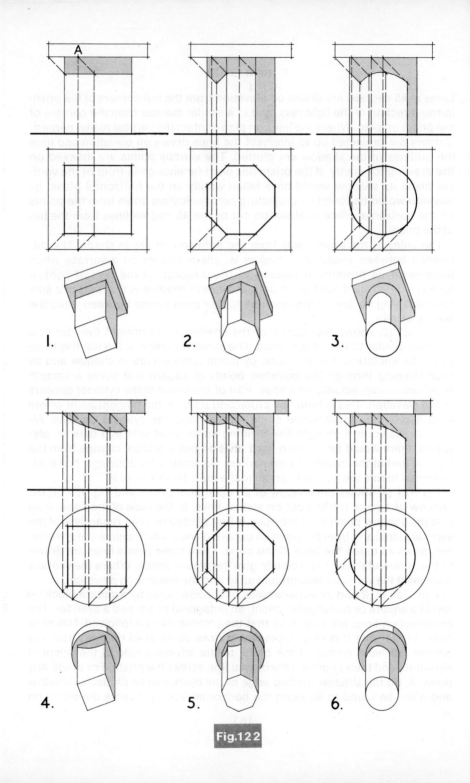

Fig.122

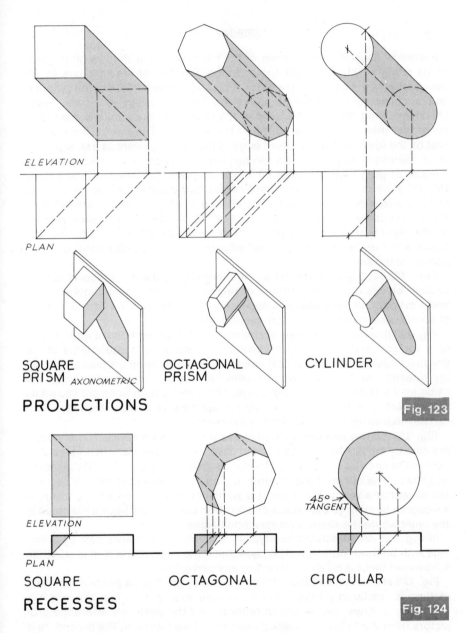

ELEVATION

PLAN

SQUARE PRISM *AXONOMETRIC*

OCTAGONAL PRISM

CYLINDER

PROJECTIONS

Fig. 123

ELEVATION

PLAN

SQUARE

OCTAGONAL

45°
TANGENT

CIRCULAR

RECESSES

Fig. 124

EXAMPLES OF SHADOW PROJECTION

the shadow caused by the corner of the block falling in shadow on the face of the prism which is at right-angles to the direction of the light rays. In (3), the shadow of the corner of the block is plotted on the surface of the cylinder, and a convenient number of points are likewise taken along the lower shadow-casting edge of the front of the block and are similarly plotted. A curve has then to be drawn through these points. The line of the shadow cast by the lower left-hand return edge of the block appears as a straight line at 45 degrees in elevation. This can be proved by casting the shadows of any number of points on the edge on to the cylinder. *The shadow cast by any straight edge projecting out at right-angles to the vertical plane and parallel to the horizontal plane always appears as a 45-degree line on elevation no matter how curved or broken the surface on which it falls.* The shadow merges on the right with the shade of the cylinder. As previously mentioned, the shade is not really defined by a hard edge but gradually fades into the lighter portion of the surface.

Figs. 122 (4, 5 and 6), similar to the foregoing, show the shadows cast by circular blocks on top of a square or rectangular prism, an octagonal prism and a cylinder. In each case it is necessary to plot the shadow from a number of points taken along the shadow-casting edge.

Fig. 123 illustrates examples of shadows cast by projections at right-angles to a surface (vertical plane) in elevation. These are the equivalents of the shadows cast by similar vertical solids as would be seen on plan, although the direction of the shadows in relation to the objects would then be the same as the direction of the light rays. The construction lines are shown as before. Note that the end of the cylinder appears as a circle in shadow and can be most easily drawn by plotting the centre.

Fig. 124 shows examples of shadows formed in recesses. The shadows are cast by the left-hand edge in each case. The simplest way to find the shadow in the circular recess is to plot the centre of the front edge of the recess as shown. The curve of the shadow in plan in this example cannot be plotted except at a very large scale; it is sufficient to plot its beginning from the 45-degree tangent to the recess on elevation and to draw back a flat curve to the point where the shadow on elevation begins.

In Fig. 125 are illustrated two typical examples of shadows cast by buildings with pitched roofs. It will be seen that if the pitch of the roof is less than 45-degrees there is no shadow cast by any part of it.

Fig. 126 shows the shadow cast by a chimney stack on a pitched roof. The plotting is similar in principle to the previous examples in Fig. 121, but it is necessary to draw the section in order to find the positions where the projectors from the top of the stack strike the inclined surface. The procedure is to find the shadow on elevation from the elevation and section, and then to project down to find the shadow on plan. Note that on elevation the inclina-

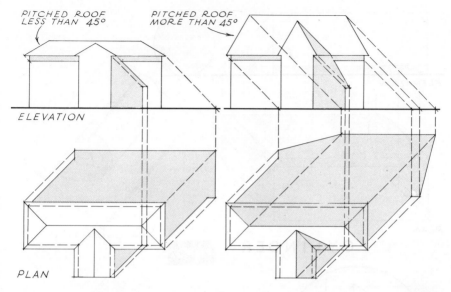

PITCHED ROOF
LESS THAN 45°

PITCHED ROOF
MORE THAN 45°

ELEVATION

PLAN

BUILDINGS WITH PITCHED ROOFS

Fig. 125

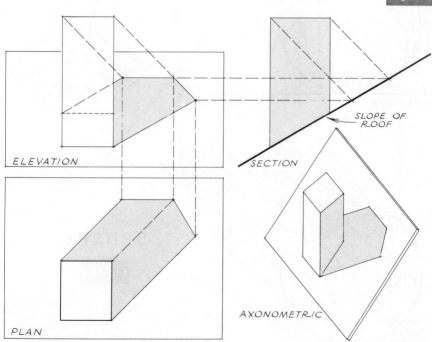

ELEVATION

SLOPE OF
ROOF

SECTION

PLAN

AXONOMETRIC

CHIMNEY STACK AND PITCHED ROOF

Fig.126

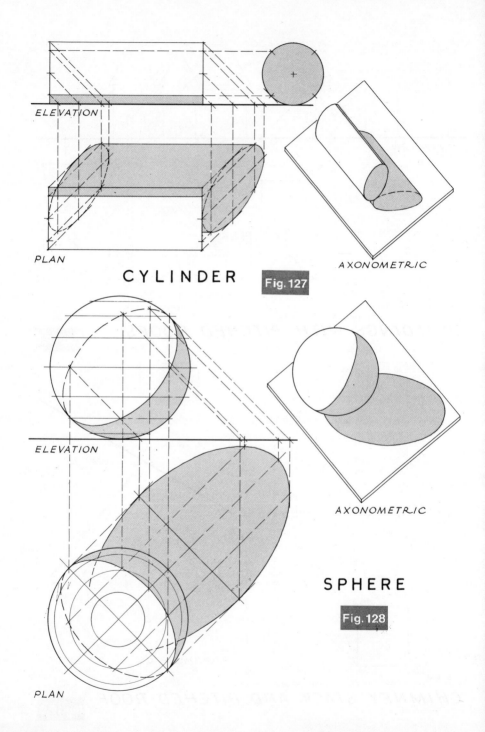

ELEVATION

PLAN

CYLINDER Fig. 127

AXONOMETRIC

ELEVATION

AXONOMETRIC

SPHERE

Fig. 128

PLAN

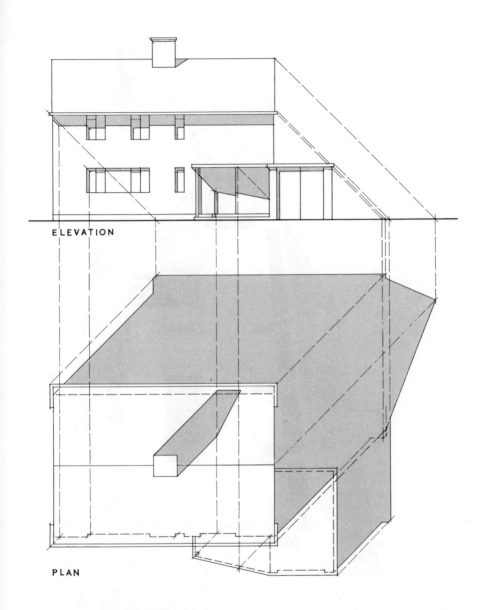

ELEVATION

PLAN

SHADOW PROJECTION

MAIN SHADOWS OF HOUSE SHOWN IN FIG. 106.
FOR CLARITY SOME CONSTRUCTION LINES ARE OMITTED

Fig. 129

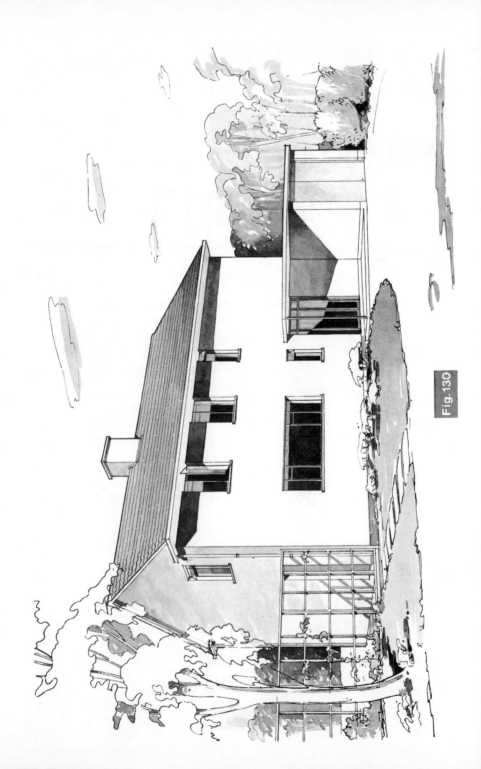

Fig.130

tion of the shadow lines of the vertical corners of the stack is the same as the pitch of the roof.

Fig. 127 shows the shade on a horizontal cylinder and the shadow cast by it on the horizontal plane.

Fig. 128 shows the shade on a sphere and the shadow cast by it on the horizontal plane. The line of shade is the line of an oblique cut through the centre of the sphere at right-angles to the rays of light. The geometrical setting-out is not shown here, but the line is drawn on plan and elevation. As in the case of shade on any curved surface this line merely marks the position of the change from diminished light to no light. The shadow cast by the sphere is found by plotting from convenient points on the shade line. The outline of the shadow is that of an ellipse.

The foregoing examples if drawn out and carefully studied provide a knowledge of shades and shadows sufficient to meet the normal requirements in the rendering of drawings of most buildings. Further examples of a complex nature would tend to carry the subject into the realm of an academic pastime without giving much further material help.

Fig. 129 shows the shadows on the elevation and plan of the small house in Fig. 110. Shadows on plan, which are often omitted, are usually taken back in the direction shown. Shadows on elevations are always shown with the sun in the same relative position to the drawing, irrespective of the actual aspects of the elevations.

Fig. 130 shows a copy of the perspective of the same house with shadows added. Shadows in perspective must be worked out in orthographic projection first and then either set up along with the rest of the perspective or added to the perspective by 'eye'.

It is always better to work out shadows on tracing paper over the top of orthographic projections and then when correct to transfer them to the finished drawing. This procedure avoids spoiling the latter by the many construction lines, etc., which are necessary. Plottings should always be made with as fine a line as possible.

Outline shadows can be completed in many ways, from carefully graded washes of water-colour to applied transfer tones. Sprayed, spattered or pastel shadows are often used on small scale drawings. Except where a bold effect is required, the transparency of shadows should not be lost. Shades and shadows are never really solid opaque areas, but are affected by the nature of the surfaces on which they occur and by reflected light as described below.

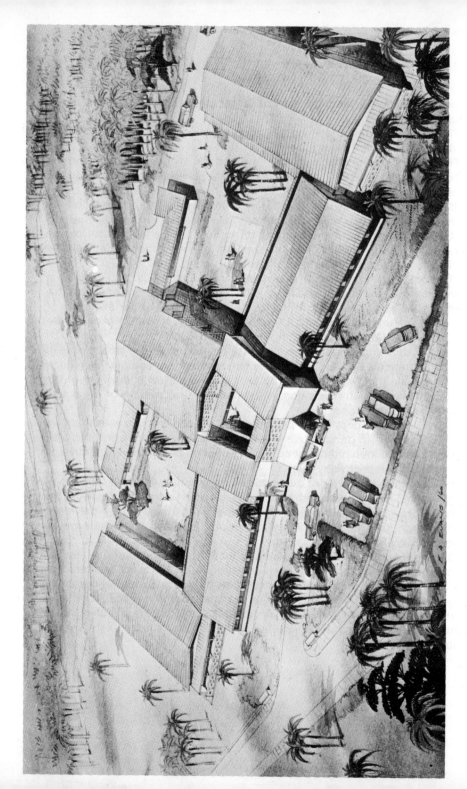

Plate 25 Aerial perspective drawing of handicapped children's home. (Architects Watkins and Partners, Trinidad.)

Reflected light

Fig. 131 gives illustrations of the principle of reflected light as used in rendering and the effect it has on shades and shadows. Every surface which receives direct light rays reflects the light to some extent and according to the angle or curvature in various directions. Consequently in bright sunlight reflected light falls on some of the surfaces which are in shade or shadow and alters their intensity and even casts shadows within shadows. The reflections are actually very complex but just as there are conventional assumptions in regard to direct light so, for architectural drawings, reflected light rays are always assumed to be exactly the reverse of primary rays and to be appreciably weaker in value.

One effect of this is illustrated in Fig. 131 (1) is to vary the tones representing the shades and shadows and, instead of their being rendered one tone all over, they are graded evenly in such a way that, in general, shadows are darker along their edges or outline and shades are darker where the surface receives no direct light and least reflected light.

Fig. 131 (2) illustrates how 'back shadows'—shadows within shadows—are cast by the rays of reflected light, and Fig. 131 (3) the effect of reflected light on the shadow within a deeply recessed opening.

As a general rule, no shade or shadow should be ungraded. Smooth grading helps considerably in giving 'life' to a rendering, and the sharper the grading and the greater the contrast between light and dark, the stronger the effect.

Long horizontal strips of shadow, e.g. under cornices, etc., which are too narrow to be graded with the lower edge darker can be successfully treated by making the left-hand end dark and grading off to the right.

Surroundings

The surroundings of a building, either actual or assumed, are often shown on rendered drawings to increase the realism of its presentation and to give 'scale', i.e. to give an impression of the real size of the building. To what extent this is necessary and in what manner it should be indicated, whether 'conventional' or 'naturalistic' for example, depends on the subject and the type of drawing desired. The simplest treatment consists in merely putting a graded background to the elevations, generally lighter towards the ground line, like a cloudless sky.

A basic conventional treatment for an isolated building is suggested by the sketches in Fig. 132. The treatment can be varied according to the technique used, scale of the drawing, etc. The first stage (1) is the putting of a dark band at the sides of the elevation to represent a hedge or fence,

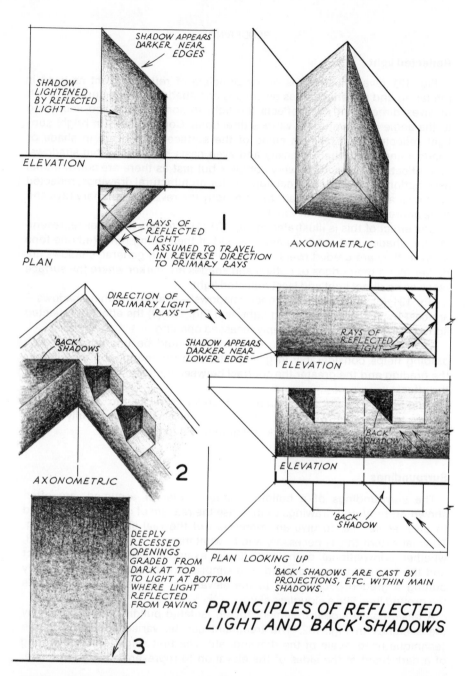

SHADOW APPEARS DARKER NEAR EDGES

SHADOW LIGHTENED BY REFLECTED LIGHT

ELEVATION

RAYS OF REFLECTED LIGHT ASSUMED TO TRAVEL IN REVERSE DIRECTION TO PRIMARY RAYS

PLAN

1

AXONOMETRIC

DIRECTION OF PRIMARY LIGHT RAYS

'BACK' SHADOWS

SHADOW APPEARS DARKER NEAR LOWER EDGE

RAYS OF REFLECTED LIGHT

ELEVATION

AXONOMETRIC

2

'BACK' SHADOW

ELEVATION

DEEPLY RECESSED OPENINGS GRADED FROM DARK AT TOP TO LIGHT AT BOTTOM WHERE LIGHT REFLECTED FROM PAVING

3

'BACK' SHADOW

PLAN LOOKING UP

'BACK' SHADOWS ARE CAST BY PROJECTIONS, ETC. WITHIN MAIN SHADOWS.

PRINCIPLES OF REFLECTED LIGHT AND 'BACK' SHADOWS

SHADOW PROJECTION

Fig. 131

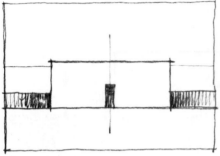

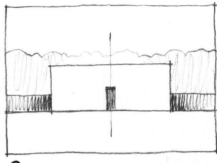

1. DARK BAND AT SIDE OF BUILDING TO REPRESENT HEDGE OR FENCE

2. ADDITION OF BROAD, LIGHT BAND TO REPRESENT BELT OF TREES BEHIND BUILDING

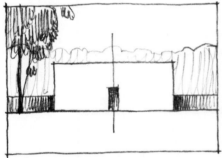

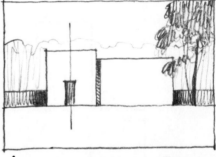

3. ADDITION OF TREE TO ONE SIDE ADDS INTEREST & GIVES CONTRAST TO BUILDING

4. APPLICATION OF 3. TO ASYMMETRICAL ELEVATION - POSITION AS REQUIRED FOR BALANCE.

5. TYPICAL PLAN REPRESENTATION OF 3. ABOVE

6. ALTERNATIVE ARRANGEMENT TO 4., ABOVE USING MASS OF DARK FOLIAGE

SURROUNDINGS *ELEVATIONS*

Fig. 132

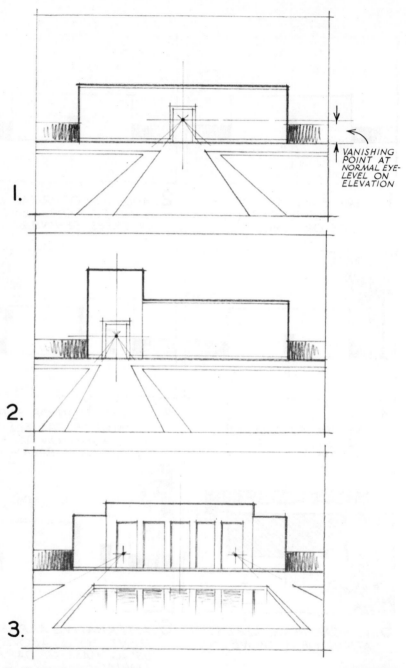

1.

VANISHING
POINT AT
NORMAL EYE-
LEVEL ON
ELEVATION

2.

3.

FOREGROUND

Fig. 133

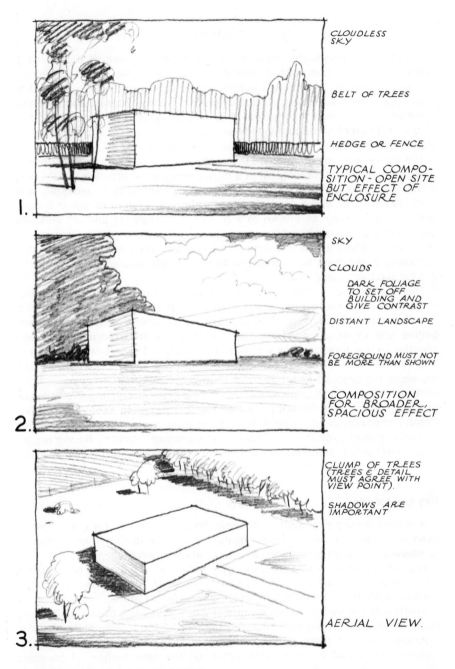

1.

CLOUDLESS SKY

BELT OF TREES

HEDGE OR FENCE

TYPICAL COMPOSITION - OPEN SITE BUT EFFECT OF ENCLOSURE

2.

SKY

CLOUDS

DARK FOLIAGE TO SET OFF BUILDING AND GIVE CONTRAST

DISTANT LANDSCAPE

FOREGROUND MUST NOT BE MORE THAN SHOWN

COMPOSITION FOR BROADER, SPACIOUS EFFECT

3.

CLUMP OF TREES (TREES & DETAIL MUST AGREE WITH VIEW POINT).

SHADOWS ARE IMPORTANT

AERIAL VIEW.

SURROUNDINGS *PERSPECTIVES*

Fig.134

etc., behind it. This band, preferably graded darkest towards the building, sets it off and in conjunction with a graded sky above is quite effective. The second stage (2) shows a lighter and broader band above the first to represent a belt of trees some distance further back. Interest and probably contrast can be given to the regularity and squareness of most buildings by the addition of a tree to one side as shown in (3) and (4) and (6). A typical plan to correspond to such an arrangement is seen in (5).

The foreground is not included in the above examples, and many consider that to do so would be illogical in a purely elevational drawing, particularly if the façade of the building has any strong projections or recesses. It is fairly common, however, to show a foreground on such drawings in a semi-perspective manner as shown in Fig. 133. Sketches (1) and (2) illustrate the use of a vanishing point for converging lines of the foreground at normal eye-level on elevation. If the perspective effect is too acute with one central vanishing point, then two vanishing points equally spaced from the centre can be used, as in sketch (3)

The treatment of surroundings in perspective drawings can be freer and, in general, of a more naturalistic kind than in elevational drawings. Fig. 134 shows sketches typical of perspective compositions although the possibilities and variations are limitless. Sketch (1) is an arrangement in perspective of the surroundings shown in Fig. 132 (3). The eye-level is more or less normal. Sketch (2), in which the eye-level is lower than normal, and therefore the amount of foreground should not be great, shows a composition for broader and more spacious effect with an interesting sky and view of distant landscape. Sketch (3) shows a building seen in aerial perspective. Careful attention must be paid here to the treatment of the ground, which receives greater prominence. Trees must be drawn correctly having regard to the view-point, and shadows are important elements in the composition.

Sky and clouds

A well-rendered sky greatly enhances the appearance of a good design, even if it will not wholly compensate for a poor design. The execution is, however, difficult at first and requires study and practice.

Fig. 135 illustrates some common types. After getting a grasp of these it is a matter of individual observation and experiment. A small pocket sketch-book is useful for noting down interesting skies from nature.

Sketch (1) shows the formal treatment usual with wash drawings. The sky is cloudless and graded from relatively dark at the top to light at the horizon. Although there are many different cloud effects in natural skies most 'architectural' skies can be dealt with either by the introduction of bunched

1. *NORMAL CLOUDLESS SKY USUALLY EVENLY GRADED FROM DARK AT TOP TO LIGHT HORIZON - FORMAL TREATMENT.*

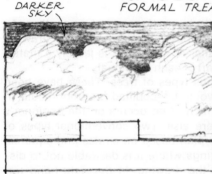

DARKER SKY

LIGHT BUT GRADED SKY

2. *ELEVATION WITH BUNCHED MASSES OF CUMULUS CLOUDS 'LIVELY' EFFECT.*

3. *ELEVATION WITH LAYERS OF STRATUS CLOUDS. 'REPOSEFUL' EFFECT.*

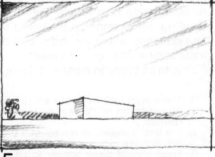

4. *PERSPECTIVE WITH CLOUDS AS IN 2.*

5. *PERSPECTIVE WITH CIRRUS-TYPE CLOUDS.*

SURROUNDINGS *SKY & CLOUDS*

Fig.135

cumulus clouds or of layers of stratus clouds. Sketch (2) shows the former; sketch (3) the latter, and illustrate the general effect of each. Sketch (4) shows a perspective with clouds similar to (2), and sketch (5) a perspective with 'cirrus' clouds of a like character to (3), but having a more lively effect. Note how the clouds follow the lines of perspective.

By whatever technique the clouds are represented there are two important points to be borne in mind: (1) the edges of clouds are invariably soft, and (2) clouds are just as much elements in the general composition as anything else—the sky must not be such a *tour de force* as to overpower the building.

Trees

Most architectural renderings include trees of one kind or another. As with clouds, there are many different types and many ways of drawing them, both conventional and naturalistic. Again, too, it is largely a matter of observation and experiment on the part of each individual.

Fig. 136 shows the drawing of various types of trees. These have been drawn in soft pencil and the drawing would be modified for other media. In the top left-hand corner is the tree which often occurs on the beginner's early drawings, but fortunately nowhere else. Two conventional types of trees are shown next in elevation and plan based on circles and squares; their use is restricted to formal renderings where it is desirable not to disturb the strictly architectural lines of the drawing. In the right-hand top corner is a more natural representation which might be described as a 'general purpose' tree.

As one of the reasons for putting trees on drawings is to help express the actual size of the building, the trees themselves must be to scale. When the representation is obviously that of a full-grown oak somewhere near to the building, for example, it is absurd to find it scaling 10 or 15 feet in height. The sketches on the second row of the figure shows sizes of certain types of trees compared to that of a man.

Points to be borne in mind in drawing trees are:

1. Trees must look as if they are growing out of the ground, not 'floating' in the air. An indication of the swelling towards the roots, and shadows, are helpful in this respect.
2. If a tree is meant to represent a particular species, it must look something like that species.
3. Trees should never appear to be growing out of roofs. Isolated trees behind a building are best omitted, unless they can be related to similar trees, the whole of which can be seen at the sides of the building.
4. The trunk and branches must seem able to support the foliage.
5. The foliage must appear to be rounded, not as if cut out of cardboard.

200

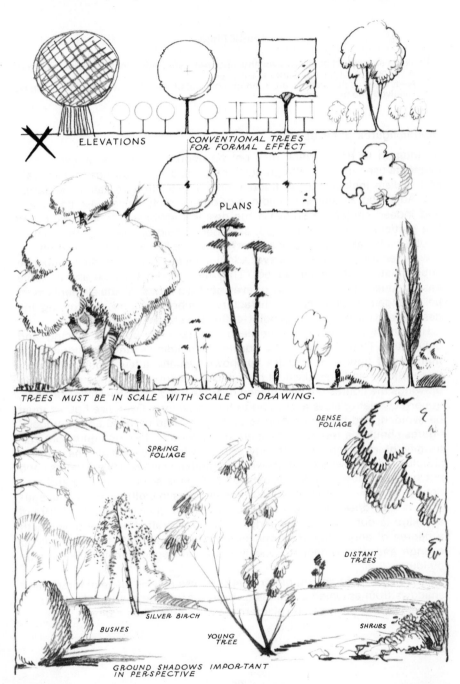

ELEVATIONS

CONVENTIONAL TREES
FOR FORMAL EFFECT

PLANS

TREES MUST BE IN SCALE WITH SCALE OF DRAWING.

DENSE
FOLIAGE

SPRING
FOLIAGE

DISTANT
TREES

SILVER BIRCH

SHRUBS

BUSHES

YOUNG
TREE

GROUND SHADOWS IMPORTANT
IN PERSPECTIVE

SURROUNDINGS *TREES*

Fig.136

6. Trees should not be overdrawn and laboured, especially if they are to be coloured. A suggestion of the main lines is sufficient.
7. Near trees in perspective are seen in more detail than distant ones, which can be resolved into mass only.

Human figures, vehicles etc.

In addition to trees, which may not be appropriate to the subject, other elements used in both orthographic and perspective drawings to give scale and realism include human figures, cars, street furniture, lamp standards, etc. Adjoining or adjacent buildings or other structures can also be shown, and indeed should be shown if the design relationship is important, and if a particular site is concerned, sketches should be made on the spot or photographs taken to provide a basis for more or less accurate indication.

As a general principle, whatever addition elements are introduced must be subordinate to the main subject. They must be kept simple and in some cases reduced to conventional or even abstract forms. All the elements must be arranged to produce a satisfactory composition and, reinforcing the design, lead the eye to a focal point—often the entrance to the building.

Human figures in particular need special care both in placing and delineation. Only if necessary to convey the building's function should large numbers of figures or vehicles be shown. Usually, a few groups of two or three figures and an individual here and there are sufficient. In perspective drawings the figures are best placed near the building, some at the entrance, in correct relative sizes according to their positions. Over-size figures must be avoided, and the temptation to add foreground or 'head and shoulders' figures should be resisted. There are many ways of drawing figures but uniformity of representation on any one drawing is essential. The student should study the work of others while developing his own style. Figures need not be amorphous blobs, but detailed realism is seldom justified and may detract from the overall effect. Extreme fashions in clothing, etc. are unsuitable as they draw too much attention, and also quickly date; caricature of any kind is out of place. Similarly, cars and aircraft should be drawn with a degree of anonymity. However, boats and sailing craft are less likely to change and can be more precisely drawn in connection with water-side buildings.

As well as the foregoing pictorial effects, use may be made of foreground shadows from assumed buildings or trees outside the picture, of reflections on wet roads or pavings, and of internal and external illumination.

TREES   elevations

plans

VEHICLES & PEOPLE   elevations

plan

Plate 26 Examples of pressure transfer trees, vehicles and people. (Reproduced by permission of Letraset Ltd; arrangement by author.)

Standard pictorial symbols

Although personally drawn trees, human figures, cars etc. have greater character, can be more satisfactorily integrated, and make possible infinite variations of treatment and style, standard graphic symbols can be used for convenience, uniformity, and sometimes speed. They may be of the pressure-transfer type (Plate 26) or applied by rubber stamp. Symbols to correspond to various scales are obtainable and can be applied equally well to final drawings in orthographic projection or to tracing media for photoprint reproduction. The tree plan symbols are particularly useful for layouts, landscape and town-planning drawings.

For elevations and sections, standard symbols must be apposite and selected with care. Indiscriminate and unrestrained use of inappropriate symbols, no matter how attractive they are in themselves, will impart at best only a superficial and temporary appeal to the drawing, and at worst will degrade the design and confuse the presentation. However, if the symbols are regarded as basic elements of pictorial composition for imaginative manipulation, they can be of considerable help to the draughtsman in preparing formal drawings.

Paper for drawings in wash

Drawings which are made in line only or which are rendered in one of the 'dry' media — pastel, crayon, etc. — can be made on paper which is pinned to the drawing board, but if washes of Chinese ink or water-colour are to be used, or if the drawing is to be sprayed, then it is necessary to use mounted or stretched paper which will not cockle when wet. Mounted papers or boards, such as Saunders and fashion-plate, are reasonably satisfactory for most work in watercolour and gouache. But they have disadvantages for both initial pencil drawing, if extensive, and prolonged rendering in wash, being less 'sympathetic' then stretched paper and less capable of standing up to sponging. Therefore, although the operation is admittedly messy and time-consuming, the method of stretching paper is described below and is illustrated in Fig. 137. The paper must be handmade, the thicker the better; HP (hot pressed) or smooth is generally suitable.

1. The right side of the paper is found by holding it up to the light so that the water-mark can be read.
2. The paper is laid on the board with the right side uppermost and the edges are turned up about 20 mm to form a shallow tray.
3. The paper is then turned over and with a sponge water is applied around the edges up to the folding mark — the 20 mm strip not being wetted as this is later to be pasted. The sponge is next applied diagonally and to the main axes, 'union jack' fashion, and these bands are thoroughly wetted. The whole sheet, except

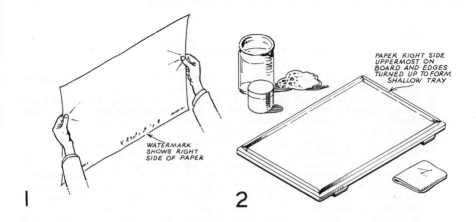

1

WATERMARK SHOWS RIGHT SIDE OF PAPER

2

PAPER RIGHT SIDE UPPERMOST ON BOARD AND EDGES TURNED UP TO FORM SHALLOW TRAY

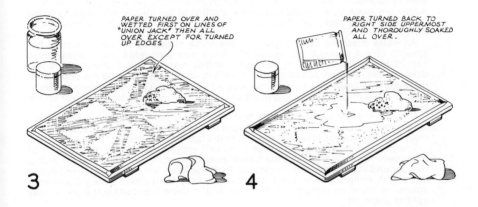

3

PAPER TURNED OVER AND WETTED FIRST ON LINES OF "UNION JACK" THEN ALL OVER EXCEPT FOR TURNED UP EDGES

4

PAPER TURNED BACK TO RIGHT SIDE UPPERMOST AND THOROUGHLY SOAKED ALL OVER.

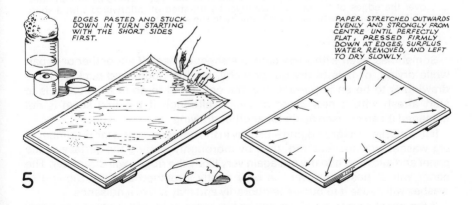

5

EDGES PASTED AND STUCK DOWN IN TURN STARTING WITH THE SHORT SIDES FIRST.

6

PAPER STRETCHED OUTWARDS EVENLY AND STRONGLY FROM CENTRE UNTIL PERFECTLY FLAT, PRESSED FIRMLY DOWN AT EDGES, SURPLUS WATER REMOVED, AND LEFT TO DRY SLOWLY.

STRETCHING PAPER

Fig. 137

the pasting strip, is then wetted and allowed two or three minutes for the water to to soak in. Any standing water is removed at the end of that time.

4. The paper is turned back right side uppermost, the edges are made square with the board, and water is liberally applied to the upper surface particularly around the edges which were not wetted on the underside. After this operation the paper should be covered with buckles and pools of water.

5. Paste is now quickly applied to the outside dry edges of the underside, starting with one of the short sides. When all the edges are pasted, some of the standing water can be removed but a pool must be left in the middle. The edges of the paper are again adjusted square with the board. The middle of the short side first pasted is then taken, pressed firmly down and with thumb and fingers pulling and pressing the edge is stuck to the board along to the corners. The opposite edge of the paper is then lifted carefully and slightly by the corners and pulled gently so as to free the underside of the paper from moisture-adhesion to the board. It is then stuck down as before, pulled strongly by the fingers first at the middle and then outwards to the corners. The two short edges now being held, the long edges are stuck down in the same way, starting at the middle and working to the corners, pulling and pressing until the whole sheet is flat and firmly stuck down all round.

An extra pressing can be given to the stuck edges by means of a hard but smooth object such as the handle of a knife or a coin edge, etc. If the paste is satisfactory nothing more is necessary in this respect, but if any doubt is felt, drawing pins can be put in at weak points or at intervals around the sheet after the edge has been dried off a little with a clean cloth. Or, alternatively, strips of adhesive paper can be stuck around the sheet, half on the paper and half on the board.

When the sheet is satisfactorily stuck down, all standing water on the surface is removed with the sponge, and the paper is mopped off gently without scrubbing from the edges inwards so that the part to dry last is the middle.

The process of drying cannot be hastened without risk, and until all signs of dampness have disappeared the board must be kept horizontal. Time for drying will depend upon a number of factors. It can be lessened by placing the board in a draught, either near an open window but away from direct sunlight and soot specks or from an electric fan. If the drying is done too quickly the paper may split or come off.

If, for any reason, the edges of the paper or the tape have to be turned down over the edges of the board, they must be trimmed off afterwards with a sharp knife or razor blade to allow the T-square to run smoothly.

Sometimes, even with every care, the sheet comes off altogether or in part while drying, or fails to dry out properly, leaving ridges and buckles. If the drawing is to be an important one, the only thing to do in such cases is to start afresh with a new sheet of paper, although if the first sheet is not damaged it can be used again for another drawing.

If it is a case of slight ridging — usually in the corners — and a large number of big washes are not required, then by thoroughly wetting the surface of the paper and allowing it to dry out again very likely the ridges will disappear. The paper will at best, however, be only lightly stretched and the running of washes will cause it to buckle temporarily and may prove a nuisance.

If the sheet comes off along one or two sides only, and is otherwise firmly held, the stretching can often be made good. The underside should first be wetted as far as possible with the exception of the pasting strip; then the top surface is thoroughly wetted and the water allowed to soak in; new paste is applied and the sheet firmly stretched and stuck down once more and allowed to dry out slowly.

Rendering in wash

As an introduction to all kinds of rendering, that using washes is of the greatest value. While its practice is less extensive than at one time it is still suitable for formal drawings of a dignified character, either alone or in combination with other techniques. Exercises in wash rendering are the surest guide to all the basic principles, and provide excellent discipline for the hand and eye.

The first step, after the completed line drawing in pencil has been carefully checked, is to clean it up if necessary, and then to give it a wash of water over the whole sheet. The purpose of this is not, as is sometimes thought, to remove the ingrained dirt from the paper, but to remove any loose pencil dust, greast from the hands, etc., and, most of all, to overcome dryness in the paper, especially if it has been exposed on the board for a long time. This water wash also has the effect of 'fixing' the pencil lines to some extent, making them more difficult to rub out, which is why the checking must be done before.

Next, the shades and shadows, see p. 180, are worked out on tracing paper and transferred to the drawing. A further water wash may then be given, but is optional. Some draughtsmen mix a very little alum with the water washes (one tablespoonful to a quart of water) as this is supposed to help remove grease and make the later washes run better.

Water washes are put on like any other wash, and the procedure is illustrated in Fig. 138. The board should be tilted slightly, not more than about 1 in 10 or about 5 degrees. The upper end is best supported on a suitable block of wood rather than on unsteady books, etc. The way up of the board depends on the area to be dealt with; generally, it is easier to work with the lesser dimension running horizontally, e.g. in the case of an over-all wash, the board would be as shown in Fig. 138.

Elementary laying of washes

Washes must always be run from the highest part to the lowest. The procedure is to fill the brush—wash brush, p. 20, for large areas—and start along the upper edge of the area, putting on a good deal of the liquid, working it carefully to the top line.[1] Then, by means of long regular horizontal brush strokes with short vertical ones at the sides, bring the wash down the sheet or area, keeping it evenly wet all the time. The brush should not 'paint' the paper but merely touch the raised edge of the wash and guide it along.

It is particularly important with washes of heavy water-colour to work slowly and smoothly or the deposit of the colour will be irregular and unpleasant.

When the wash has been brought to the bottom of the area it must be finished off carefully along the line, and this is sometimes more easily effected with a smaller size of brush, say No. 6. The wash will tend to collect at the bottom, and the surplus must be gently removed by holding a squeezed-out brush just touching it so that the liquid is drawn up into the hairs. This operation is repeated as many times as necessary to ensure that the wash dries evenly from the top downwards.

If properly put on, a wash should show a perfectly regular tone, colour or mottle over the whole area.

If the wash is in two parts for a distance, e.g. passing on either side of an elevation, as in Fig. 139, the two parts must be kept moving equally and evenly. It is easier in such cases to start with the divided parts, doing a bit to each in turn.

Brushes loaded with water or wash should not be carried over the drawing any more than necessary because of possible drops. Fig. 138.

Above all, washes must be run 'wet'. There must be enough wash mixed up at the beginning to cover the whole area; it is fatal to success to have to stop in the middle of putting on a wash to mix up some more.

Defects in wash rendering

The following are the defects most likely to occur in wash rendering. They should be guarded against so far as possible, but can sometimes be remedied as described.

1. *Untidy Edges* — Caused when the wash over-runs or falls short of the enclosing lines. To remedy, when the wash is dry, take a small brush, dip it in clean water and dampen the edges affected and blot them off with clean blotting paper several times until all traces of the over-run or the sharp edges of the short wash are removed. This matter should be attended to after every wash and the defects not allowed to accumulate. Stubborn over-runs can be quickly cleaned off by holding a piece of thin card (post-card) along the true edge of the wash and taking a small piece of sponge dipped in clean water, wiping away gently the over-run.

[1]It is, of course, unnecessary to work to border lines if the sheet is to be cut off along them afterwards.

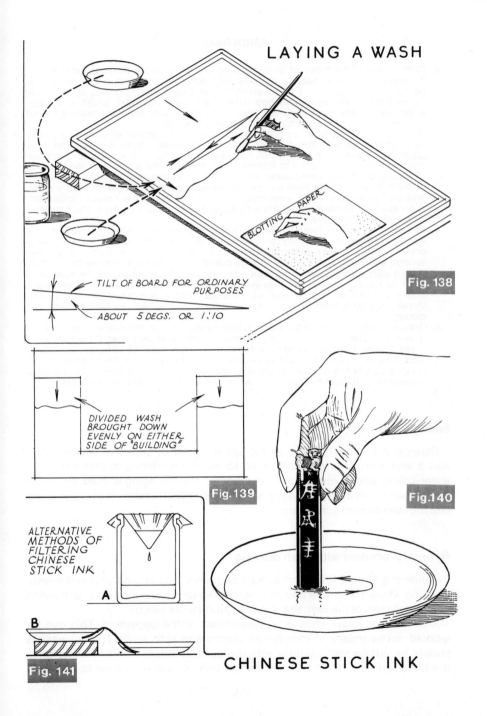

LAYING A WASH

TILT OF BOARD FOR ORDINARY PURPOSES

ABOUT 5 DEGS. OR 1:10

BLOTTING PAPER

Fig. 138

DIVIDED WASH BROUGHT DOWN EVENLY ON EITHER SIDE OF "BUILDING"

Fig. 139

Fig. 140

ALTERNATIVE METHODS OF FILTERING CHINESE STICK INK

A

B

Fig. 141

CHINESE STICK INK

2. *Blots* — Caused by drops of colour falling on the rendered parts of the drawing. If blotted up immediately — a piece of clean blotting paper should always be handy, but sacrifice a handkerchief if necessary — nothing may show. If the marks have been overlooked and have dried, take a bluntish brush and clean water and gently wash over the spots repeatedly with alternate blottings until they are light enough to be blended in as described later.

3. *Run-backs* — Result from a collection of wash at the bottom of an area seeping back up the partially dried upper part or, sometimes, from the addition of a quantity of wash to an area which has been run rather on the dry side. If serious nothing much can be done to remedy this defect and the whole area may have to be sponged out with clean water when quite dry. In less serious cases, the specks of pigment which float back can be picked out carefully with the point of a brush and the worst effects are somewhat mitigated. In free water-colour renderings, run-backs are sometimes deliberately sought to build up a striking effect, but this if no trick for beginners.

4. *Streaks* — Horizontal lines of darker colour are usually caused by running the wash too slowly or unevently, or by a defect in the paper — spoiled surface due to previous rubbing out — or impurities in the wash. If serious, lift the board and with sponge and clean water gently sponge over the area, trying to remove the streaks. Do not start sponging until the area is dry all over. Avoid scrubbing the surface or it will be ruined. Streaks are less likely to occur with light washes, and for formal drawings tones should be built up by a succession of washes. Sometimes the streaks can be turned to account, if occurring in the 'sky', by being made into clouds.

5. *Grease Spots* — Small spots which refuse to take colour are due to some sort of grease or water-repellent having affected the fibres of the paper. If not too large, these can be patched up to match the rest of the wash by stippling on colour with the point of a small brush or by cross hatching, also with the point of a small brush much in the manner of darning. With patience and a steady hand almost 'invisible repairs' can be made. The air-brush can also be used for this work.

Sponging off

Reference has been made to the sponging off of defective washes; it is also a useful procedure to soften the tones of a rendering in chinese ink or water-colour and to remove any hard edges. The sponging should always be done when the drawing is evenly dry all over, with a maximum of clean water and the minimum of scrubbing.

General procedure with wash drawing

Rendering should follow an orderly sequence and should proceed evenly over the whole sheet. It is bad practice to render up one portion of a drawing completely before the rest, the result is bound to be patchy.

A scheme ot tones should be determined at the beginning. This can be worked out by means of thumb-nail sketches in soft pencil. The big washes should be put on first, starting with the general tones, then the lesser ones gradually working down to the final accents. A light even tone to establish

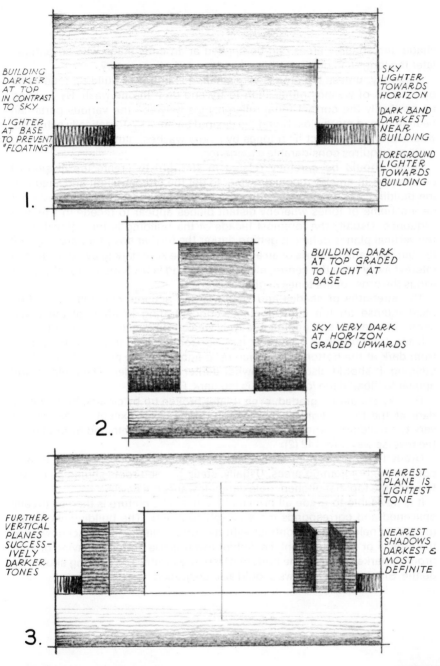

1.

BUILDING DARKER AT TOP IN CONTRAST TO SKY

LIGHTER AT BASE TO PREVENT "FLOATING"

SKY LIGHTER TOWARDS HORIZON

DARK BAND DARKEST NEAR BUILDING

FOREGROUND LIGHTER TOWARDS BUILDING

2.

BUILDING DARK AT TOP GRADED TO LIGHT AT BASE

SKY VERY DARK AT HORIZON GRADED UPWARDS

3.

NEAREST PLANE IS LIGHTEST TONE

FURTHER VERTICAL PLANES SUCCESSIVELY DARKER TONES

NEAREST SHADOWS DARKEST & MOST DEFINITE

TONE VALUE

Fig.142

shade and shadow areas can be applied at an early stage with advantage; later the tones can be strengthened and graded as necessary.

Generally, unless the area is very small, it is better to build up tone value by a series of washes rather than to try and do it in one wash. By building up gradually the correct tonal relationships between the various parts can be maintained more closely and the desired balance systematically achieved, whereas to get correct final tones by single washes, although possible and quicker, requires considerable experience.

Tones should be carefully related in strength to create the illusion of perspective in an elevational drawing, to get the effect of light and shade on the building, and to emphasise the composition of the picture. There should be a scheme of tones whereby distant planes appear to recede in a logical sequence. Usually the foremost façade of the building is the lightest tone, the vertical planes behind it getting darker the further away they are, Fig. 142 (3), but the flanking parts of an elevation may be kept dark to avoid taking the interest away from the centre, e.g. if the building is U-shaped with projecting wings the order of the tones might be reversed.

The strengths of shades and shadows and accents generally should be most intense on the lightest plane, concentrating in effort at the visual centre of interest, and getting relatively weaker on successive darker planes.

If the foreground is a more or less horizontal plane it should be graded from dark at the bottom of the picture to light near the principal face of the building. It should also be somewhat darker at the sides. The building will appear to 'float' if the foreground is too dark, Fig. 142.

The sky should be graded, even if later broken up by clouds, for relatively dark at the top to light at the horizon, Fig. 142 (1) except in the case of very tall buildings, when a better effect is sometimes obtained by grading in the reverse way, Fig. 142 (2).

Graded washes should be applied to inclined planes, e.g. roofs, to give contrast with adjoining areas. Usually, steep pitched roofs should be darker towards the top; flat pitched roofs darker towards the eaves.

It is advisable to grade all principal washes. The picture is thereby greatly enlivened and corresponds more closely to reality. The building should be graded to heighten the contrast with its surroundings and to acknowledge the effects or reflected light, i.e. lighter towards the bottom if paving or light ground, darker towards the bottom if dark grass, etc. The grading should be gentle. Shades and shadows should also be graded.

Plate 27   Drawing in pencil and chinese ink washes.

Sylvia Payne

Media

The principal media used for rendering drawings are:

1. Chinese ink washes.
2. Water-colours.
3. Gouache and Poster colours.
4. Pastel.
5. Coloured pencils.
6. Pencil only or black ink only.
7. Dry transfer tones and colours.

All of these can be used by themselves or in combination with one or more of the others. It must be emphasised again that it is by personal handling of these materials and the study of actual drawings that the full possibilities of each will be realised. It is not attempted here to do more than give a few suggestions and hints.

Chinese ink

Chinese ink is obtained in sticks usually marked with Chinese characters. There are various sizes, but quite a small one will last some time. The quality also varies, the cheaper being rather harsh and cold in tint; the more expensive is warmer and is always to be preferred. The particular value of the ink is its transparency, which gives to a formal wash drawing a finish difficult to obtain by other means. It is especially useful for early exercises in wash rendering and for neutral washes on any kind of drawing.

The ink is prepared for use by being rubbed down with a little water on a slate slab or in a saucer, Fig. 140. If a quantity of wash is required it is advisable to rub down a strong mixture — almost black in intensity when tried out on a piece of paper — which can be subsequently diluted as needed. The liquid must be filtered after being rubbed down, by being passed through fine muslin or coarse filter paper until all specks are removed. An alternative filtering process is to soak a small piece of string in water and, by putting one end in a saucer at a lower level and the other end in a saucer of the ink at a higher level, to allow it to pass through by capillary attraction. This action filters it at the same time, Fig. 141.

The filtering process is of the greatest importance and must be carefully carried out. The filtered ink can be stored in a clean bottle with a clean stopper or covered over with damp blotting paper for several days.

After use the stick should be wiped dry or it will crack and become useless.

The ink should be used in light washes, dark tones being gradually built up, the general procedure being as described for wash rendering. The ink dries much lighter than it appears when wet. Water-colours, such as cobalt

214

blue, viridian, burnt sienna, raw sienna, and carmine, can be added in small quantities to tint the ink if desired.

Water-colours

Some reference has already been made to water-colours, page 19. For formal rendering in wash it is usual to work with mixtures of burnt sienna and french ultramarine, or raw sienna and ivory black, or cobalt blue and light red. These mixtures should be definitely inclined in hue towards one or other of the constituents. In all cases, the colours are deposited as the wash is run, forming what is termed a 'mottle', and it is by the speed and manipulation of the brush that the most interesting effects are obtained. Knowledge of this can only come by experiment. It is essential, of course, that the wash is put on evenly and kept very wet. And, as the pigments tend to be deposited in the jar or dish, the wash must be stirred up every time a brushful is taken. As with chinese ink, if a good quantity of colour is required, it is better to mix the whole lot at the beginning rather than have the difficult task of mixing new washes to match the original at various times.

It is not possible to discuss free water-colour rendering in detail. Water-colour is perhaps the most flexible media of all, and can be used with success for every type of drawing. Experiments should be made at first with a few colours, and then new ones can be added to the palette and others discarded according to individual preference. A wide range is seldom necessary; many successful water-colourists manage with about half a dozen only.

A few hints are: avoid prussian blue and vandyke brown which stain the fibres of the paper and cannot be sponged out if anything goes wrong. Never mix ultramarine and vermilion; a chemical reaction produces a black sediment. Always put the colours on wet, except for an occasional dry brush stroke for foreground treatment or other special effect. Try to let the colours do the work; avoid 'painting' them on thickly and muddily, let the white of the paper show here and there for high-lights and sparkle. Vivid colours should be reserved for accents and spots of interest; large patches of them are garish. Cobalt is the best blue for skies. Burnt sienna with a little ultramarine is better for brickwork than any red. Raw sienna is a useful colour for light tones on stonework, etc.

Gouache and poster colours

Opaque colours, see page 20, are the equivalent of water-colours mixed with Chinese white. They dry with a flat matt surface of even tone if properly

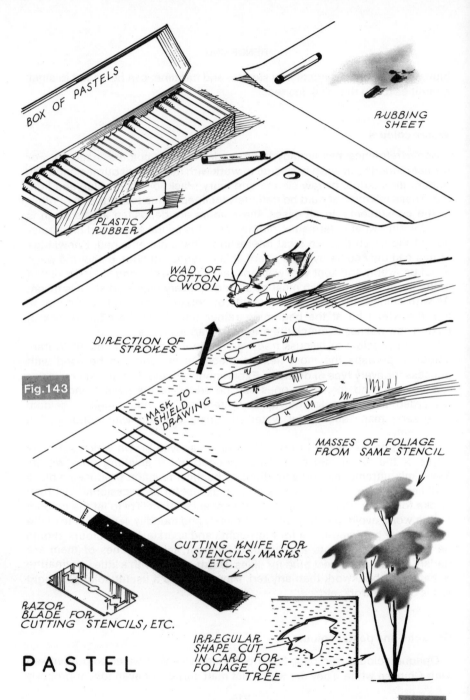

BOX OF PASTELS

RUBBING SHEET

PLASTIC RUBBER

WAD OF COTTON WOOL

DIRECTION OF STROKES

Fig.143

MASK TO SHIELD DRAWING

MASSES OF FOLIAGE FROM SAME STENCIL

CUTTING KNIFE FOR STENCILS, MASKS ETC.

RAZOR BLADE FOR CUTTING STENCILS, ETC.

IRREGULAR SHAPE CUT IN CARD FOR FOLIAGE OF TREE

PASTEL

Fig. 144

applied, and because of this are often used to represent buildings of simple form and sharp outlines, and particularly for interior design drawings. It is essentially a medium for strong if not bold effects.

The colours can be used in combination with water-colour or with pastel, e.g. a building largely coloured in poster colour with a water-colour or pastel sky. The colour must not be too wet when applied to the paper or it will not dry evenly. A second coat must be applied fairly dry or excess water will be absorbed by the first, which will mix with the second or be pulled off by the brush. For large areas of thick colour which are to be gone over owing to alterations, it is safer to remove the first coat with a knife or with a wet brush and blotting paper. If the colour is applied too thickly it may flake off when dry. Small but regular areas of colour can be outlined with the ruling pen and filled in with the brush before the lines are dry. Brick courses can also be ruled in to small scales. Poster colour or chinese white can be superimposed over indian ink, but indian ink cannot be superimposed on either of the former. Fine detail can often be effectively added to poster colour by drawing on it with a sharp HB pencil, the line appearing with unusual brilliancy. Although poster colour covers up original pencil lines, this should not be made on excuse for careless draughtsmanship.

If designers' colours are used, the following are useful colours which will meet most requirements: black, white, indigo, lemon yellow, red ochre, raw sienna, vandyke brown, geranium red.

Pastel

Pastel is used in architectural rendering for applying soft, graded tones and colours to the comparatively larger areas of the drawing. The method in general, see Fig. 143, is to scrape off with a penknife or to crush a small quantity of pastel on to a sheet of cartridge paper, known as the rubbing sheet, until a very fine powder is obtained, and then to pick it up with a piece of cotton-wool and apply it to the drawing by firm even rubbing, the parts of the drawing not to be pastelled being masked by thin card or stiff paper.

Only the best pastels of finest grain should be used. There are many different colours and tones, so many that it is best to start with a representative selection and add and discard as suggested for water-colours. Strong, vivid colours are little used; useful ones are: raw sienna, autumn brown, green grey, indian red, prussian green, white and black. The colours can be blended together on the rubbing sheet.

The medium lends itself well to sky effects, a wide range of soft tones being easily obtained. 'Breaks' can be made in the clouds by removing some of the pastel with a plastic rubber. The main tones on buildings can also be applied lightly with grading, and a suggestion of foreground can be given by rubbing off a little pastel downwards from the ground line of the elevation.

Pastel by itself is seldom sufficient and the accents of the rendering can be given by touches of poster colour, e.g. ruled window-bars, flowers, trees, figures, etc.

Trees can, however, be pastelled by cutting an irregular shape in a thin card and by rubbing through this to build up a mass of foliage, as shown in Fig. 144, the trunk and branches of the tree being added by thin brush strokes of dry poster colour dragged upwards from the ground.

The chief disadvantage of pastel is the amount of dust which gets on to hands, clothes and, sometimes, the wrong parts of the drawing.

Coloured pencils, etc.

The use of coloured pencils is restricted in the main to good-sized drawings to a fairly large scale, although in combination with ordinary pencil or indian ink detail can be satisfactorily tackled. The advantage of using coloured pencils lies in the ease and speed of the medium and the wide range of tone values according to pressure. The technique can vary from free coloured sketching to quite formal renderings wherein regular, even tones are obtained by carefully ruled, close, parallel lines. The applying of colour and tone by indiscriminate scribbling must be avoided.

Crayons and chalks and felt-tipped pens can be similarly employed. For rapid, broad effects the best medium is charcoal. The sticks should be held almost parallel to the paper in use and not like a pencil. Tones can be obtained by smudging with the fingers.

Drawings in charcoal, crayon, or any powdery medium need to be protected on completion by being sprayed with a fixing liquid.

Pencil

Pencil renderings in general consist of the addition of shadows and surroundings in line; shadows, for example, often being indicated by close parallel lines, either horizontal or vertical, according to the area concerned. Gradations of tone can be obtained by varying the pressure on the pencil and sometimes by cross-hatching. A little smudging by the finger, however, can be done to add indefinite tones for clouds, foliage, etc.

Lines of indian ink to the silhouette of the building or for accents and points of emphasis can be used on otherwise pencil drawings.

Pen and ink

Formal drawings completed wholly in pen and ink are very infrequent, the technique being more often used for freehand sketches on the lines described in Chapter 10. Small-scale elevations, however, can be effectively shown in ink with blacked-in openings and the addition of very simple surroundings in line.

Perspectives also must be fairly small to be successfully executed in ink. Large drawings in the medium, unless the brush supplements the pen, tend to look laboured and restless. The mapping pen, incidentally, generally gives too fine a line for any but the smallest drawings.

As variations of tone cannot be obtained directly with ink, greater use has to be made of different thickness of line, cross-hatching, dots, dashes and areas of solid black, and the possibilities of these should be thoroughly studied.

Sepia ink is a possible alternative to indian ink, and wash—sepia or ivory black water-colour—combined with ink drawing opens up wider fields of expression.

Spatter, spray, and air-brush techniques

Water-colour and Chinese ink, instead of being washed on with a brush, can be applied to drawings in the form of minute particles by the following methods:

Spatter

For small areas, especially shadows on 1:100 and 1:200 scale elevations, colour can be spattered on using a tooth-brush or similar stiff brush and a piece of fine wire mesh, as shown in Fig. 145. The ink—indian ink is commonly used for shadows—or poster colour is mixed in a dish and picked up by the brush, which is then rubbed backwards and forwards over the mesh, held horizontally a short distance away from the paper. The brush must not be too wet or splashes will mar the fine texture which can otherwise be obtained. It is comparatively easy to grade evenly quite small areas by this method. Great care must be taken to mask all parts of the drawing not to be spattered, even those some distance away from the operation. The usual practice is to fit pieces of stiff paper carefully to the outlines concerned and to hold the edges flat with coins or similar small heavy articles. The slightest separation of the surfaces of the drawing and the mask will allow the spatter to find its way in and spoil the sharpness of the edge to which it should be confined.

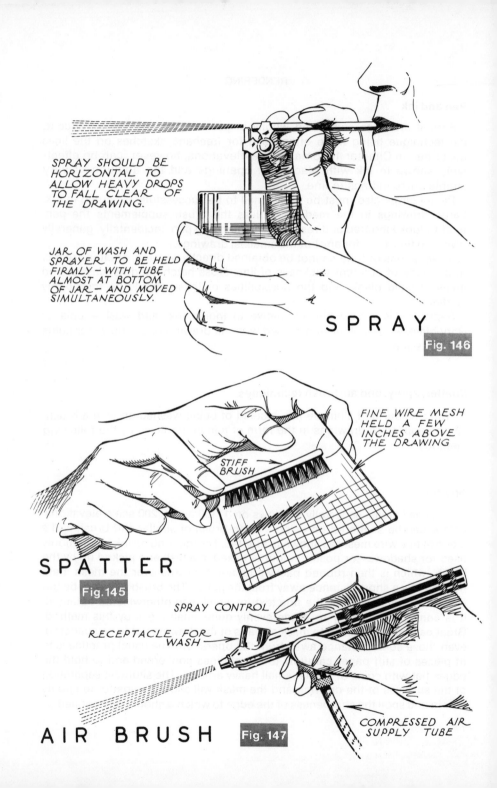

SPRAY SHOULD BE HORIZONTAL TO ALLOW HEAVY DROPS TO FALL CLEAR OF THE DRAWING.

JAR OF WASH AND SPRAYER TO BE HELD FIRMLY – WITH TUBE ALMOST AT BOTTOM OF JAR – AND MOVED SIMULTANEOUSLY.

SPRAY

Fig. 146

FINE WIRE MESH HELD A FEW INCHES ABOVE THE DRAWING

STIFF BRUSH

SPATTER

Fig. 145

SPRAY CONTROL

RECEPTACLE FOR WASH

AIR BRUSH

Fig. 147

COMPRESSED AIR SUPPLY TUBE

Spray

For large areas, particularly skies, water-colour can be sprayed on, using a metal spray of the type sold for spraying fixing liquid on to charcoal drawings and costing only a few pence, as illustrated in Fig. 146, or an atomiser such as a throat spray. The particles of colour are much larger by this method; this may be an advantage for bold drawings.

It is again necessary to cover the parts of the drawing not to be sprayed, but as it is better to stand the board vertically, a mask or template is cut out of thick tracing paper or detail paper and held in position by ordinary pins about an inch apart close to the edge. The pins must be carefully placed so that the prick marks, which should be very slight, do not show afterwards. For small areas, which cannot be easily masked in this way, a coating of diluted rubber cement can be painted on and later removed quite cleanly.

The spray should be blown horizontally to the drawing from two or three feet away at least, so that any large, heavy drops fall clear of the drawing and only the finer particles impinge on the surface.

The spray should be kept steady in force and should be moved about to prevent any one part of the surface becoming too wet and causing the particles to run together. The process should not be rushed, but the mask must not be allowed to cockle or shrink. If the spray does, however, fall outside its intended limits, it can usually be washed off afterwards with a brush and clean water. It is said that a little alcohol added to the liquid gives a finer spray and quickens the drying.

The strength of the spray is difficult to judge until the mask is removed, but a corner can always be turned down at intervals and affords some guide.

Any colour can, of course, be sprayed on. By spraying with alternate constituent colours a brighter combination on the paper can be obtained than by mixing them together first in the wash. Settlement of the pigments in the wash must not take place or the colour of the spray will vary.

Air brush

For large and small areas and for fine and regular sprays there is nothing to surpass the air-brush, which is operated by compressed air, see Fig. 147, although the expense is probably only justified when a considerable number of drawings are being dealt with continually. The compressed air is supplied from a cylinder charged by means of a foot-pump or electric compressor, through a rubber hose to the 'brush', which has a receptacle for ink, colour, etc., and a control button for varying the spray. With a little practice interesting and beautiful renderings can be carried out. The main danger to guard against is the somewhat 'artificial' air which the mechanical perfection of the

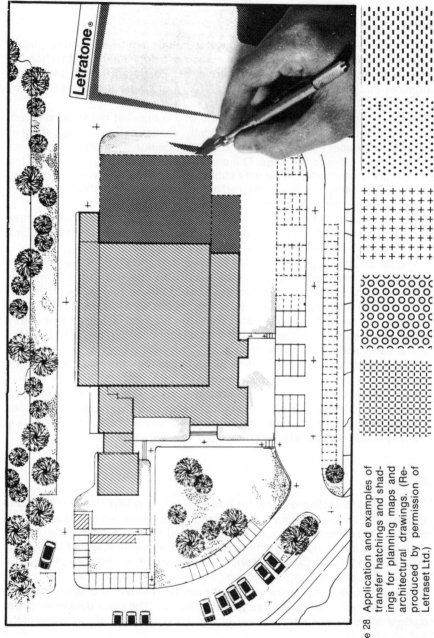

Plate 28 Application and examples of transfer hatchings and shadings for planning maps and architectural drawings. (Reproduced by permission of Letraset Ltd.)

spray tends to give. Masks or templates have to be used as before, but drawings need not necessarily be vertical.

Transfer tones and colours

Various kinds of mechanical tones or tints, e.g. hatching and shadings, closely-spaced lines, dots, and other patterns, can be applied to final drawings and tracing media by pressure transfer from standard paper-backed sheets of acetate film printed in black in a manner similar to pressure transfer lettering described in Chapter 4. The usual procedure, however, is to place the selected sheet over the required area of the drawing with the backing paper underneath; using a sharp knife, a piece of film slightly larger than the area is then cut out, care being taken not to cut the backing paper; the piece of film is removed from the backing sheet and is put in position and pressed gently onto the drawing; the surplus film is removed by cutting away or scraping; and finally the film is covered with paper and firmly burnished for positive adhesion. The adhesive is heat-resistant and the drawing can be safely reproduced by the dyeline process. Plate 28 illustrates an example. The tones can be used to indicate shades and shadows, to distinguish plan areas, and to represent different materials, etc.

Matt and glossy colours can also be applied to final drawings by a similar technique, although the methods of application differ; the makers' current directions should be carefully followed.

Perspective rendering

The following notes on his personal method of rendering perspective drawings have been kindly supplied by Frank A. Evans, MBE, FRSA, AFAS, several of whose works are illustrated in this book:

'It is wise to employ a system that, barring accidents, will ensure success, and for this reason I use paper pre-mounted on boards rather than stretched paper to save time. I use a dry technique for the sky such as pastel, which can be manipulated more easily than water colour. The use of a carbon pencil, not too soft, for line drawing reproduces well. It is not 'deadened' by water colour, that is, it shows through the colour. I also use opaque colours in moderation to emphasize focal points, foliage, etc. I consider it always essential to make an accurate setting up of perspectives in the first place.'
(Mr. Evans' method of setting up perspectives is similar to that described earlier in this chapter.)

Presentation

There are so many ways of presenting rendered and all types of display drawings that only a brief guide can be given. Exhibitions, whether specifically architectural or of any kind of a graphic nature, provide examples and ideas that can be adopted, adapted or used to suggest new methods. The intention behind the presentation will influence its mode, which must be appropriate.

Presentation may involve added lettering, symbols, etc. Almost all presentation drawings, unless prepared on pre-mounted paper, have to be mounted on stiff card or, if large, on hardboard, although lightness as well as rigidity for ease of handling and transport is a consideration. Slow-drying, non-penetrating pastes or spray adhesives are best for complete contact mounting as this enables the drawing to be manipulated into position and then smoothed out and made perfectly flat. This can be done by placing a sheet of tracing paper over it and then pushing hard with the edge of a scale or roller outwards from the centre to the edges to remove air bubbles and ridges. Care should be taken to avoid using too much adhesive.

The drawing thus mounted should be left on a horizontal surface, covered with a clean sheet of tracing paper and weighted down with evenly distributed piles of journals or books until dry. Subsequently, a cut-out surround can be added with or without a border.

Alternatively, but more costly, drawings can be commercially mounted and, if required, framed and glazed.

However, drawings, whether mounted or not, can be readily protected by covering them with transparent self-adhesive film, which is obtainable in sheets and rolls. In addition to affording protection against the hazards of handling – and this applies particularly to drawings used in workshops or on construction sites – the film imparts brightness. The film comes with an 'easy-peel' removable backing printed with guide 'squares' for convenience of alignment and cutting and with instructions for application. There are two kinds of film: gloss for normal purposes and matt for use where lines in felt-tip pen or other media may have to be added. Relatively small drawings, if to be covered by film, can be affixed to card merely by arrowmounts (p. 28).

Plate 29 Realistic perspective drawing of Bank Building, Barbados. Note importance of shadows in clarifying form. (Architects Watkins & Partners.)

F. A. Evans

Plate 30 Full colour aerial perspective of Mount Hope Hospital. Trinidad. (Architects Whiting Associates International and Watkins Phillips Bynoe & Partners.)

F. A. Evans

10
Freehand Drawing

The ability to make freehand drawings simply and quickly is of value to anyone; to architects, planners and everybody connected with design and construction of buildings it is well-nigh indispensable. By means of such drawings ideas and explanations can be far more rapidly conveyed than by words, and can, moreover, be more easily understood. No study of planning architecture and building can be undertaken without the making of intelligible diagrams and drawings and the technique should therefore be one of the first things to be practised by the student, who will thereby subsequently save much time and labour.

Training in freehand drawing consists of (1) training the 'eye', including the 'mind's eye' or imagination, and (2) training the 'hand' to express what is seen. The two things proceed simultaneously, but it is no use trying to train the hand if the vision or the visualisation are defective.

Elementary technique

In looking at a building or any object, or in imagining it, it is helpful to analyse it into (1) shapes bounded by lines, and (2) axes.

1. Whatever the sketch is to be — a plan, elevation, section, perspective — it can be resolved into its essential simple geometrical shapes, as seen in one plane.

2. At the same time, any prominent axial lines (lines of symmetry) can be noted. Almost every subject, whether strictly symmetrical or not, has axial lines of some kind or, failing these, outstanding horizontal or vertical lines. Such lines are the first to be drawn, and using them as a basis the various geometrical figures can be built up in correct proportion. When the skeleton of lines is complete, the most important features are sketched in and after these, the next important, and so on, to details as may be necessary. All the drawing is done in the first instance by lines; shades

227

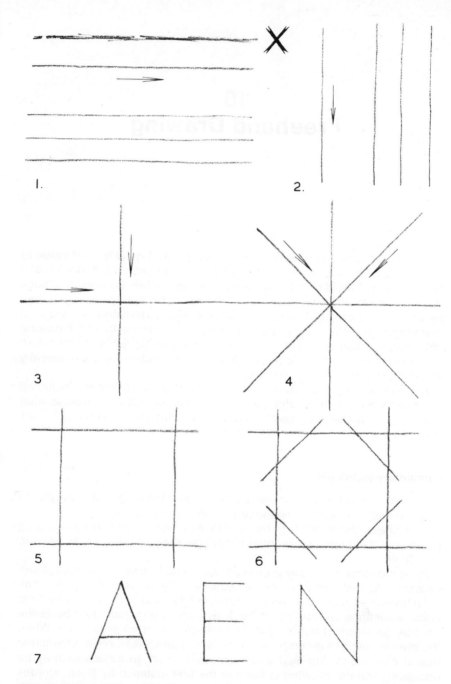

1.   2.   3   4   5   6   7

FREEHAND DRAWING
ELEMENTARY EXERCISES   STRAIGHT LINES

Fig.148

and shadows being added only if essential for the purposes of the sketch. By practice it will be found that a great deal can be expressed by straight, curved and squiggly lines and by dots, making further elaboration unnecessary.

Preliminary exercises

The majority of preliminary sketches are best made in pencil. The pencil should be fairly soft, well sharpened, and firm under pressure on smooth paper.

Exercise 1 — Straight lines

Fig. 148 illustrates examples which should be practised. All lines must be drawn freehand and must be as straight and even in quality as possible. A slight wobble is not serious, but there is no virtue in trying to make an irregular line.

1. Horizontal lines drawn from left to right. To help in keeping them horizontal try making them equidistant from the edge of the paper (use paper with straight square edges, it is easier). A line 50 mm long is good enough at first; longer lines can always be made up of a succession of short lines. After a single line has been drawn satisfactorily, draw several horizontal lines parallel and equally spaced to one another — all, of course, by eye.
2. Vertical lines drawn from top to bottom. Keep parallel to the side of the paper.
3. Lines at right-angles. Draw either the horizontal or the vertical first, then the other to cross at right-angles through a determined point.
4. Lines at 45 degrees. First draw lines at 45 degrees to pass in both directions through the intersection of lines at right-angles drawn as in (3). Then try drawing 45-degree lines by themselves. Check for accuracy afterwards with set-square.
5. Square. Drawn with horizontal and vertical lines, starting with different sides first. Check for accuracy.
6. Octagon. Drawn by adding 45-degree lines to square.
7. Lettering, patterns, etc., composed of straight lines.

If it is found that the vertical lines persistently slant in one direction, try to correct the tendency by deliberately making such lines lean a little (as you see them) to the other side. If the difficulty is serious vision is defective.

Exercise 2 — Curved lines

Fig. 149 illustrates examples.

1. and (2) Circle. Easiest way is to draw two lines lightly at right-angles, mark on them points equally spaced from the intersection and draw the curve to pass

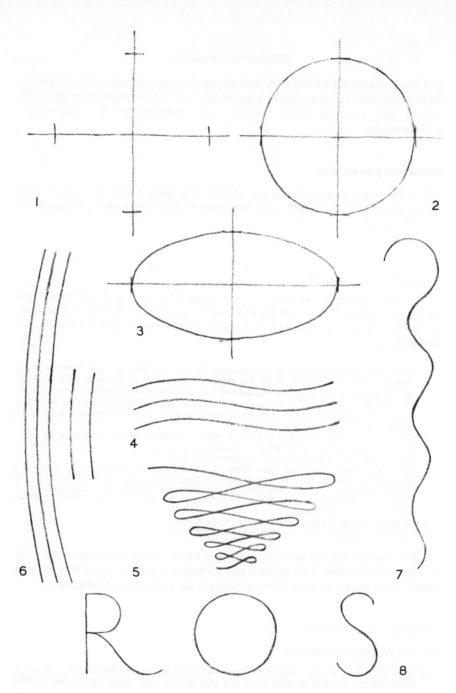

FREEHAND DRAWING
ELEMENTARY EXERCISES   *CURVED LINES*

Fig. 149

through the points. The fullness of the curve will be assisted if the points are marked by short cross lines.
3. Ellipse. Similar procedure to circle.
4. Line of double curvature. Draw them to various sizes.
5. Continuous diminishing looped line. Practice for smoothness and regularity.
6. Flat arcs.
7. Free curves.
8. Lettering or simple pattern composed of curved or curved and straight lines.

When the above exercises have been practised and present no difficulty, then any building or object can be sketched provided the eye has been trained to pick out the essential lines.

Fig. 150 shows examples of the setting-up and finished sketches of a number of plans: (1) and (2) the plan of the house in Fig. 110. This consists of straight lines mainly at right-angles, as do most building plans. Note the 'filling-in' of walls; centre lines through openings, arrows at entrances, etc., all conventions to help legibility. (3) Plans of a Greek temple. Note drawing of line and marking of centres of columns in setting-up. (4) Bramante's plan for St. Peter's Church, Rome. Note the stages in the setting-up. In such an axial plan only one-quarter needs to be fully completed. (5) Irregular shape. Note representatin of water in pool and of grass by short dashes.

Fig. 151 shows examples of the setting-up and indication of elevations. (1) is the elevation of the house in Fig. 111, showing the main lines. (2) is a smaller thumb-nail sketch of the same subject. (3) and (4) St. Paul's, London. Note the setting-up of the main lines. The first line drawn is the ground line, then the vertical axes, then the main horizontal divisions. This sequence is suitable for most elevations. Note also the rapid suggestion of detail in the completed half of the sketch. (5) Sketch of a detail. Note how main shape and outline are established first, and the thickening of some lines to suggest form.

For most uses the above type of sketch is adquate, but a greater degree of finish can be given. By adding conventional shadows, by eye, the third dimension can be brought out more strongly, and the sketch passes from the diagrammatic to the semi-pictorial. By the addition of surroundings and an indication of material, texture, etc., attractive pictorial sketches can be made if necessary. All this is excellent practice for the development of a personal style of free sketching in which the preliminary stages are done automatically and the initial setting-up on paper is omitted, Fig. 152.

Freehand perspective

Perspective or metric freehand drawings can be made on exactly the same lines as described above for plans and elevations. There is no

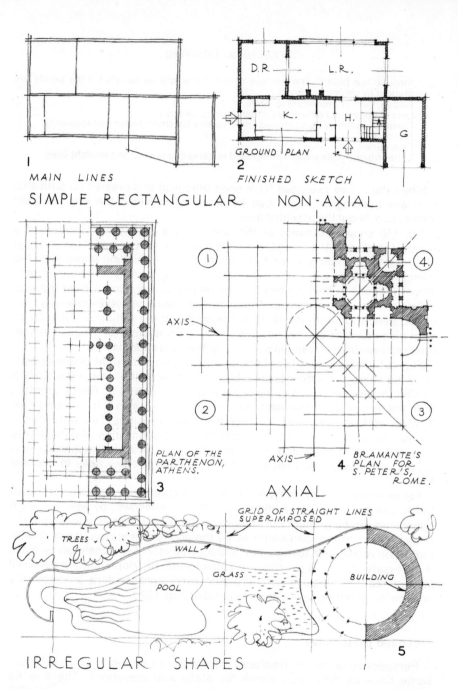

1

MAIN LINES

2

GROUND PLAN

FINISHED SKETCH

D.R.   L.R.   K.   H.   G

SIMPLE RECTANGULAR   NON-AXIAL

1

AXIS

2

3

AXIS

4.

4

PLAN OF THE
PARTHENON,
ATHENS.

3

BRAMANTE'S
PLAN FOR
S. PETER'S,
ROME.

AXIAL

GRID OF STRAIGHT LINES
SUPERIMPOSED

TREES

WALL

GRASS

POOL

BUILDING

5

IRREGULAR   SHAPES

FREEHAND DRAWING
SETTING UP AND INDICATION OF PLANS

Fig. 150

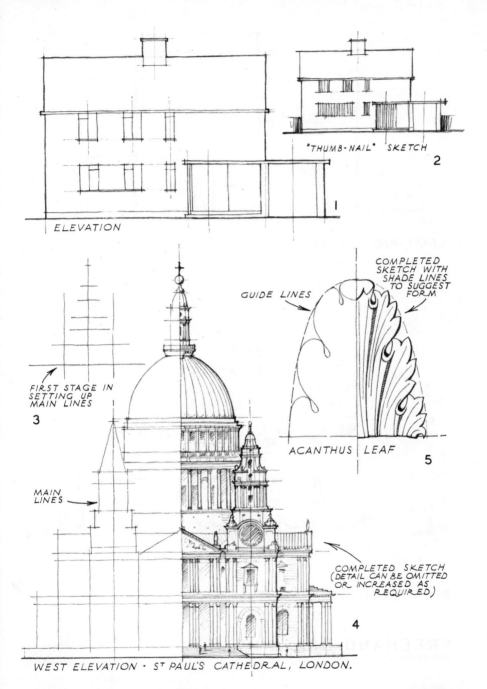

"THUMB-NAIL" SKETCH

2

ELEVATION

1

COMPLETED
SKETCH WITH
SHADE LINES
TO SUGGEST
FORM

GUIDE LINES

FIRST STAGE IN
SETTING UP
MAIN LINES

3

ACANTHUS LEAF

5

MAIN
LINES

COMPLETED SKETCH
(DETAIL CAN BE OMITTED
OR INCREASED AS
REQUIRED)

4

WEST ELEVATION · ST PAUL'S CATHEDRAL, LONDON.

FREEHAND DRAWING
SETTING UP AND INDICATION OF ELEVATIONS

Fig. 151

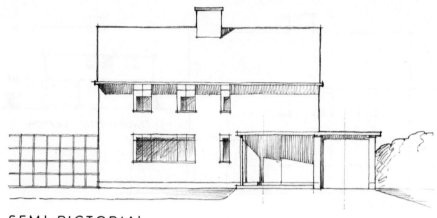

SEMI-PICTORIAL

PICTORIAL

FREEHAND DRAWING
RENDERING OF ELEVATIONS

Fig. 152

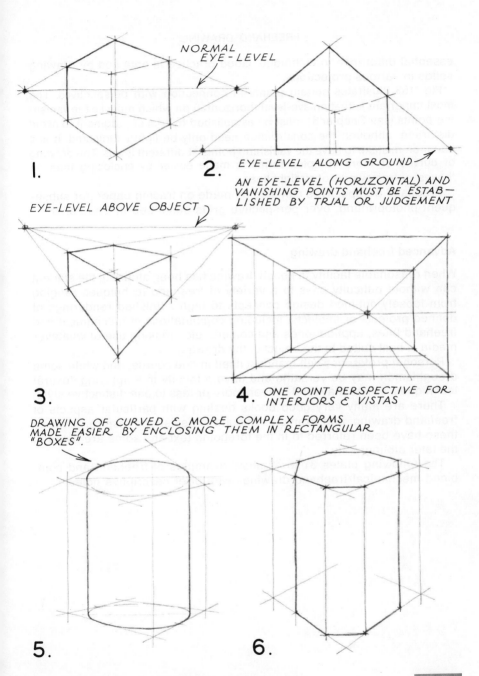

NORMAL EYE-LEVEL

1.

2. EYE-LEVEL ALONG GROUND

AN EYE-LEVEL (HORIZONTAL) AND VANISHING POINTS MUST BE ESTABLISHED BY TRIAL OR JUDGEMENT

EYE-LEVEL ABOVE OBJECT

3.

4. ONE POINT PERSPECTIVE FOR INTERIORS & VISTAS

DRAWING OF CURVED & MORE COMPLEX FORMS MADE EASIER BY ENCLOSING THEM IN RECTANGULAR "BOXES".

5. **6.**

SKETCH PERSPECTIVE

Fig. 153

essential difference in technique. Good practice is obtained by drawing solids in various projections.

Fig. 153 illustrates certain points in connection with perspectives. The most important is that an eye-level (horizontal) on which must lie the vanishing points (see Chapter 8) must be established by trial or judgment to avoid distortion, although the construction need only be lightly indicated. It is a common mistake to have the vanishing points at different levels. The drawing of curved or more complex forms is made easier by enclosing them in 'boxes' or frameworks of straight lines.

Freehand perspectives can also be made on tracing paper, for subsequent photoprinting, over perspective grids described in Chapter 8.

Advanced freehand drawing

When reasonable facility in pencil drawing has been attained, the student can without difficulty pass to a variety of freehand techniques ranging from loosely-outlined design concepts to highly finished renderings of defined projects or subjects, including combinations of mechanical and freehand lines, applied tones and colours, etc., making use of whatever media is best suited to the object of the drawing.

Personal preference will manifest itself in due course, and while some draughtsmen may be versatile and have a facility in employing several techniques, others may tend to keep more or less to one distinctive style.

There are many very good books dealing with particular aspects of freehand drawing, and examples abound to assist and inspire. Some of these have been referred to in the foregoing text and some are listed in the later bibliography.

The following plates 31 to 42 show examples of freehand and combined mechanical/freehand drawings with brief descriptive notes.

Plate 31 Freehand drawing in black ink on white paper of rococo facade. *Norah R. Glover.*
The technique is admirably suited to the subject.

interior design sketches

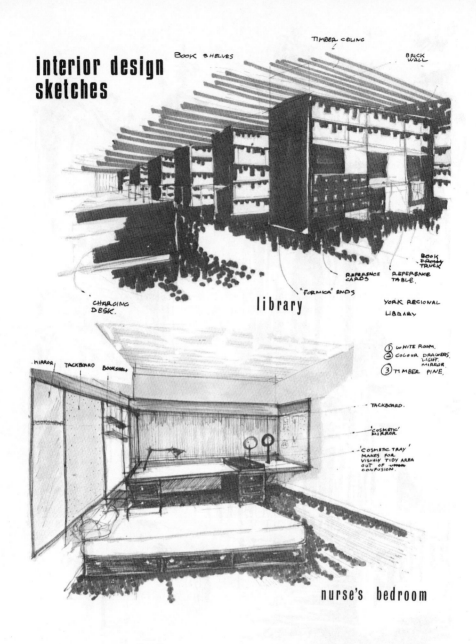

TIMBER CEILING

BOOK SHELVES

BRICK WALL

BOOK TROLLY TRUCK

REFERENCE CARDS

REFERENCE TABLE

"FORMICA" ENDS

CHARGING DESK.

library

YORK REGIONAL LIBRARY

① WHITE ROOM.
② COLOUR DRAWERS.
   LIGHT.
   MIRROR.
③ TIMBER PINE.

MIRROR TACKBOARD BOOKSHELF

TACKBOARD.

'COSMETIC' MIRROR

'COSMETIC TRAY' MAKES FOR VISUALY TIDY AREA OUT OF CONFUSION.

nurse's bedroom

Plate 32 Rapid freehand sketches of interior designs in ballpoint pen coloured by felt-tipped watercolour pens.

John F. Reekie

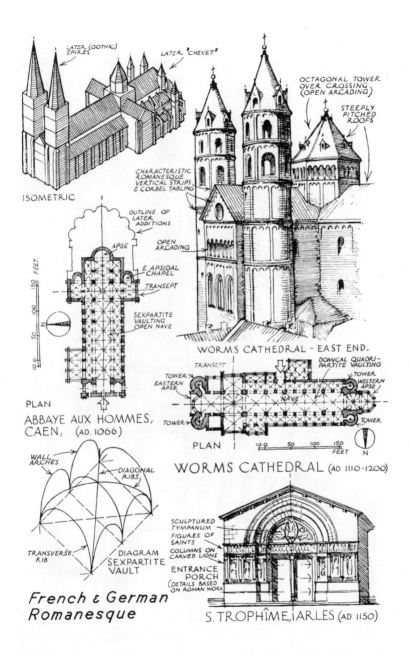

LATER (GOTHIC) SPIRES

LATER "CHEVET"

OCTAGONAL TOWER OVER CROSSING (OPEN ARCADING)

STEEPLY PITCHED ROOFS

CHARACTERISTIC ROMANESQUE VERTICAL STRIPS & CORBEL TABLING

ISOMETRIC

OUTLINE OF LATER ADDITIONS

APSE

OPEN ARCADING

E. APSIDAL CHAPEL

TRANSEPT

150 FEET

100

50

0

N

SEXPARTITE VAULTING OPEN NAVE

WORMS CATHEDRAL – EAST END.

PLAN

ABBAYE AUX HOMMES, CAEN, (AD. 1066)

TRANSEPT

TOWER

EASTERN APSE

TOWER

WESTERN APSE

DOMICAL QUADRI-PARTITE VAULTING

NAVE

TOWER

TOWER

PLAN

10 0   50   100   150 FEET   N

WORMS CATHEDRAL (AD 1110-1200)

WALL ARCHES

DIAGONAL RIBS

TRANSVERSE RIB

DIAGRAM SEXPARTITE VAULT

SCULPTURED TYMPANUM

FIGURES OF SAINTS

COLUMNS ON CARVED LIONS

ENTRANCE PORCH (DETAILS BASED ON ROMAN WORK)

French & German Romanesque

S. TROPHÎME, ARLES (AD 1150)

Plate 33 Architectural history sketches in pen and ink over pencil guide lines.

sketch from viaduct level

Plate 34 Coloured sketch perspective of bus station and car-parking building.
(Student's drawing in pencil and felt pens.)

M. Coleridge

Plate 35 Freehand pen and ink drawing over outline pencil perspective of semi-detached houses. (Architects Tranter Associates.)

L. Solomon

Plate 36 Perspective sketch in pencil and ink of memorial chapel. (Design and drawing by author.)

Fraser Reekie

Plate 37 Freehand drawing: black ink drawing on white paper on one-point perspective basis. A lively example of an individual technique. High Kingsdown Development, Bristol, reproduced by permission of J. T. Building Service Ltd.

Plate 38 Careful freehand pen and black ink drawing on white card combining variety of indications with strong unity of style and composition. Interest heightened by judicious use of sharp contrasts. Reproduced about quarter actual size. *F. A. Evans*

Plate 39 Black pencil sketch over some lightly ruled guidelines set up on site by eye. Note effective use of dark, graded shadows. An excellent example of pencil technique. Reproduced about half actual size.

F. A. Evans

Plate 40 Example of a quick sketch made on site using felt-tip pen on ordinary loose-leaf
pad paper. A simple but effective technique for various architectural and planning
study purposes. Reproduced about half actual size.   *A. K. McCarthy*

Plate 41 Example of rapidly executed sketch made on site using black felt-tip pen on cartridge paper. Reproduced about one-seventh actual size.

A. K. McCarthy

Plate 42 Black ink drawing of Place Vendôme made using 0.2 Rapidograph drawing pen on tracing sheet over carefully set up pencil perspective (from old Parisian sequence map). Openings and road surface darkened by even application of HB pencil to back of tracing sheet. A technique well suited to dyeline and photographic reproduction.

Graham Moss

Bibliography

In addition to references in the text, the following publications are sources of further technical information on the preparation of various kinds of drawings:

Recommendations for Building Drawing Practice BS1192: 1969, British Standards Institution. This is a useful guide for all concerned with production drawings for buildings, including drawings for modular coordination. It contains examples of graphical symbols and schedules.

RIBA Handbook of Architectural Practice and Management: Section 3410, Royal Institute of British Architects.

The Detailing of Reinforced Concrete, Concrete Society and Institution of Structural Engineers, London.

Coordination of Dimensions for Buildings, Royal Institute of British Architects.

CI/SfB Project Manual, Alan Ray-Jones and Wilfred McCann, Architectural Press, London.

Working Drawings, *Building Research Establishment Digest* 172, 1974.

Redland Guide to the Construction Industry, Redland Ltd., Reigate.

Development Plans: A Manual of Form and Content, HMSO.

Techniques of Landscape Architecture, edited by A. E. Weddle, Heinemann.

Architectural Rendering, Albert O. Halse, McGraw-Hill Book Co.

Architectural Drawings, New Architectural Drawings, New Techniques of Architectural Rendering, Helmut Jacoby, Thames & Hudson.

Architectural Delineation, A Photographic Approach, Ernest Burden, McGraw-Hill Book Co.

Ways with Water Color, Ted Kautzky, Rheinhold Publishing Corporation, New York.

To keep abreast of changes and developments such periodicals as: *Architects' Journal, Architectural Review, The Architect, Building, Building Design, RIBA Journal, The Planner* (Journal of the Royal Town Planning Institute), *Planning, Built Environment, Journal of the Institute of Landscape Architects*, and similar publications in the USA, Canada, Australia and other countries often contain illustrations of drawings and frequently print articles on graphic and related techniques. The librarians of the major professional institutes and societies will usually assist in locating relevant material on any particular aspect.